Haile-Selassie's Government

Haile-Selassie's Government

by Christopher Clapham

with a Foreword by Dame Margery Perham,

PRAEGER, PUBLISHERS
New York · Washington

BOOKS THAT MATTER

Published in the United States of America in 1969
by Praeger Publishers, Inc.
111 Fourth Avenue, New York, N.Y. 10003

Second printing 1970

© 1969, in England, by Longman Group Ltd (formerly
Longmans, Green and Co. Ltd) London

Library of Congress Catalog Card Number: 68–54000

Printed in Great Britain

To those who have helped

Table of Contents

Acknowledgements		x
Foreword by Dame Margery Perham		xi
Preface		xii
Technical Notes		xiii

Chapter 1 **Land and People** 1

The Ethiopian Setting 1
Society and Government 4

Chapter 2 **The Ethiopian Polity and its Development** 8

The Political Tradition 8
The Emergence of the Modern Empire, 1855–1907 12
The Rise of Haile-Selassie, 1907–1941 15
The Supremacy of Haile-Selassie, 1941–1968 21

Chapter 3 **The Imperial System** 28

A Palace Government at Work 28

Chapter 4 **The Constitutional Framework** 34

The Constitution of 1931 34
The Revised Constitution of 1955 36
The Formal Structure of the Central Executive 44

Chapter 5 **The Emperor** 47

Haile-Selassie 47
Emperor and Government 51
The Imperial Family 59

Chapter 6 **Political Groupings** 64

The Political Class 64
The Nobility 65
Non-Noble Groupings 71
Regional and Ethnic Groups 75
Church and Religion 82
The Influence of Education 87

Chapter 7 **The High Officials**   92

    The Way to Power   92
    The Ministers   98
    Foreigners in the Government   103

Chapter 8 **The Imperial Secretariat and its Decline**   108

    Imperial Orders and the *Aqabé Sä'at*   108
    The Supremacy of the Secretariat, 1941–1955   110
    The Secretariat in Decline, 1955–1968   117
    His Imperial Majesty's Private Cabinet   120
    The Crown Council   123

Chapter 9 **The Growth of Central Institutions**   126

    The Council of Ministers   126
    The Prime Minister's Office, 1943–1957   129
    The Development of the Prime Ministry since 1958   130

Chapter 10 **Parliament and Legislation**   135

    The Legislative Process   135
    The Infancy of Parliament, 1931–1957   140
    Parliament since 1957   142

Chapter 11 **Government Spending**   155

    Appropriations, 1941–1960   155
    Budget and Appropriations since 1960   164
    The Italian Loan, a Case Study   175

Chapter 12 **Concluding Review**   181

    The Working of the Government   181
    Government and Country   184
    The Present and the Future   188

    Biographical Appendix   193

    Notes   200

    Select Bibliography   206

Tables

1 The fate of Ethiopians educated abroad and of Senior
Government Officials during the Italian Occupation   20
2 Ethiopian Political Chronology, 1941–1968   27
3 Number of Individuals from Different Regions holding high office in the Central Government, 1941–1966   77
4 Education of Senior Central Government Officials,
1941–1966   88

Figures

                                               facing page
1 Ethiopia: Administrative Divisions and Major Towns   2
2 Chart of the Ethiopian Government, *c.* 1947   170
3 Chart of the Ethiopian Government, *c.* 1967   191
4 The Dynasties of Shoa and Tegré   210
5 Family Connections between Ministers   211

Plates

                                               facing page
Haile-Selassie I   34
The Imperial Family   35
The Liberation, 1941   50
The Anglo-Ethiopian Agreement of 1944   51
The Federation with Eritrea, 1952   51
The Emperor and his Ministers   130
Ministers of the Crown   131
A Church Occasion   146
The Parliament Building, Addis Ababa   147

Acknowledgements

The author and publishers are grateful to the following for permission to reproduce the photographs in this book:

René Groebli, Black Star, London, for photograph of the Emperor (facing p. 34); Associated Press Ltd., London, for that of the imperial family 1932 and of the Crown Prince (facing p. 35), for both photographs facing p. 51 and for that of the Parliament Building (facing p. 147); Central Press Photos Ltd., London, for that of Prince Makonnen (facing p. 35); Camera Press Ltd., London, for that facing p. 50 and for those of the Prime Minister and the Ministers of Justice and of Information (facing p. 131); the Ministry of Information, Imperial Ethiopian Government, for that of the Emperor and his Ministers (facing p. 130); Paul Popper Ltd., London, for the photograph which appears on the jacket and also faces p. 146.

Foreword

by Dame Margery Perham, D.C.M.G., D.Litt.

Ethiopia is not a land of mystery quite comparable with Tibet before—and indeed since—the recent Chinese invasion. Especially since this ancient and unique African state was violated by the Italian conquest it has been increasingly opened to economic and cultural relations with the outer world. Even more recently it has made such effective contact with its own continent, upon which it had turned its back all through the centuries, that it has now become something like a political capital for Africa, especially tropical Africa. Yet one aspect of Ethiopia remains obscure, the nature of the central government. This is the subject Christopher Clapham courageously set himself to study some five years ago. Courageously, because the matrix of this two thousand year old state is largely hidden under the mantle of imperial power which descended, some forty years ago, on one great and famous man, Haile-Selassie.

Is he still an African Louis XIV? How does he control a state, rapidly proliferating in modern services and world-wide contacts for many of which he is his own roving ambassador? If, behind the appearance of centralisation, there is delegation, what directions does it take—to the newly promoted Prime Minister and Cabinet, to the extending Civil Service, to the Senate or the House of Representatives? Have the *rases* and the older territorial nobility been wholly undermined? What should be read into the so-called 'coup of 1960'? Some observers would say that only a very well-placed Ethiopian could answer these irreverent questions. But what Ethiopian, under the present régime, would presume to do so? It is for these reasons that Dr Clapham's initiative and persistence, shown in the course of five years of study, with three periods in Ethiopia, are so valuable.

He has penetrated a long way into the secrets of the Emperor's authority, his methods of dealing with the complex circles, old and new, which surround the throne; the subtle web of medieval and modern forms of influence and control, and the degree to which these are being relaxed. Here is a fascinating analysis of the ways in which a great ruler, with an immense historical inheritance, has tried, with much success, to bring his state and people into active relationship with the modern world. All those interested not only in Ethiopia but also in the new and contrasting Africa in which the Emperor plays such a vigorous part, should read this book. It is at once a picture of the present and an introduction to a future which must in no long time confront Haile-Selassie's Empire.

Oxford July, 1968   *Margery Perham*

Preface

This book attempts to describe and analyse Ethiopia's central government and its development, between the Liberation from Italian occupation in 1941, and the end of 1967. I hope that it will interest both Ethiopians and others who are drawn to their country, and also students of government who will find here an account of an indigenous African polity faced by modern pressures for change.

The research for this study has taken me four years, two and a half of them in Ethiopia, from 1963 to 1967. It has grown from a doctoral thesis for Oxford University, called *The Institutions of the Central Ethiopian Government*, which is now buried in the inaccessible depths of the Bodleian Library. Where I have been able to draw on published work or publicly available materials, I have referred to them in the footnotes. But I have relied far more on innumerable conversations with Ethiopians in the government, and also foreigners in Ethiopia, who have let me ask all manner of questions and have sometimes answered them. Since there are many whose names I am not free to give, I will mention none; but should any of them notice here a thought or fact which he has given me, I hope he will accept it as a measure of my thanks. This book is dedicated to them.

To my supervisor in Oxford, Dame Margery Perham, I am most grateful for moral support, kindly criticism of successive drafts, and her understanding of the difficulties of writing a book about Ethiopia. My debt to my two universities is also great: to the Board of the Faculty of Social Studies at Oxford, for letting me embark on a project of research which must at the time have seemed pretty far-fetched; to the Institute of Ethiopian Studies and the Faculty of Law of Haile Sellassie I University, Addis Ababa, for giving me a home and a welcome in Ethiopia; and finally, to the Department of Education in London for giving me the State Studentship and travel allowances which paid for this research, and for meeting my problems with unfailing helpfulness. None of these institutions is responsible for the publication of this book or for any of the opinions in it.

C. S. C.
African Studies Centre,
Cambridge.
July 1968.

Technical Notes

Spelling

In spelling Ethiopian names and other words, I have followed the system of transliteration devised by Mr Stephen Wright, in the *Journal of Ethiopian Studies*, Vol. II, No. 1, though with a few simplifications. In particular, palatalised consonants are rendered as 'sh', 'ch' and so on, and no diacritical mark is used to distinguish explosive consonants; Ethiopicists will doubtless discover occasional mistakes, but since this is not a linguistic treatise I hope they will forgive me. I have also followed the *Journal of Ethiopian Studies* in retaining conventional spellings for Haile-Selassie (see below), Imru, Makonnen and Shoa; otherwise, names have been transliterated even when their owners have adopted particular spellings.

Ethiopian Names

An Ethiopian's name consists of his own personal name, followed by that of his father. Thus, Eskender Dästa's personal name is Eskender, and his father was called Dästa; the patronymic exists only to prevent confusion with namesakes, and where no confusion is likely, it is quite correct to refer to him simply as Eskender, without any hint of familiarity. On the other hand, it is a mistake to call him Dästa, as this confuses him with his father; it is a mistake often made by those who assume that an Ethiopian's second name is a surname, and follow European usage. Where the full name and patronymic have not been necessary, I have therefore used the first name alone, and so Aklilu Habtä-Wäld, the Prime Minister, is often referred to as Aklilu.

Many Ethiopian religious names are compounds of two words; Gäbrä-Mäsqäl, for example, means Servant of the Cross, and Haile-Selassie means Power of the Trinity. In general usage, such names are sometimes written as one word, sometimes as two, and sometimes hyphenated; I have hyphenated them whenever they occur, even with Haile-Selassie which is usually spelt as two words. It is a mistake to use either part of such a name without the other, and the all too common journalists' habit of calling the Emperor 'Selassie' confuses him with the Father, Son and Holy Ghost.

Ethiopian Titles

Ethiopian titles have been described in several books, including Perham's *The Government of Ethiopia* and Levine's *Wax & Gold*, and so they are not enumerated here. In the text, those with the title of *Ras* have retained it whenever they are mentioned, but other titles have usually been given only for clarification.

Dates

The Ethiopian year begins on September 11th, and the system of numbering is between seven and eight years behind the Gregorian calendar; the Ethiopian 1961, for instance, runs from September 11th, 1968 to September 10th, 1969. To avoid confusion, I have used the Gregorian calendar throughout, and when the Ethiopian has been used in quotations, I have added the Gregorian equivalent in brackets.

Reference Numbers

For ease of reference among often confusing Ethiopian names, the most important politicians are distinguished by numbers, placed in brackets after their names where they are mentioned; these numbers refer to their place, in alphabetical order, in the Biographical Appendix at the end.

Chapter 1
Land and People

The Ethiopian Setting

In the hot new continent of Africa, Ethiopia comes as a surprise and an exception. It is an ancient country, built on the high mountains of the Horn of Africa, and alone among African nations it successfully resisted the incursions of colonial powers, and so has survived to the present day as an independent state. Here the past lies with peculiar weight. Ethiopia has not been rudely divorced from its history by the successive shocks of colonial rule and independence which have shaken the rest of Africa; and so the traditional attitudes and institutions of the Ethiopian Empire have remained comparatively undisturbed, protected by the high mountains—slashed by ravines and surrounded by deserts—which guarded Ethiopia's independence in the past, and which remain as standing obstacles to its development in the present. As Ethiopia stands among African countries, so does the Emperor Haile-Selassie among their leaders. He has been Ethiopia's ruler for over fifty years, Emperor for nearly forty, and for all this time the country has depended heavily on his leadership.

It is a country of some 400,000 square miles and some twenty million people.[1] Its heartland is the great plateau which stretches from Addis Ababa in the centre of the country north to the ancient cities of Lalibela, Gondar and Aksum. Most of this is rich farmland, with rolling uplands broken by sudden valleys and strangely contoured hills, dotted all over with little hamlets and hilltop churches, each with its clump of trees. At night it is cold, sometimes freezing, and the heavy annual rains leave it green and sodden from June until October. This plateau has been Ethiopian territory for over a thousand years, and here live the two dominant peoples of the Empire, the Amharas and the Tegreans. Closely related, they are descended from the fusion of local Hamitic stock with immigrants from South Arabia in the centuries before the birth of Christ, and they form the common core of both historical and modern Ethiopia. The Tegreans occupy the northern part of the plateau, in the modern provinces of Tegré and Eritrea, where the Ethiopian Empire had its origins, some two thousand years ago, in the kingdom of Aksum. But over

I

the centuries, the centre of power has shifted south, and for the last seven hundred years the initiative has almost always lain with the Amharas. The Amharas cover most of the provinces of Bägémdär, Gojam and Shoa, with much of Wälo, and since 1889 Ethiopia has been ruled from Shoa, the very southernmost Amhara province, which surrounds the modern capital of Addis Ababa.

The Amharas, and especially those from Shoa, have thus become the country's leading ethnic group, and they have partly imposed their language and culture on other areas. Both they and the Tegreans have since early times been Orthodox Christians, with a devotion to their faith which, aided by the powerful unifying influence of the Emperor, has enabled them to maintain a national identity and a common political system down the centuries. The political power of the Church is latent, except in time of crisis, but it is a vital element in the Ethiopian state; conversion to Christianity has been an almost essential condition for admission to any important function in the government.

Most of southern Ethiopia is the territory of the Gallas, the third important ethnic group in modern Ethiopia. They were originally nomads, akin to the Somalis, and invaded the Empire from the south in the sixteenth and seventeenth centuries. They settled in a semi-circle round the Amharas, extending from Wäläga in the west to the old walled city of Harär in the east, and driving a wedge up the great eastern escarpment of the plateau. Today, they occupy most of the great area of highland and thorn scrub from the centre of the country down to the Kenya border, and they account for nearly half of Ethiopia's population. They have been absorbed into the Ethiopian political system in small numbers over the last two hundred and fifty years, but most of them were incorporated only in the late nineteenth-century expansion, when the Empire spread out from its Amhara/Tegrean base to take in much surrounding territory. The Gallas have usually been a fairly passive element in political affairs, partly assimilated to the Amharas. They divide into many regional groups, differing from one another in religion, political organisation and the amount of assimilation to the Amharas, though there have been some recent signs of the growth of a common Galla consciousness.

The remaining peoples of Ethiopia mostly live in the peripheral lowlands, or in isolated pockets elsewhere, and have been brought into the Empire by conquest over the last century. They include the nomadic Danakil of the Red Sea plains, and the Somalis who follow the seasonal grazing through the barren scrubland of the south-east and the neighbouring Republic of Somalia. Since Somalia became independent in 1960, this area has been a constant source of friction between the two countries, as the nationalist claims of Somalia have met the steadfast Ethiopian determination to hold on to their territory. There are many

Figure 1

Ethiopia: Administrative Divisions and Major Towns

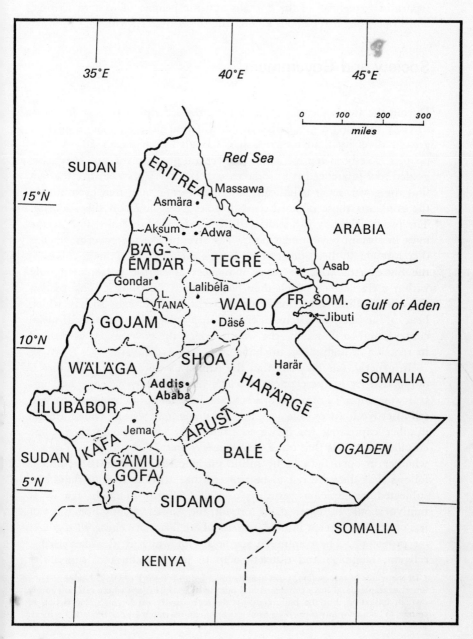

small tribes in south-western Ethiopia, and down the long western frontier with the Sudan. But these outlying areas have scarcely been represented in the government, for they lack ethnic, religious or historical connections with the established core. Their political importance lies largely in the separatist tendencies of the Somalis and the peoples of western Eritrea, and in occasional rebellions among the south-western tribes.

Society and Government*

During the two millennia of its history, the Ethiopian Empire has consistently included a great diversity of different peoples, though never a greater diversity than today. Some, though by no means all, of these peoples have been represented in the central government, and they have guided and influenced it to some extent. But this does not alter the fact that the government is basically an Amhara one, and that even among the Amharas those of northern Shoa are very much in the majority. The present dynasty is Shoan, and Shoans have also tended to hold the most important government posts. The structure of the government has therefore chiefly been determined by the society and common values of the Shoan Amharas, for other influences affect the government only within a framework which they have already laid down. This section therefore outlines some major characteristics of Amhara society which bear on the political system, in order both to place the system in its social context, and to illuminate the way in which the government works and its reaction or adaptation to change.

'In general, one may say that the Amhara's view of human nature is dominated by his perception of man's inherent aggressiveness and untrustworthiness.'[2] From his earliest years, he is taught to be aggressive and self-assertive towards outsiders, and his name may well be one of a large number expressing his desire to smite, cow or dominate them. The corollary of this is that other people are equally ready to do you down, whether in open fight or by subtle intrigue behind your back; and it follows that they are not to be trusted, that all their actions should be subjected to suspicious scrutiny, and that in case of doubt the worst motives should be assumed. As a result, the Amhara family lives more or less on its own, except in border areas where farms are clustered together for protection. The communal symbols with which it identifies itself— religion, language and district—help to justify feelings of superiority

* In the whole of this section, I am heavily indebted to the work of D. N. Levine. I have found examples, and have confirmed and adapted his conclusions where relevant to my own investigation, but the basic concepts depend heavily on Levine's. He is not, of course, to blame for any distortions or oversimplifications which I have made to his ideas.

4

against strangers and outsiders, without providing much sense of community among those who share them.

These attitudes are well illustrated by several characteristics of Amhara society. Constant litigation is used not only for resolving the disputes which aggression naturally causes, but also as a vehicle for self-assertiveness itself, providing a golden opportunity for declamation before an attentive audience. Much time and effort may be spent in giving insults to others, or taking offence at those directed against oneself, and the speed with which a crowd gathers when an argument breaks out bears witness to the subject's fascination. Co-operative action is therefore rare, except in brief periods of emergency. Such activities as singing, dancing and even war-making are largely unco-ordinated, with an emphasis on individual prowess; the failure of the Ethiopian national football team in 1964 was explained by the existence of a bitter personal feud between its two star players,[3] and any institution is similarly liable to be split by animosities which swiftly descend to personal intrigue and backbiting. The weakness of communal bonds makes it fairly easy to cut oneself off from society altogether, by becoming a monk or hermit, or taking as an outlaw to the hills.

These tendencies are naturally reflected in the government. Unity is found largely as a temporary response to a strong external threat, illustrated by the way that an impending major conference or royal visit may galvanise the Addis Ababa city authorities into a brief stint of feverish activity; the crisis past, they revert to their normal dilatory progress. The government itself is split by feuds and factions, some based simply on the convenience of the moment and some on more permanent differences which obstruct co-operative action and collective responsibility.

Those sociable and co-operative attitudes which do exist among the Amhara are in themselves by no means strong enough to hold together any social organisation, let alone one which has shown such stability over such a long period. But that combination of qualities which hampers communal activity also forms the basis of a system founded on authority, in which vertical lines of communication largely replace horizontal ones. Authority in itself is generally regarded as good; not only is the Amhara at his happiest when bossing someone around, but the language provides many forms for flattery, adulation and expressions of deference towards those in authority. Relationships tend to fall into the pattern of authority and subservience, and it has often been noted that at the top of the social hierarchy stands the Big Man or *teleq säw*;[4] he is the authority figure *par excellence*, by virtue of his high birth or individual prowess, and is accorded universal respect. Even a nobleman must prove his capacity for leadership in order to achieve this status, and anyone with sufficient ability can reach the highest rank, especially in wartime; the strong hierarchical structure thus leaves important channels for social mobility. These authority figures, ranging from minor chiefs to the Emperor himself, hold the society together; and when the bond of authority is snapped, as happened in Addis Ababa after Haile-Selassie's flight in May 1936, anarchy results. In the same way, an Ethiopian army often falls apart and flees the battlefield once its leader is dead.

The leader himself loses status if he shares his authority with an inferior, and this, with the inferior's reluctance to seem presumptuous, contributes to that failure to delegate which has been one of the most marked features of Ethiopian administration. Authority cannot be effectively delegated because it is personal to the individual, and any political position, likewise, is essentially a personal position rather than an impersonal office. This has been a constant barrier to the development of institutional government, and one of the main reasons why Emperors have failed, until recent times, to 'build up any kind of administrative framework'[5] through which to exercise their power. Instead, power has depended on personal relationships, and differences within the government tend to take the form of personal likes and dislikes, rather than of policies. Discussions of the political situation, for instance, constantly turn on whether one politician has quarrelled with another and on who is 'close' to whom, especially who is 'closest' to the Emperor.

In the conservative society of the Amhara, authority also provides the major source of impetus for change. Important innovations have had to come from the Emperor himself, the only man with status enough to introduce them, and have had to be filtered down through successive levels of local governors and chiefs. Without such initiative, innovations are generally greeted with suspicion, while the evils which they are meant to counter are accepted with the heavy fatalism often found in static societies. Anything beyond one's immediate knowledge may be ascribed to fate, and this attitude encourages people to accept whatever is handed down from earlier times.

The respect for authority makes it very difficult to express any open opposition to a superior short of outright rebellion, for there has been no place for reasoned criticism of his proposals—a trait which has added to the difficulties of junior educated officials trying to suggest improvements in the government. There are, however, subtler ways of softening the impact of authority. It is certainly almost unthinkable for an inferior to refuse to obey an order, except as a prelude to revolt, but it is very common for him to profess his obedience and then do nothing about it, or else provide a range of excuses for delaying its execution until the morrow; or he may carefully 'interpret' the order until very little of its spirit remains, using the ambiguities of the Amharic language to do so. Opposition can also be expressed through the obscurities of witty repartee, or by appeal to another figure of still greater authority. Thus the decision of a judge may be acquiesced in only until the loser has a chance to take his case to a higher court. Further, a leader can make himself obeyed only so long as he is successful, and no Ethiopian can be sure of retaining his followers when he falls on evil days. The dexterity with which these contrive to abandon a falling star and attach themselves to a rising one is at times quite remarkable, and several senior members of the present government have reached high rank by such judicious changing of alliances. In former times, it was by no means unusual for the soldiers of an outnumbered army to desert *en masse* to the enemy before a battle.

This adaptability to circumstances leads at times to astonishing divergencies between theory and practice. In the government, the theoretical omnipotence of the Emperor has been asserted even at times when he had no actual power at all; in the Church, indissoluble Christian marriage is recognised as the ideal, but another form of marriage with easy divorce is also available. This divergence is recognised in the contrast, consciously made, between the surface appearance of things and their underlying reality. So in Amharic poetry, the immediate meaning may only be a mask for the poet's subtler points; in social behaviour, aggression and distrust may lie beneath the outward forms of courtesy and camaraderie. This way in which the significant actions often lie beneath the surface gives Amhara society its complexity and ambiguity; within the government, it furnishes the secrecy and subtlety which combine with the tendencies to suspicion and personal rivalry to give Ethiopian politics its peculiar aura of rumour and intrigue, and to provide a setting in which neither Othello nor Iago seems in the least implausible.

These traditional traits have naturally been modified, in present-day Ethiopia, by modern education, with its emphasis on different forms of organisation and different combinations of values; they certainly cannot be applied to every member of the government. But their influence is always present, both in the traditional forms of government which retain much of their force, and in those, of whom the present Emperor is the first, who have been strongly affected by them. Their relevance to Haile-Selassie's government will be clear in every chapter.

Chapter 2
The Ethiopian Polity and its Development

The Political Tradition

The Ethiopian state traces its origins back for some two thousand years, even discounting the legends which add another millennium or two to the story. To the kingdom of Aksum, which flourished and decayed in the first seven centuries of the Christian era, it owes the foundation of the two great institutions which have since guided Ethiopia's course: the office of Emperor, and the Ethiopian Orthodox Church. Following the expansion of Islam in the seventh century, Ethiopia was cut off from the outside world, but these twin pillars of the state were both firmly established throughout the central plateau by the thirteenth century; and in about 1270, the so-called 'restoration' of the Solomonic dynasty opened the second great flowering of historic Ethiopia which occupied the next three hundred years. These centuries of history are important not only as a memory of which to build a modern nationalism, like that of ancient Ghana or Zimbabwe, but also because they established traditional political forms which are still highly relevant today.

By 'traditional' characteristics are here meant simply those derived from indigenous Ethiopian (and especially Amhara) forms and values, as opposed to the recent impact of 'western' or 'modern' ones introduced from outside. This distinction is easier to maintain than one might expect from experience of other polities. First, the isolation of Ethiopia has led to the peculiar and homogeneous system whose social bases have just been examined; this is both readily identifiable, and easily contrasted with outside forms. Second, though there was a certain amount of change within the traditional government, there was very little 'development', in the sense understood in Europe; the system has basically been static, and it is therefore possible to examine it as a whole, rather than in some given period. Third, the examination of the 'traditional' is made easier by the continuity between ancient times and the present day; we are not trying to ferret out indigenous traits from a political framework imposed from outside, but are following such traits within the indigenous system itself.

We do not have to look far to find the nucleus of this traditional system. The king of kings has been the centre and moving force of the Ethiopian government for as far back as records will take us. From the era of Aksum onwards, the government has been founded on his authority, and even in the period of puppet Emperors between 1769 and 1855, the ideal of the monarchy remained intact, to be realised by the modern Emperors.

The Emperor's position is firmly rooted in the Amhara social structure. In a sense, he is simply a product of this structure, which calls for a Leviathan who is the ultimate authority figure; and in any event, imperial rule could not long have been maintained over so large an area, with its primitive economy and communications, but for the powerful support which Amhara attitudes to authority provide. And since horizontal links are so weak, it is the Emperor who holds the state together. He is looked up to as the source of every benefit, and praised and flattered by the many means which exist for the purpose.

The Emperor has been surrounded by a strong semi-religious mystique, indicated by his position as the lieutenant of God on earth. His title *Seyumä Egzi'abhér*, or Elect of God, carries far more active implications than the purely permissory *Dei Gratia*, and Emperors have had an important part to play as defenders of the faith. The Church has transmitted legitimacy to the Emperor by anointment, and has generally upheld his authority, though in turn it has demanded his support. In the few cases where an Emperor has abandoned the Orthodox Church for Roman Catholicism, and once apparently Islam, he has been killed, deposed or forced to abdicate.

A second source of legitimacy has been the Solomonic legend, which not only raises Ethiopians to the status of children of Israel, but places the Emperor, as heir of Solomon, in a special relationship with the Almighty.[1] For five centuries after the 'Solomonic restoration', Emperors had to be descended in the male line from the dynasty then established. The succession was further guided by a rough and ready system of natural selection between genealogically qualified candidates, involving choice by the major notables at accession, and modification by palace revolts or provincial rebellions thereafter; for long periods in Ethiopian history, potential rivals to the throne have been confined on one of the barely accessible flat-topped mountains which provide distinctive landmarks in the northern highlands. The need for membership of the Solomonic line lapsed with the growing feebleness of eighteenth-century Emperors, and since 1855 has scarcely influenced the succession, though Emperors once made have been quick to maintain their connection with the dynasty; Haile-Selassie's descent from Solomon is asserted in the 1955 Constitution.

The Emperor has been the only person with the authority to rule over the whole of Ethiopia, and it has been unthinkable to place any formal restraint on his powers. In constitutional theory, at any rate, these have until modern times been absolute. They have included the claim that he is the owner of all the land in the Empire, and complete master of all its inhabitants.[2] The Emperor receives petitions and dispenses justice, issues decrees, makes and revokes appointments, grants titles, and directs all government affairs. But in practice, these great powers have constantly had to be made good by effective leadership, and enforced through military strength.

It follows equally from traditional attitudes that only the Emperor, at least in the central government, has been able to take major decisions. The Emperor's authority has been vested directly in his own person; it could neither be delegated nor shared. His personal initiative has therefore been needed for any innovation or improvement. This requirement is indicated by the chronicles of medieval emperors, but it has been especially marked in the modernising reigns of the last hundred years or so. Such imperial initiative was naturally essential for any reform of the system of government, and Haile-Selassie's monopolisation of the processes of change has been quite in keeping with the traditional powers of his office.

But the Emperor's effective powers have often been far less than his formal supremacy would lead one to suppose, and this wide and oft-noted divergence between his theoretical and his actual position was also implicit in the traditional bases of his rule. The religious backing for his authority was, as we have seen, balanced by the need for adherence to the Orthodox Church. The Amhara social hierarchy by which he was supported also helped to establish provincial rulers and dynasties, which tried to remain independent of the Crown and provided the most effective opposition to it. The very personal nature of the Emperor's power on the one hand placed him on a pinnacle of prestige, but on the other hand prevented the establishment of institutional administrative forms through which this power could be systematically exercised. The difficulties which this concept of authority places in the way of institutional development are constantly evident in the government of Haile-Selassie.

Emperors of Ethiopia have accordingly been remarkably free from limitations on their power by any surrounding group of great officers of state. Not only has the nature of their office cast those around it into the twilight, but provincial lords have tended to wield power by direct action in their home areas, rather than by influencing decisions at the centre. This has not prevented powerful lords from dominating the throne at times of imperial weakness, but it has prevented the growth of any powerful office other than that of the Emperor. Such offices as existed were simply extensions of the Emperor's own personal power. The *Tsähafé T'ezaz* (Writer of Orders) was responsible for transmitting imperial commands—an important function, especially when the

Emperor could only be approached with difficulty; to the *Afä Negus* (Breath of the King) were delegated some of his judicial powers; the *Ligaba* and a host of other officials dealt with the ceremonial of the court. But such posts were held by imperial nominees, rather than by individuals with independent political backing,[3] and they did not develop into established offices. Nor were collective responsibility or government by council in the least suited to Ethiopian methods, and one therefore looks in vain for any office or institution which could, on the English model, gradually take over the functions of the Emperor. Weak emperors have often been the victims of palace plots which help to ensure through a process of survival of the fittest that the man at the top retains the capacity for leadership which the system demands of him; but such plots have merely replaced the individuals in power without altering the basic structure of the government.

The Emperor's authority has therefore been challenged not so much at the centre as in the provinces. While a strong Emperor has been needed to hold the Empire together, considerable delegation has been needed to govern it; and so the centralising prestige of the Emperor has been balanced by the local strength of provincial governors, who themselves have benefited from the Amhara respect for authority figures and have tended, if given the chance, to establish themselves as petty kings in their own domains. These conflicting tendencies have resulted in a continuous struggle between successive Emperors and governors, with the former trying to turn the latter into obedient servants, the latter trying to assert their independence. Strong Emperors have been able to appoint their own nominees, with little regard for whether they came from the area which they were governing; but the nominees of a weak Emperor could not hold their own, and so men with some local standing in their governates had to be appointed. These notables have sometimes been so well established that installation by the Emperor was simply a formality.[4]

At the height of the medieval Empire, the Emperor held the initiative in this tussle with his governors, for in the early sixteenth century we find him in Shoa, granting and revoking appointments at will to an important governorship in distant Eritrea.[5] But soon afterwards, a series of political disasters toppled the imperial power into a three-hundred year decline. First, military defeat: from 1529, Moslem invasions under Ahmad Grañ (the left-handed) ravaged the plateau almost unchecked for twelve years, until in 1541 Grañ was killed and his forces dispersed, with the help of a small band of Portuguese sent to succour a fellow Christian kingdom. Next, population movements: the weakened Ethiopians were in no state to repel the tidal wave of Galla invasion which, starting in the mid-sixteenth century, flowed over much that had previously been Ethiopian territory, and pushed back the Ethiopian state to frontiers from which it only re-expanded in the nineteenth century. Then religious controversy: the Portuguese remained in Ethiopia after Grañ's defeat, and brought Jesuit missionaries who succeeded in converting two Emperors, and so produced civil wars which ended only with the Jesuits' expulsion in 1632. And finally, the establishment of a permanent capital at Gondar, just north of Lake Tana, in the middle of the seventeenth century; in the days of their greatness, Emperors had maintained their power from a tented capital, which moved from one province to another, policing and extending the frontiers and subduing rebellious vassals. Once the capital city was fixed, however, the Emperor's domain shrunk to the area surrounding it, and other provinces beyond his reach came under the control of local dynasties. From the mid-eighteenth century, Ethiopia was no more than a collection of independent principalities, and even in Gondar the Emperor became the puppet of a local warlord. For the next hundred years, no central Ethiopian government existed.

The Emergence of the Modern Empire, 1855–1907

By 1850, the disintegrated Empire had reached its lowest ebb. Yet within fifty years, a united Ethiopia was to defeat a European invasion and more than double its territory. This is the measure of the late nineteenth-century resurgence which laid the foundations of modern Ethiopia.

It began with the meteoric reign of the Emperor Téwodros (1855–1868). Téwodros had no genealogical claim to the throne. He started his career as a minor local chieftain, at times almost a bandit; but he fought his way up, gathering followers after each successful action, until he was strong enough to defeat each in turn of the great provincial lords, and so reach for the Crown. As Emperor, Téwodros was not content with the passive role of his immediate predecessors. He was driven by a burning vocation to unite his country, which he then hoped to lead, in true medieval fashion, in a crusade to liberate Jerusalem. He founded his policy of reunification on a growth in imperial power, coupled with a conscious appeal to memories of past glories and prophecies of future greatness, and so demonstrated the resilience of an imperial tradition which had long been in abeyance. But though the rise of Téwodros was thus in some ways a revival, he also tried to use his office to further ambitious plans for modernisation, striking that balance between tradition and innovation which has since characterised Ethiopian emperors.

The reign is, however, memorable more for its aspirations than for its achievements, for Téwodros lacked the resources needed to realise his plans. As he conquered each province, he replaced the local ruler by his own viceroy, but these were too weak to hold their own, and within a few years local dynasties reasserted themselves. Téwodros himself had no territorial base on which to build his army and administration, and by 1865 he retained control over only a sixth of what was then Ethiopia.[6] The frustration of his ambitions drove him close to madness, and he contributed to his own downfall as he first alienated the Church, and then imprisoned the British Consul and other foreigners at his court. A British expeditionary force, sent to rescue the captives, was helped in its march through Ethiopia by Téwodros' rivals, and in 1868 defeated his by then much diminished army. His subsequent suicide only put an end to a reign which was already in ruins.

The provincial rulers then fought one another for the throne, and the resulting power struggles ensured strong leadership during the rest of the nineteenth century. The eventual successor was Yohanes IV (1872–1889), the only Emperor in modern times to come from the northern province of Tegré. He was more realistic and less ambitious than Téwodros, and was willing to tolerate provincial dynasties so long as they recognised him as Emperor. In particular, he conceded considerable autonomy to Menilek, King of Shoa, who had himself claimed the imperial throne when Téwodros died; but within this federal framework the imperial power increased. It had need to, for Yohanes was faced by the first serious dangers to Ethiopian independence since the time of Ahmad Grañ. The Suez Canal was opened in 1869, transforming the Red Sea into an international waterway, and European powers made their appearance on its shores. The first attempts at conquest came from Egypt, and were repulsed by Yohanes in 1875 and 1876. A decade later, he found himself threatened both by the Mahdists in the Sudan, and by the Italians, who occupied Massawa on the Eritrean coast in 1885. He marched first against the Mahdists, and was killed in the resulting battle at Metemma in 1889.

With Yohanes dead, Menilek II (1889–1913) made good his claim to the throne. He was a capable ruler and a crafty diplomat, and as King of Shoa since 1865 he had long been aware of the importance of firearms. He imported them in huge numbers, both from the French in the Gulf of Tajura and from the Italians, who regarded him as an ally against Yohanes.[7] Shortly after his accession, indeed, Menilek signed a treaty with the Italians which they claimed (wrongly) gave them a protectorate over Ethiopia.[8] But when they tried to make good their claim, Menilek marched against them with an army superior both in numbers and in firepower, and in 1896 crushed them at the decisive battle of Adwa, which preserved Ethiopia's independence for a crucial forty years.

Ethiopia owes much to Menilek and his predecessors, for the country today is in large measure the product of that formative half-century.

First, Ethiopia remained independent, alone among the indigenous states of sub-Saharan Africa, and so developed as an African Empire, and not as the colony of a European power; when the Italians tried again, in 1935, their five-year occupation was too short to invalidate this independence. But the Italians did keep their colony of Eritrea, formed in 1890 from the Red Sea coast and the northernmost part of the highlands, with the result that Eritrea has been subjected to very different influences from the rest of Ethiopia, which it rejoined in 1952.

Second, Ethiopia was united more closely than ever before. The leading chieftains of every province fought by Menilek's side at Adwa, and the victory expressed a national unity which was achieved only just in time. Since Téwodros' accession, these local notables had gradually lost power, until by 1900 they had reached a point where, though influential in their home areas, they could no longer offer a direct and successful challenge to the Crown. This reunification was achieved by a succession of increasingly powerful Emperors, and in this way the strength and unity of modern Ethiopia has been built around the throne.

Third, the Empire was centred on the new Shoan capital at Addis Ababa, and it has since 1889 been dominated by the Amhara of Shoa. Twentieth-century Emperors have all so far been chosen in Addis Ababa, and have belonged to the Shoan royal house. Dynastic claimants are now limited to members of this dynasty, and possibly to the Tegrean descendants of Yohanes IV.

Fourth, Ethiopia expanded well beyond its original central highland core. This process began under Yohanes, but his concern with foreign threats and the respective positions of Shoa and Tegré meant that it was largely carried out, even then, from Shoa. So vigorously did Menilek and his generals campaign in the territories around them that Shoa, once the southernmost province of the country, is now at its centre; large populations of non-Amhara/Tegré peoples were added to the Empire, among whom the Gallas were the most numerous. The expansion made Ethiopia's frontiers, but for Eritrea, virtually what they are today, and was accompanied by an assumption of Amhara supremacy and a policy of Amharisation which still continue.

Fifth, Ethiopia started to adopt new instruments and techniques brought in from abroad, combining tenacity to her imperial traditions with a gradual modernisation. Firearms were the European invention most eagerly seized on, but Menilek also used foreign advisers, established a modern school in Addis Ababa, and authorised a railway to be built from the French port at Jibuti to his new capital.

But these developments, though immense, did not immediately bring with them any changes in government machinery. Téwodros and Yohanes ruled in traditional fashion through the imperial court, and not until late in his reign did Menilek feel it necessary to set up western-inspired administrative institutions through which to exercise his government's expanded tasks. While the foundations of the modern government are grounded in the nineteenth century, therefore, its formal framework is entirely a product of the twentieth.

The Rise of Haile-Selassie, 1907-1941

In August 1907, Menilek suffered a stroke, the first of a number which paralysed him for the closing years of his reign.[9] That October, he announced that a Council of Ministers was to be established, clearly hoping that it would offset his own deteriorating health.[10] Nine, later eleven, ministers were appointed, and given lists of functions for their ministries to carry out. To some extent, this was simply giving new titles to old officials: the *Afä Negus* became Minister of Justice, and the *Tsähafé T'ezaz*, Minister of the Pen. Other portfolios, like Foreign Affairs and Posts and Telegraphs, reflected increased contacts with the outside world. But their ministers, like the rest, performed their functions as personal servants of the Crown; one duty of the Minister of Posts and Telegraphs was to deliver telegrams to the Emperor.[11] In this way, the modern institutions of the central government have evolved directly from the imperial entourage.

Important men were appointed as ministers, but their installation marked a decline in the efficacy of the government. Not surprisingly, the embryo Council was in no condition to take over from the Emperor. The ministers split into competing factions and could not reach decisions, as usually happens in Ethiopia when the leader is out of action, and by 1909 Menilek was too ill to be of much account; he remained a helpless invalid until his death in 1913. After two years of confusion, Menilek's grandson Lej Iyasu became Regent, but he was then only fifteen, and acted under the tutelage of his father, the Galla King Mika'él of Wälo, and some of the Shoan lords. This brought little improvement, for the ministers were no more in agreement than before, and had to refer decisions to Lej Iyasu, who was seldom in Addis Ababa and showed little interest in affairs of state even when in the capital. Even if Iyasu was not the out-and-out villain which he is sometimes painted,[12] he had not the least capacity for administration, and it is surprising that five years without effective central government went by before his overthrow. It was only in September 1916, after his apparent conversion to Islam had alienated the Church and given new impetus to the opposition, that he was deposed by a group of Shoan noblemen and high Church officials in

Addis Ababa, with the support of the Italian, French and British legations.[13] The whole period from 1907 to 1916 emphasises the Ethiopian political system's complete dependence on effective leadership.

Under the new régime, Menilek's daughter Zäwditu became Empress; she was conservative by inclination, but concerned more with religion than with politics, and the key post of Regent and heir to the throne was given to Ras Täfäri, the son of Menilek's cousin Ras Makonnen, who was later to reign as Haile-Selassie. At this time he was about twenty-five, and to counteract his youth and modernising tendencies, he had to rule in concert with several elder statesmen. After the Wälo Galla supporters of Lej Iyasu had been defeated, and a few plots against Ras Täfäri foiled,[14] the country was run by an uneasy coalition of conservative and reforming forces, with two powerful figures, the Archbishop and the Minister of War, holding the balance between the two.[15] The modernising party was thus held in check, but the Regent did succeed in opening a new school, named after himself, and in securing Ethiopia's admission to the League of Nations. In 1918, Täfäri tried to free himself from the control of the more conservative ministers by having them banished to their provincial estates, an operation carried out under the guise of a popular petition to the Empress, but they were able to return and re-establish themselves when he was seriously ill later in the year.[16] Thereafter, there seems to have been little attempt by the major politicians to upset the balance of forces, and in 1924 Täfäri was secure enough to leave Ethiopia for a four-month tour of Europe.

This period of balance ended when the Archbishop and the Minister of War both died in 1926. Täfäri then took control of the army, and exiled the deputy head of the Church, who had been one of his most conservative opponents. Early in 1927, one foreign observer noted that 'the power of the Regent is steadily increasing',[17] and this consolidation of his position at the centre was completed in 1928, when his opponents attempted a *coup d'état*; in the wake of its failure, Täfäri was strong enough to demand the title of *Negus*, or King, and assume complete control over the central government. When Zäwditu died in April 1930, he succeeded her without difficulty as Haile-Selassie I.

The reign of Zäwditu contributed little to the growth of government institutions. The weakness of the monarch did not help officials to become more independent, as has sometimes happened elsewhere, since Ras Täfäri as Regent took the detailed administration into his own hands. His opponents, in so far as one can surmise from the obscure and ill-documented events of the reign, grouped themselves around the Empress, and tried to block the Regent through delays in the imperial assent; there are also fleeting references to various councils, which appear to have done little, except possibly as blocking agencies.[18] On his accession, therefore,

Haile-Selassie already controlled a central government which functioned in the traditional manner as an extension of the palace.

The first part of Haile-Selassie's reign lasted only half a dozen years, before the invasion by Mussolini's Italy in 1935, and the occupation which began the following year. But this truncated period forms a natural bridge between the Regency and the post-war government, and shows clearly the continuity of Haile-Selassie's half-century in power. As Emperor, he continued the cautiously modernising policies developed during the Regency, coupled with an extreme centralisation in himself which prevented the growth of effective institutions outside the palace compound. No Council of Ministers could do much when its members were all imperial nominees used to dealing directly with the throne, and their inability to act without Haile-Selassie was revealed when they were left in charge in Addis Ababa during his absence with the army at the front in 1936.[19] The ministries were similarly affected by the fact that no decisions could be taken in them, and only two seem to have been at all active:[20] the Ministry of Foreign Affairs drafted diplomatic notes for submission to the Emperor, and that of Commerce supervised customs dues, which were the main source of central government revenue.

As a result, government took place in the palace, and a politician's importance depended on the influence which he could exert there. During the Regency, Ras Täfäri's most trusted adviser had been Blatengéta Heruy Wäldä-Selassie, a churchman by training, who became Minister of Foreign Affairs in 1930. By then he was becoming old, and his influence diminished. The Emperor's closest confidants in the 1930s were mostly younger men, some of whom were to gain great power after the war; these included a palace secretary, Ato Wäldä-Giyorgis Wäldä-Yohanes, and Ato Makonnen Habtä-Wäld of the Ministry of Commerce.[21]

Within the largely traditional form of the pre-war government, there were some modernising departures. In July 1931, Haile-Selassie promulgated a written Constitution,* under which Ethiopia's first Parliament convened four months later, as yet with only advisory powers.† These innovations took root no more immediately than did Menilek's ministries, but they were useful at least in symbolising the Emperor's modernising intentions. Fresh ideas were introduced by the first generation of Ethiopian graduates, sent to foreign universities during the Regency, who joined the government on their return. By 1935, however, few of them had yet reached major posts, and of fifty-two senior central government officials in that year, only five had been educated abroad, with six more in diplomatic positions;[22] the only important politician among them was

* See Chapter 4.   † See Chapter 10.

Ato Lorénzo T'ezaz, an able and liberal-minded Eritrean who was to draft the Emperor's famous appeal to the League of Nations in 1936. Foreign advisers were also first systematically brought into the government in the pre-war period, though individual Europeans had helped earlier Emperors; they were attached to the ministries, without executive functions, and were largely employed on technicalities such as drafting legislation, and on contacts between the government and the foreign community.

In some fields, notably foreign affairs and military organisation, the urgency of impending war gave force to modernising proposals. But before the war, as after it, the Emperor was by no means prepared to give a free hand to the agents of change. He was quite willing to listen to the arguments presented by foreigners and Ethiopian graduates, but only rarely came down on their side in any controversy with an important traditionally-reared politician.[23] The frustrations of those trying to force a faster pace than he deemed desirable were certainly not confined to the post-war years, though he did seem, in the earlier period, to have a greater personal commitment to modernisation. The difference lay in that before the war Haile-Selassie was cautiously leading the process of change, whereas after it he was cautiously being led.

There was no such ambivalence in his attitude to the provincial lords. Central control had weakened with Menilek's decline, and many local rulers, especially in the north, tried to reassert their independence; they were helped by the virtual absence of a central government under Lej Iyasu, and by the divided control of the Regency. This trend was reversed once Ras Täfäri had established his supremacy in Addis Ababa, and made it his business to reduce the provinces to dependence on the centre. The first step was largely achieved between 1928 and 1932, with the replacement of the great lords who had governed provinces in their own right since before 1916. One by one they died, or else staked their fortunes on revolt and lost; and of the powerful chieftains of former days, only Däjazmach Ayalew Biru of Semén was still there at the Italian invasion. The others were replaced by imperial supporters, or by local noblemen allied by marriage with the imperial family. Haile-Selassie's reforming cousin, Ras Imru, was sent to Gojam, whose ruler Ras Haylu had tried and failed to restore Lej Iyasu in 1932. Tegré was governed by Ras Seyum, grandson of Yohanes IV, whose daughter was married to the Crown Prince. And in Shoa, the Emperor had the constant support of Ras Kasa, a senior member of the royal line who in 1916 had waived his claims to the throne in Ras Täfäri's favour, and who retained the confidence of conservatives to an extent which the reforming Emperor never achieved.

When the war came in the autumn of 1935, then, Haile-Selassie led a united Ethiopia against the invaders, and only one major nobleman, the

Tegrean Haile-Selassie Gugsa, deserted to the Italians. But this unity was not enough. The Ethiopians were overwhelmed by the Italians' vastly superior weapons, and in May 1936 the Emperor went into exile with a small band of followers. The ensuing occupation is the only period of recorded Ethiopian history for which the country's independence has been lost, and several members of the former government worked for the Italian régime. But the government in exile and a strong resistance movement sustained the continuity of the Ethiopian state, and the eventual liberation therefore led to a restoration, very different from the successor states to colonial rule elsewhere in Africa.

The Occupation did not long survive Italy's entry into the Second World War in December 1940. A British expeditionary force, aided by the Ethiopian resistance, liberated the country in an astonishingly short time, and in May 1941 Haile-Selassie re-entered his capital.

So far as the central government is concerned, the effects of the Occupation were essentially indirect. There was no transition from one régime to the next, and virtually nothing in the field of administrative organisation which the restored imperial government of 1941 took over from its predecessor. The effects of the Occupation are therefore to be looked for in the changed conditions under which the Emperor and his government had to work.

Haile-Selassie re-established himself remarkably quickly in 1941, though he needed his considerable political gifts in order to do so, and so the Occupation in no way weakened his supremacy in the central government. Most important for the maintenance of continuity was the fact that not only the Emperor himself, but also many of the most influential members of his entourage, were the same as before the war. On the side of change, a fresh start was made possible by the clean break with the earlier period and the presence of British advisers for a few years immediately after 1941, and the administrative machinery was completely overhauled. An official gazette, the *Negarit Gazeta*, was published, and replaced the rather rough and ready pre-war system for promulgating legislation. The Ministers (Definition of Powers) Order of 1943 formally established the Council of Ministers, and determined the fields of competence of the various ministries. The financial system was reformed, and the structure at least of a standardised method of accounting and tax-collecting provided. The effect of these changes was, however, far greater on the administration's formal structure than on its actual working.

It is often asserted that the Italians systematically liquidated educated Ethiopians, so that there were practically none to help run the government in 1941.[24] This charge needs to be examined carefully. The available figures are therefore given in the accompanying table, with corresponding information for senior government officials and soldiers. The totals for graduates are incomplete, but they do show that reports of wholesale massacre of the educated are greatly exaggerated. This impression is confirmed by the figures for senior officials, which are almost complete.[25]

Table 1

The fate of Ethiopians educated abroad and of Senior Government Officials during the Italian Occupation

	Gradu- ates	Diplo- mats	Central Govt.	Army	Gover- nors
Died before 1941	22	1	2	1	8
Killed in action	9	–	5	5	10
Liquidated	19	–	1	–	2
Post-war Officials	55	4	21	3	14
Other survivors	76	8	15	2	11
Unknown	67	–	4	2	7
Totals	248	13	48	13	52

On the other hand, no Ethiopians received advanced education during the Occupation, except for a few in exile abroad, and this had a far greater effect than the massacres on the number of educated officials. This gap in education and recruitment to the government led to a division between pre-war and post-war generations, which is considered in a later chapter. Nor did Ethiopians acquire much practical experience of government under the Italians. They were mostly employed in very junior posts, and though several collaborators joined the government after the war, they lacked any great independence or idealism, and were unable to take much initiative in introducing European administrative efficiency.

Overall, the effects of the Occupation on the central government seem to have been surprisingly slight. The Emperor continued, more or less, where he had left off in 1936, with the same personal supremacy, very similar gradually modernising policies, and much the same group of officials; we have noted some changes as being due to the Occupation or the conditions of the Liberation, but these do not amount to very much more than would probably have taken place anyhow had Haile-Selassie remained in power between 1936 and 1941.

Its effects on the nobility and the provincial government were much greater. Several powerful noblemen were killed in the war, and more died in the resistance, including the three elder sons of Ras Kasa. Others so compromised themselves by collaboration with the Italians that at the Liberation they could safely be excluded from the government. Provincial leaders were the main losers from the centralised Italian administration which, imposed by force and backed by a new network of Italian-built roads, was able to destroy far more of their autonomy than would have been possible for an indigenous ruler.

When Haile-Selassie returned to Ethiopia, his position was therefore in many ways stronger than when he had left, and he consolidated his advantage by changes which cut at the roots of the nobility's administrative control over the provinces. Its military functions were removed by training a professional army, under the Emperor's command, which replaced the feudal levies and private armies of pre-war days; its power to raise tribute was severely reduced by creating a centralised system of taxation administered by the Ministry of Finance; and the old provincial boundaries were systematised into a hierarchy of province, sub-province, district and sub-district, which was controlled from Addis Ababa, and to which appointments were made directly by the Emperor. Noblemen who might have given trouble if left in their home areas were brought to Addis Ababa, and many of them were given unimportant posts in Parliament and elsewhere. Haile-Selassie has thus been able to control the nobility and provincial government far more effectively than he could before 1936.

The Supremacy of Haile-Selassie, 1941-1968

Haile-Selassie immediately set about rebuilding his administration, and he appointed his first ministers within a week of returning to Addis Ababa. In the next year or two, the army was built up, Parliament was recalled, and a spate of legislation issued to regulate the central government, the provincial administration, the Church and the financial system. Another urgent task was to settle the position of the British in Ethiopia, for the British Army had liberated the country, and some of its commanders regarded Ethiopia as occupied enemy territory. Their status was defined by an agreement in January 1942, which recognised Ethiopian independence under the Emperor, but gave the British a favoured position *vis-à-vis* other foreigners. British advisers accordingly remained, both to help re-establish the government and because of Ethiopia's strategic situation beside the Red Sea supply route to the army in North Africa. The Ethiopians resented this special status as a slight on their country's independence, and it was given up by a second agreement in 1944.

Throughout the 1940s, Haile-Selassie was chiefly concerned with consolidating his own centralised power. He extended his hold on the provinces by the means already described, and crushed revolts in Gojam and Tegré, though he needed help from the British Royal Air Force to put down the Tegrean uprising of 1943. Several palace plots were uncovered in Addis Ababa, the most dangerous of which were attempts to depose Haile-Selassie in 1947 and to assassinate him in 1951. The leaders of the wartime resistance were closely involved in these, and since they commanded both high prestige and independent military power, they had to be especially closely watched. One of them, Ras Abäbä Arägay (1), became Minister of War and later Interior, but most of the others received only minor posts. Content with extending his personal power, Haile-Selassie did not further antagonise conservatives by any hasty modernisation, and the eight years or so after 1943 were the most uneventful of his reign. In that time, virtually no new officials entered the government, owing to the lack of education during the occupation and the Second World War, and so there was none of the impetus which fresh blood could have provided.

Although a Prime Ministry and a Council of Ministers had been set up in 1943, the dominating institution of the period was the Ministry of the Pen, direct successor of the ancient office of *Tsähafé T'ezaz*, which sent out the Emperor's orders. It was so close to the Emperor that its operations were often quite indistinguishable from his own, and it therefore formed a suitable focus for the process of centralisation. Its Minister, Ato Wäldä-Giyorgis Wäldä-Yohanes (33), was the outstanding figure of the time, and probably the most powerful politician in Ethiopia since the Liberation. Not least among the Emperor's achievements was the way in which he caused the resentment both of the nobility and of frustrated reformers to be directed against Wäldä-Giyorgis rather than himself, thus remaining detached from policies for which he was essentially responsible. Other key offices were also held by the Emperor's *protégés*, including Makonnen Habtä-Wäld (19) at his pre-war post in the Ministry of Commerce and later Finance, and the Galla General Mulugéta Buli (26) in command of the Imperial Bodyguard. The Shoan noblemen, among whom the Emperor's cousin Ras Kasa (13) was still the outstanding figure, were loosely opposed to them.

The early 1950s brought changed political conditions. In 1952, Eritrea was federated with Ethiopia. This former Italian colony had been under provisional British administration since 1941, pending disposal by the

United Nations, and Ethiopia made vociferous claims to it. Much of Eritrea had before 1890 belonged to the Ethiopian Empire, but after sixty years as a colony it was more strongly affected by foreign influences than other parts of Ethiopia, and the Ethiopians had to make good their claims to be able to govern it; since the Federation, Eritrea has had a consistently modernising influence on the rest of the country, for example over constitutional reform in 1955 and the legalisation of trades unions. By the terms of the Federal Act which defined the union, the central Ethiopian government dealt with foreign affairs, defence and trade, while residual powers over local affairs were vested in an elected Eritrean Government in Asmara. The Ethiopians never regarded the Federation as more than a stopgap, and they worked steadily to undermine the Eritrean Government; in 1962 they achieved their aim of completely absorbing Eritrea into the centralised administrative system which applied to the rest of the Empire. Many Eritreans resented this treatment, and a separatist movement, the Eritrean Liberation Front, has been especially active in the Moslem lowland parts of the province which have fewest links with the central government.

The Federation coincided with other events which helped to end Ethiopia's isolation. In 1951 the University College of Addis Ababa was founded, and at about the same time the first batch of post-war Ethiopian graduates returned from abroad and took posts in the government. These graduates have been the moving force behind most of the political changes in Ethiopia since 1950, forming a loose pressure group for modernisation and furnishing the techniques needed to run the government along lines which had earlier been impossible. Increased contacts with abroad followed the despatch of an Ethiopian contingent to Korea in 1951 and the Emperor's state visits to Europe and the United States in 1954, and about this time the American presence in Ethiopia also started to grow.

Conditions were therefore ripe for political changes. A Revised Constitution was promulgated at the Emperor's Silver Jubilee in 1955, and the first popular parliamentary elections followed in accordance with it two years later. New legal codes, initiated in 1954, were issued in 1957 and 1960. A Five Year Plan for economic development was started in 1957. But these developments were designed more to give a reforming face to the régime than to change its actual working, and the dismissal in 1955 of Wäldä-Giyorgis (33) had a greater immediate effect. His centralising functions had been carried out, and different methods would be needed to meet the new challenge from the modernising sector of Ethiopian society. The imperial secretariat consequently declined, but no alternative agency, apart from the Emperor himself, developed to exercise the co-ordinating powers previously wielded by the Minister of the Pen. As a result, the period from 1955 to 1960 was the most unstable in Ethiopian government since the war. There was no single dominating politician, as Wäldä-Giyorgis had been, and the Emperor held an uneasy balance between several major politicians. These included Makonnen Habtä-Wäld (19) at the Ministry of Finance, Ras Abäbä Arägay (1) as Minister of Defence, and the Emperor's son-in-law Ras Andargé (4), who was for some time Minister of the Interior. They fenced for power both among themselves and with two influential soldiers, Mulugéta Buli (26) who had left the Bodyguard to become Chief of Staff, and Colonel Wärqenah Gäbäyähu (34) of the Emperor's personal security service. The ups and downs of competing cliques and individuals were reflected in constant government reshuffles, in which each group tried to manœuvre its men into the most important offices.

But there was as yet little place in the government for the newly returned graduates. They succeeded better than traditional groups like the nobility in staying independent of the Emperor, but they could neither exert much influence on the political system nor, for the most part, adapt themselves to it. The most powerful politicians were still men without western education, and would-be modernisers found themselves lost in a world of dubious intrigues, where initiatives were discouraged and attempts at reform were blocked.

Their frustrations were partly responsible for the Imperial Bodyguard revolt of December 1960, though chance and personal factors also came into it. While Haile-Selassie was away on a state visit to Brazil, the Bodyguard seized most of Addis Ababa and proclaimed a new régime under Crown Prince Asfa-Wäsän, the Emperor's eldest son, with the liberal Ras Imru (12) as Prime Minister. The *coup* was led by General Mängestu Neway, Commander of the Bodyguard, and master-minded by his radical graduate brother Germamé; they were joined by the chiefs of police and security, and made a policy proclamation which concentrated on economic development, though the privileges of the armed forces were also mentioned.[26] But the revolt lasted for only a few days; several loyalist leaders were left at large, including the commanders of the army—a force quite separate from the Imperial Bodyguard—which declared for Haile-Selassie and crushed the rebels in a short battle. Haile-Selassie returned to a tumultuous welcome.

The attempt illustrates both the foundations and the failures of the imperial régime. The government had not only failed to meet pressures for change, but had also had no idea, until the revolt, of their strength and urgency. On the other side, the abiding power of traditional sources of legitimacy showed through at several points: the rebels themselves appealed to traditional authority figures like Ras Imru and the Crown Prince, and, most strikingly, they completely avoided any direct attack on Haile-Selassie; the loyalists circulated a leaflet denouncing the rebels which was signed by the Patriarch and seems to have had a powerful influence; and even in Addis Ababa, the rebels received little support except from automatic radicals such as the university students. Cynical observers note the success of Haile-Selassie's divide-and-rule political techniques, and the way in which many politicians, both young graduates and conservative officials, refrained from committing themselves to either side until the outcome was clear.

The revolt gave a short and violent jolt to the even uneventfulness of Ethiopian politics, and left a drastically changed situation in its wake. The rebels had held hostage as many of the ministers as they could lay their hands on, and turned a machine-gun on them in the closing minutes of the fighting. Ras Abäbä (1), Makonnen Habtä-Wäld (19) and Mulugéta Buli (26) all died in the massacre; so did Ras Seyum (28), the old lord of Tegré. Colonel Wärqenäh Gäbäyähu (34) declared for the rebels, and committed suicide when the battle was lost, emulating his hero the Emperor Téwodros. In the unsettled vacuum which followed, Ras Kasa's son Asratä (6) and other conservatives urged repressive measures against suspects and others who had acquiesced in the revolt; it is to Haile-Selassie's credit that he strove instead to maintain a consensus with reformers, through a policy of increased though still gradual modernisation. The government was reconstructed under the premiership of Aklilu Habtä-Wäld (3), francophile brother of Makonnen, who had been Minister of Foreign Affairs almost continuously since 1943 and deputy Prime Minister since 1957. Several of the younger graduates were given portfolios, though the more active among them left the government within a year or two, and the Emperor made a speech urging ministers to take decisions themselves, rather than bring them to the palace.

In March 1961, the armed forces showed their increased political strength by enforcing demands for higher pay on a reluctant Emperor and civil government, and they did so again in September 1964. Political public opinion in Addis Ababa is another legacy of the attempted *coup d'état*, and it has been fostered by the greatly increased contacts with the outside world which have followed Ethiopia's entry into African politics, and Addis Ababa's growing importance as an international centre.

As the government weathered the aftermath of the revolt, much of its old inertia returned and many plans for reform were shelved; a series of committees had been set up in 1961 to suggest changes in the constitution, the judiciary, land tenure and other subjects, but little has yet been done to implement their reports. Yet unobtrusive pressures in the 1960s have led to corresponding gradual changes. By 1968, university graduates have come to occupy most major government offices, and the rise of younger men to responsible posts has improved the administration and relieved some of the earlier tensions. The elected Chamber of Deputies, and sometimes even the appointed Senate, have become increasingly willing to criticise the government, and the personal rivalries which divided politicians before 1960 have declined. The Emperor has slowly withdrawn from many day-to-day administrative matters, and has become increasingly concerned with foreign affairs. These changes have enabled Aklilu Habtä-Wäld (3) to systematise the administration around the Prime Minister's Office. He has been a conciliator, neither forceful nor ambitious, but he has presided over a gradual and still very incomplete institutionalisation of government. This was marked in March 1966 by the delegation to the Prime Minister of the power to choose other ministers and vice-ministers, who until then had been appointed directly by the Emperor; the Prime Minister's first Cabinet, consisting mostly of existing ministers, was installed a few weeks later.

Looked at in this way, Ethiopia has certainly changed a good deal since 1941, and later chapters will detail these changes in terms of the men and institutions which make up the government. But all the same, one comes away with the impression not so much of development as of stagnation: despite changes, the *ancien régime* is still basically with us; and the various reforms have not yet got down to essentials. The new conditions which will presumably follow Haile-Selassie's death, and which are now rather apprehensively awaited, will no doubt prove to have been latent in the present situation, and will call on existing developments in the economy, the political structure and, perhaps most of all, the armed forces. But the abiding impression is still not so much of a stage in a continuing process of development, as of an era slowly reaching its end.

Table 2

Ethiopian Political Chronology, 1941–1968

5	May	1941	Liberation: Haile-Selassie enters Addis Ababa
10	May	1941	First list of ministerial appointments
31	Jan	1942	First Anglo-Ethiopian Agreement
30	Mar	1942	First issue of *Negarit Gazeta*, the official gazette
27	Aug	1942	Slavery (Abolition) Proclamation
2	Nov	1942	Re-opening of Parliament
30	Nov	1942	Regulations for the Administration of the Church
29	Jan	1943	Council of Ministers formally established
	Sep	1943	Revolt in Tegré
30	Sep	1943	Prime Minister's Office established
19	Dec	1944	Second Anglo-Ethiopian Agreement
2	Dec	1950	U.N. Resolution to federate Eritrea with Ethiopia
27	Feb	1951	University College of Addis Ababa inaugurated
5	Jul	1951	Plot to assassinate the Emperor discovered
9	Oct	1951	First post-war graduate appointed to the government
16	Sep	1952	Federation of Eritrea with Ethiopia
26	Mar	1954	Codification Commission established
19	May	1954	Start of the Emperor's first foreign tour
25	Apr	1955	Wäldä-Giyorgis dismissed as Minister of the Pen
4	Nov	1955	Revised Constitution promulgated
14	Nov	1956	Death of Ras Kasa
12	May	1957	Death of Duke of Harar, the Emperor's second son
23	Jul	1957	New Penal Code promulgated
2	Nov	1957	Opening of the first popularly elected Parliament
		1957	Start of the First Five Year Plan
	Dec	1959	The Emperor's Private Cabinet established
5	May	1960	New Civil, Commercial and Maritime Codes promulgated
	June	1960	Independence of Somalia
14	Dec	1960	Start of the attempted *coup d'état*
17	Dec	1960	Failure of the revolt; Haile-Selassie returns
23	Mar	1961	Successful army demand for higher pay
14	Apr	1961	Emperor's speech on ministerial responsibility
11	Oct	1962	Second Five Year Plan promulgated
14	Nov	1962	Complete integration of Eritrea into Ethiopia
22	May	1963	African summit conference opens in Addis Ababa
27	Jun	1964	Parliament rejects proposed loan from Italy
4	Sep	1964	Successful army demand for higher pay
22	Mar	1966	Prime Minister empowered to select other ministers
11	Apr	1966	Prime Minister's Cabinet installed
	Nov	1966	Leaders of Galla political movement arrested
	Jan	1967	Emperor in Eritrea to combat separatism

Chapter 3
The Imperial System

A Palace Government at Work

Haile-Selassie rules from the palace, and there is no better place to watch his government at work than the old red-roofed palace of Menilek, which stands as a living monument to the continuity of imperial rule. Here Menilek pitched his camp when he founded Addis Ababa, and here Haile-Selassie still works, though he lives in the Jubilee Palace a few hundred yards away.* It is built on a little hill overlooking much of the city, and is ringed with successive gates and compounds after the manner of Ethiopian palaces and encampments down the centuries.[1] The first gate, at the bottom of the hill, is open for anyone to go through, and beyond it is the outer circle of the palace, with a few of the minor offices. Further up, the hill gets steeper and the gates harder to pass, and at the top stands the cluster of shady, dignified buildings of sixty years ago, each with its allotted function. The Emperor's office looks out north towards the Parliament house, with a tall flagpole in front of it; just below is the imperial Chelot, the personal court where the Emperor stands in judgement, in the Solomonic style, at twelve noon sharp each day. The Ministry of the Pen, the long-influential agency of the imperial secretariat, is close beside the Emperor's office. Behind are the Council of Ministers chambers and the Crown Council building, once the private quarters of the Empress Zäwditu, where Haile-Selassie receives petitioners and the Crown Prince has his office. Beyond them, on the other side of the hill, lie the ceremonial buildings, the Throne Room which is used for state occasions, and the Banqueting Hall in which Lej Iyasu was deposed. And on the very summit is the delightful colonnaded *unkulal bét*,† from which the watchful Menilek, a telescope to his eye, surveyed the daily doings of the city below. Thus the central agencies of government are gathered round the throne,

---

* For much of his reign, Haile-Selassie lived and worked at the Gänät Le'ul Palace, now the university, which he left after the massacre of hostages there in December 1960; he then returned to the Menilek Palace, or Grand Palace as it is officially called, which had been the seat of government under Menilek, Iyasu and Zäwditu. The Jubilee Palace was built to commemorate Haile-Selassie's Silver Jubilee in 1955.
† Literally 'egg house', so called because of its shape.

and only in the last few years have the Prime Minister's Office and the Supreme Court moved out of the palace compound to their own quarters elsewhere.

The place is deserted when the Emperor is away; one can walk all round it, and meet no one but some minor functionaries and a few officious guards. But when he is there, the bottom of the hill glitters with parked cars cooking in the sun; even the outer compound is packed with petitioners, and favoured individuals ascending to the higher level. When Haile-Selassie is abroad on one of his many state visits, the administration is still carried on in ministerial offices, and the Prime Minister and the Crown Prince co-ordinate day-to-day affairs; but the vitality is missing, for only the Emperor is in a position to supply it.

From time to time, the crowds at the palace gate clear a way for some high official, sweeping up to see His Imperial Majesty, or coming down again with his business done or put off until another day. It is worth watching to see who these visitors are, for these are the men who, together with the Emperor, compose the Ethiopian polity. Some of them are simply personal servants, like Ato Täfärä-Wärq Kidanä-Wäld (31), Minister of the Palace, whose plump deferential features are usually to be seen close beside the imperial throne. Others are favoured *protégés* who 'have the Emperor's ear', or simply departmental ministers who have come to clear decisions or explain some project to the Emperor—every politician has to be there at some time or other, for they all owe their places to Haile-Selassie's favour, and there is none whom he could not dispense with if he chose. Most of the ministers have little if any political standing of their own, and such authority as they possess is derived from the Crown. Even the Prime Minister, Aklilu Habtä-Wäld (3), is an imperial chief of staff rather than an executive leader, and he is at the palace for an hour or two most mornings.

Yet some officials do partially embody the various traditional and modernising elements which are represented in the present Ethiopian state. Despite intensive centralisation, noblemen are still needed in certain posts for the status and authority which they retain. Among these are Ras Asratä (6) and Ras Mängäsha (21), powerful governors of the northern provinces of Eritrea and Tegré; they are the only surviving sons of Ras Kasa (13) and Ras Seyum (28) respectively, and Mängäsha also commands deference as the chief of the Tegreans and great-grandson of the Emperor Yohanes. Other visitors to the palace also have provincial connections, like Ato Yelma Derésa (35), the astute Wäläga Galla who is Minister of Finance, and several Eritreans, though most politicians come from Shoa. Ato Kätäma Yefru (14), Minister of Foreign Affairs, is at present the main spokesman among ministers for the new graduate élite.

The political pressures which are thus brought into the government work through elusive personal connections and through tendencies for individuals to collaborate or think along similar lines; and each division cuts across others. Connections do not harden into organised parties, and indeed there are no political parties in Ethiopia, not even a single governmental one. In their absence, the integrating and co-ordinating functions which parties usually perform in other countries are carried out instead through the palace. Three main elements can be distinguished in the resulting interplay of forces: the Emperor's attempts to reduce everything to his control; the centrifugal pull exerted by other partly independent sources of authority; and the steady influence of development—as the Emperor and his associates grow older, new men come into the government, and the administration expands.

Haile-Selassie has adapted the traditional political system to his purpose by emphasising those aspects of it which favoured the imperial power, while eroding other forces which made the traditional government, for all its theoretical insistence on imperial supremacy, one of balance between powers. His unique position, and the Amhara respect for authority figures, have helped him to establish himself as sole arbiter between competing factions and individuals in the government, so that each depends on him, and comes to him both to obtain his authority for decisions, and to report on rivals. He alone has remained above the factions, leaning now to one side and now to another, so that none is so placed as to challenge his authority. Noblemen have thus been played off against self-made men, former resistance fighters against former collaborators, Shoans against Eritreans, and so on. In each case, he has used a central group more dependent on him—the commoners, the collaborators, the Shoans—as an instrument for taming factions which have some authority of their own.

There are many examples of the way in which this process works. The two main military forces in the country, the Army and the Imperial Bodyguard, have been kept completely separate, and their leaders have often been chosen from men at odds with one another—the 1960 revolt, when the two forces took opposing sides, shows the usefulness of this device. Rivalries between individuals have been encouraged by letting junior officials report directly to the Emperor over their superiors' heads, or by placing former friends in positions where competition between them is inevitable. Thus between 1962 and 1966 Kätäma Yefru (14) as acting Minister of Foreign Affairs was almost bound to clash with his former *protégé* Dr Menasé Haylé (24), whom the Emperor made his personal adviser on the subject. Independent officials, like independent groups, have been subordinated to the Emperor, sometimes by being offered temptations of power or money, acceptance of which may force them into

30

subservience. One notable example here was Ras Abäbä Arägay (1), who had gained great independent stature as a resistance leader during the occupation, and who after the war was involved, as Minister of Defence, in questionable arms deals.[2]

This system has strengthened the traditional tendency to look up to the throne, and has hampered the growth of institutional government by obliging officials to take a great many decisions to the Emperor. Officials taking personal initiatives have been demoted or reshuffled, though like many of the Emperor's methods this is a traditional stratagem, long known as *shum-shir*. Nor has the imperial office itself been formalised, and Haile-Selassie prefers to grant requests as special favours to particular individuals, rather than simply let his approval subside into administrative routine.

It is often suggested that decisions are taken to the Emperor because officials are unwilling to accept the responsibility which he tries to force upon them. As he himself has said:[3]

Our Ministers came to Us with their problems and questions. Always We said: 'But the power has been given to you to do this yourself.' Frequently, Our words went unheeded. Responsibility was shirked, decisions were avoided and thrust back upon Us.

But while decisions have indeed been avoided and thrust back upon the Emperor, he has to a large extent been responsible for this state of affairs himself. He has not often chosen as ministers men who would take responsibility; nor has he left them, once chosen, to get on with their work, but has always been ready to intervene in the running of a ministry. In particular, he has not been prepared to let ministers put into effect decisions with which he disagrees, and he has encouraged rather than penalised those who brought decisions to him. Any ministerial initiative, to be effective, needs the Emperor's approval; he cannot be circumvented and he certainly cannot be defied. Officials have therefore risked nothing by taking decisions to the Emperor, and much by taking them themselves, and even should the Emperor have wished to delegate authority, he has acted in a way which has prevented it.

The balance between centralising Emperor and semi-independent groups is clearly seen in the position of certain officials torn between their subordination to the Emperor and their advocacy of particular interests. If they come too close to the Emperor, they may be compromised in the eyes of the interests which they support; if they remain too independent, they lose influence with the Emperor, and may lose their posts. At times, the effect of this two-way pull is to reduce groups increasingly to imperial supervision, and Haile-Selassie has been especially successful with traditionally based groups such as the nobility. He has also largely controlled the pre-war generation of foreign-educated Ethiopians. The post-war graduates have been notably more independent, and one who subordinates himself to the Emperor enough to take an important part in government may find himself repudiated by his contemporaries. Few of this generation in high office have retained untarnished reputations among graduates outside government; Kätäma Yefru (14) has succeeded best because, as Minister of Foreign Affairs, he has avoided entanglement in domestic controversies.

But if the Emperor influences the groups, they also influence him, for he can only keep them under his authority if he can maintain a consensus by granting something to each. The process works both ways, and decisions tend to resolve themselves into competitions between factions to win the support of the Emperor and a consensus within the government. This is true both of individual policy decisions and of the often more important struggles over appointments to high office. The strength of groups is reflected both in policies and in appointments. As the nobility has declined in power, so has the number of noblemen in the government; and as the influence of modernising groups has increased, their members have been brought into the government, and some reforms have been granted in order to retain their support or acquiescence.

In this way, developments in political pressures have been reflected in the government, and the equilibrium of the political system has been maintained. But the imperial system is very far from being a simple transformer of social interests into government action. First, the government structure itself is an active element in the political process, for different interests are selected, combined and subordinated so as to preserve the existing political framework and the imperial supremacy on which it rests. Second, the representation of interests in the government is personal, uneven and at times ineffective. It is at this point that the absence of a party system is most clearly felt. Interests are incorporated in the government by individual politicians, like those mentioned above. But such politicians only 'represent' interests in a very attenuated sense. A minister who comes from a particular region, for example, is not chosen by that region; he has no local political organisation there, indeed he may never even go there, or try to provide the area with government benefits. In the absence of parties, it is hard for him to establish a political power base, or to forge links between the government and outside forces. A minister must look first to the throne, and only second, if at all, to some other interest which he embodies. And since the Emperor effectively sets the point of balance between interests, he can (and does) favour those which are most amenable. As a result, it is very easy for important elements to be excluded from the political process; such exclusion was partly responsible for the attempted *coup d'état* in 1960.

Based on the palace and lacking direct institutional links with outside pressures, the government takes on an almost domestic atmosphere. It is carried on through a criss-cross of personal connections within a fairly self-contained élite, many of whose members are related to one another.* Politicians are very little known outside the government, for only very rarely does one take a stand on any controversial issue; instead, he is far more likely to work, behind a smokescreen of contradictory rumours, through subsurface discussions with the Emperor or other politicians. The domestic atmosphere is emphasised by the smallness of the political society which maintains the government and provides its major officials, though this is true of almost any developing country. Then again, members of the upper élite are constantly meeting one another at the palace and elsewhere, and they have often been working together for twenty-five years and more; they therefore usually know one another very well, and can work in personal terms which would be impossible in a larger system. Beyond this, the ever-presence of the palace as both a political and a social focus gives a certain homogeneity even to political factions which are at daggers drawn with one another, and brings them together in common dependence on the throne.

Developments in the political system have to adapt themselves to this dependence. Although the Prime Minister has been given the power to choose his own ministers, for example, the effect of this delegation is in practice greatly weakened by his lack of any platform or power base separate from the Emperor. The Council of Ministers has to take account of the fact that each of its members has individual access to the throne. The financial machinery has developed between the conflicting pressures of administrative efficiency and imperial control. Since 1957, the Chamber of Deputies has been popularly elected, and it has come to represent provincial opinion far more clearly than any distribution of ethnic groups within the executive government; but it is balanced by a second chamber still directly appointed by the Emperor, and it has been kept separate from the executive by the need to avoid open conflict between electoral and imperial sources of authority. The role of the palace is the key to the 'two steps forward, one step back' which characterise political development under Haile-Selassie.

* See the chart of family connections facing page 211.

Chapter 4
The Constitutional Framework

The Constitution of 1931[1]

The first written Constitution of Ethiopia was promulgated by Haile-Selassie in July 1931, fifteen months after his accession. It stayed in effect without amendment for twenty-four years, and was replaced by the Revised Constitution which is still in force, at the Emperor's Silver Jubilee in 1955. These Constitutions deserve attention not only because they furnish the formal basis for government during our period, but also because they illustrate both theoretical and practical problems of integrating the traditional political system with the needs of modernisation and the centralising policies of the Emperor.

The Constitution of 1931 was one of a number of modernising initiatives taken by Haile-Selassie on ascending the throne, and one of its purposes was undoubtedly to emphasise, both at home and abroad, the reputation which he had built up during the Regency as an enlightened and reforming ruler. At the same time, it was thought desirable to provide a formal framework both for the consolidation of imperial power, and for the increasingly complex machinery of government which was then being developed. There was no sign of any popular pressure for such a document, and by many of the more traditionally minded figures, especially in the nobility, it was opposed rather than supported; there is thus no reason to doubt the claim, endlessly reiterated by Ethiopian writers, that the Emperor granted the Constitution 'unasked and of His own free will', though it must in fairness be remembered that its chief immediate beneficiary was the Emperor himself.

This Constitution was largely drafted by the foreign-educated Minister of Finance, Bäjerond Täklä-Hawariyat. His version of the affair is that he urged the Emperor to grant a Constitution, and was thereupon ordered to write it himself, and did so with the aid of copies of other constitutions provided by foreign legations in Addis Ababa.[2] This would explain the considerable borrowing from the Imperial Japanese Constitution of 1889, since of all the countries then represented in Addis Ababa, Japan, as a modernising Empire, was by far the closest in political position to

Ethiopia. There are nevertheless many changes from the Japanese, the general tendency which is to simplify the document and increase the Emperor's powers. The draft was submitted to the major noblemen of the country, and was promulgated only after they had discussed and approved it. It is noteworthy that the nobility was brought into the constitution-making process, to add weight to the Constitution and help secure its acceptance in areas where it retained great influence; but the noblemen were unable to alter those parts of it which limited their own powers.

At the same time, Täklä-Hawariyat prepared a law expanding and implementing parts of the Constitution. In particular, this contained the Law of the Imperial House referred to in the Constitution; it gave further powers to Parliament, and it granted a few minor privileges to the great lords which may well have been exacted by them as the price of their support. It was not published at the time, and its legal status is obscure.[3]

The Constitution of 1931 was, first and foremost, an instrument for securing national unity under the centralised rule of the Emperor, reflecting the traditional principle of imperial supremacy without the limitations which in practice modified it. This central principle was constantly emphasised both in the Constitution itself, and in the speeches which accompanied its promulgation. The Emperor received the entire executive power over both central and provincial government, and powers amounting to control of both the legislature and the judiciary; certain popular rights were recognised by the Emperor, but could be disregarded by him in emergencies. In this, the Constitution reflected the centralising policies of the period, and provided the formal basis for a process of centralisation which was necessary both for national unity and for effective modernisation.

Second, the Constitution was an instrument of modernisation, and here also it followed the tendencies of the time by adopting a cautious and gradualist approach. A two-chamber Parliament was founded, and was given the power to discuss laws, except those on subjects including government organisation, the armed forces and foreign affairs, which were reserved to the Emperor; the Senate was appointed directly by the Emperor, and the Chamber of Deputies was elected by local notables. The rights which were recognised, subject to limitation by law and the Emperor's emergency powers, included freedom from illegal arrest, imprisonment and expropriation, and from searches of domiciles and correspondence; but provisions on freedom of speech, association and religion, contained in the Japanese model, were left out. A democratic or liberal constitution, however, could not at that time have been implemented, and at least it could be claimed that a start had been made; some element of modernisation was implicit in having a Constitution at all, defining powers which had previously been left to the all-sufficient imperial prerogative.

In both its centralising and its modernising aspects, nevertheless, the Constitution of 1931 echoed the developments of the time without doing anything to cause them. Its sole direct result was the foundation of the Parliament, and in no other field was there administrative or legal machinery available to implement it. It was subject to no judicial interpretation, and the provisions on rights can have had little relevance to a people to whose traditions they were largely alien; the power of the Emperor over the provinces was expanded by the gradual process already outlined, rather than by any constitutional provision; and the organisation of the executive branch of government was left so vague in the Constitution that none of the developments in that field can be ascribed to it. The rest of the document mostly confirmed in the Emperor powers which he would in any case have exercised, and while it was often cited in preambles to laws, it made little difference to the actual business of government. *The Ethiopian Herald* could therefore say, in July 1944, that:[4] 'It is doubtful if it is generally known that Ethiopia's written Constitution has served as the primary basis for the government of the Empire since 1931.'

The Revised Constitution of 1955[5]

Inadequacies in the 1931 Constitution became apparent with the changing political climate of the early nineteen-fifties, and especially with the Federation with Eritrea in 1952. It contrasted unfavourably with the liberal Constitution bestowed on Eritrea by the United Nations, and there were also doubts about its applicability to Eritrea, and hopes that a new Constitution might be used to bring Eritrea more closely under the control of the central government in Addis Ababa. Supporters of reform further urged that Ethiopia was being criticised for the illiberality of the existing Constitution both abroad and by the growing number of educated Ethiopians, and that it would be wisest to anticipate demands for change before it became obvious that the government was giving in to pressure. The revision of the Constitution thus followed closely from the political developments of the time.

This Revised Constitution was a long time in preparation; the Emperor has said that the process took six years, and it was noted in July 1952 that the revision was under way.[6] The lengthy procedure itself marks a considerable development from the informal drafting of 1931. The first formal step appears to have been the setting up of a committee of ministers under the chairmanship of the then Prime Minister, Bitwädäd Makonnen Endalkachäw (18). This committee suggested a number of changes to the existing Constitution, including provisions on the status of the family, non-retroactivity of legislation, and freedom of speech and assembly; on the liability at law of ministers and civil servants; on additional parliamentary representation of large cities; and on a Senate with partial renewal of membership every three years.

These suggestions in turn served as a base for the work of the Constitutional Commission, an expert body charged with drawing up a draft Constitution. The Commission worked in a house in the palace grounds, beneath the close supervision of the Emperor. Most of its detailed work was done by three American legal advisers, notably Mr J. H. Spencer, but although the draftsmanship was largely theirs, they worked beneath the close supervision of Ethiopian officials. The Commission started intensive work in the summer of 1953, and its first completed draft was dated February 2nd, 1954; it was written in English, and was translated into Amharic by the Imperial Chronicles Department. Twenty-one months were to elapse between this draft and the final promulgation of the Revised Constitution, a fact which indicates the leisurely pace at which the revision was carried out, and also that the government was under no urgent pressure for reform.

The draft was then submitted for revision and review to the Emperor, the leaders of the Church and the nobility, and important officials; five amended versions were produced between February 1954 and June 1955, adapting the original to their suggestions. As in 1931, the agreement of the major figures of the country was needed to secure general acceptance of the new Constitution, and in particular, conservative nobles and churchmen had to be persuaded to accept its more liberal aspects. This process was carried out more institutionally than in 1931, through the Crown Council,* whose key figure was the Emperor's cousin Ras Kasa (13). He was one of the great lords who had considered the Constitution of 1931, and so great was the respect in which he was held by the Church and the older noblemen that his support was essential for a general consensus.

The process of persuasion is illustrated by the report of the Constitutional Commission, which argues for liberal provisions in a way calculated to attract the support of elder statesmen and the more conservative members of the Emperor's entourage. The prohibition of gerrymandering, for instance, is presented as a device to prevent Moslem domination of Christians, while the human rights provisions are put forward as a means of increasing Ethiopian control over the affairs of Eritrea.[7] Such arguments were presumably designed to convince officials afraid that the Constitution was giving too much away.

* The Council is an advisory body to the Emperor, which is considered in Chapter 8.

Though the final text of the Constitution broadly agreed with the Commission's first draft, there are enough important changes to show that this review stage was more than a formality. Several of these changes prevented the Emperor from by-passing Parliament or the Constitution itself. The articles on Regency and succession to the throne, previously detached as an organic law, were brought into the Constitution and thus subjected to the ordinary process of amendment; the Emperor's residual and emergency powers were made subject to the rest of the Constitution; a provision giving the Emperor complete control of foreign affairs was modified to require parliamentary approval of certain types of treaty; and articles were deleted which allowed the Emperor to legislate by decree when the two chambers of Parliament disagreed on an important matter, which allowed Parliament to delegate all legislative power to the Emperor in emergencies, and which allowed the Council of Ministers to raise loans of up to fifteen per cent of the year's budget without Parliamentary approval. Other changes, however, increased the Emperor's powers of appointment to the legislature and the judiciary. A suggested territorial qualification for the Senate was removed; and judges were to be disciplined not, as in the first draft, by a standing judicial committee, but by the Emperor, subject to a special law, one of several occasions on which an implementing law was used as a device to postpone decisions on controversial matters. The reasons for these changes cannot be analysed without more detailed information on the political groupings of the time, though it is clear that the Emperor must have been personally concerned in amendments which dealt so much with his own powers.

The Constitution was also approved by Parliament before its promulgation, but the Parliament of that time is most unlikely to have done more than give its formal blessing to a project with which the Emperor was so closely concerned.

The Revised Constitution is considerably longer than that of 1931, having 131 articles in 8 chapters, against the 55 articles and 7 chapters of its predecessor. The first chapter, as in 1931, was devoted to 'The Ethiopian Empire and the Succession to the Throne'. The first article defines the Empire as the area 'under the sovereignty of the Ethiopian Crown', repeating exactly the wording of the Federal Act which defined the relationship of Eritrea to Ethiopia, and thus bringing Eritrea firmly within the bounds of the Constitution. After reciting the Emperor's descent from Solomon and Sheba (Article 2), the Constitution lays down the order of succession (Article 5). This is by primogeniture and only males may ascend the throne, thus excluding the possibility of another reigning Empress like Zäwditu, but the position of sons of princesses is not satisfactorily defined. The rest of the chapter covers such matters as Regency, the imperial family, and coronation oaths.

The second chapter, 'The Powers and Prerogatives of the Emperor', vests considerable powers in the Crown. The vesting of sovereignty in the Emperor (Article 26) was probably, like the wording of Article 1, determined by the Eritrean situation, and seems to grant no substantive powers. Article 27 enables the Emperor to determine the organisation, powers and duties of all government departments, and to appoint and dismiss government officials; this article provides the principal basis for legislation by imperial Order, which does not go before Parliament. Article 29 gives the Emperor complete control of the armed forces, though Parliament must consent to a declaration of war, and provides the Emperor with wide emergency powers. By Article 30, he receives complete control of foreign relations, except that Parliament must approve treaties on various matters which would have come within its jurisdiction if covered by ordinary legislation. Article 33 enables him to dissolve Parliament, and Article 35 gives him general supervision of the courts, including the power to grant pardons. Article 36 makes the Emperor 'as Sovereign' responsible for the welfare of the Empire and its inhabitants, and provides him with broad though very vaguely defined powers in order to perform this duty.

Chapter III, 'Rights and Duties of the People', grants a large number of specific rights, including freedom of religion, speech and assembly, and the guarantee that 'No one within the Empire may be deprived of life, liberty or property without due process of law' (Article 43). Many of the rights, however, are granted only 'in accordance with the law', subject to the general conditions that laws limiting them must be justified by 'respect for the rights and freedoms of others and the requirements of public order and the general welfare' (Article 65); this rather vague provision leaves room for a great many different opinions, and makes it difficult to challenge restrictive legislation on constitutional grounds.

Since the executive powers are already vested in the Emperor, Chapter IV, 'The Ministers of the Empire', gives ministers no powers beyond that of attending Parliament when they wish or are requested to. It recites the responsibility of ministers to the Emperor, both individually and in the Council of Ministers, and formally establishes the Crown Council, an advisory body to the Emperor which in practice already existed. Article 74 prohibits ministers and civil servants from certain activities which might conflict with their official duties, though it is too vague to do much justice to the problem, and Article 75 lays down special 'impeachment' procedures for ministers committing offences in connection with their official functions.

Chapter V, 'The Legislative Chambers', establishes a Chamber of

Deputies popularly elected every four years, and a Senate still appointed by the Emperor. The powers of Parliament are greatly increased by comparison with 1931, for laws have to be approved, and not merely discussed, by both chambers. But these powers are limited by the controversial Article 92, which enables the Emperor to legislate by decree in cases of emergency arising during the parliamentary recess, on most of the matters which would otherwise be dealt with by Parliament; such decrees continue in effect unless subsequently disapproved by both chambers.

Chapter VI, 'The Judicial Power', vests this in the courts established by law, and provides formal guarantees of judicial independence, though these are vitiated by the fact that the Emperor continues to appoint judges. Chapter VII, 'Finance', is notable for the extent of the financial powers given to Parliament, of which the most important have been the budgetary power, and the requirement of parliamentary approval of government loans; Parliament also has to grant taxation, and receives some supervision over government accounts, though all of these powers are in practice weakened by the inadequacies of government financial machinery. Chapter VIII, 'General Provisions', includes the supremacy provisions of Article 122, one of several occasions on which the wording echoes the United States Constitution:

> The present revised Constitution, together with those international treaties, conventions and obligations to which Ethiopia shall be party, shall be the Supreme Law of the Empire, and all future legislation, decrees, orders, judgements, decisions and acts inconsistent therewith, shall be null and void.

The word 'future' has raised controversy over whether past legislation inconsistent with the Constitution still remains in effect. The rest of this chapter provides for amendment procedures (Article 131), for the establishment of the Ethiopian Orthodox Church (Article 126), for certain natural resources to be State Domain (Article 130), and for various less important matters.

The Revised Constitution develops the centralising and modernising themes already present in its predecessor, though with the differences in content and emphasis involved by changes since 1931.

The policy of centralisation, for instance, took on a new aspect with the federation with Eritrea. Eritrea and its Constitution were subject to central control by making the Revised Constitution the 'Supreme Law' of the area 'under the Sovereignty of the Ethiopian Crown', and the powers of the Eritrean Government were more directly limited by preventing it from raising loans without the consent of the Emperor and the Addis Ababa Parliament, by removing from it the control of natural resources in Eritrea, and in other ways. All of these limitations were imposed without any reference to the existence of a Federation from one end of the document to the other.

The central position of the Emperor could be taken for granted, and in vesting the executive powers of government in him rather than in the Prime Minister, the Constitution was simply stating the existing situation. It further followed the *status quo* in treating the ministers as imperial advisers and assistants, and in leaving vague the administrative relationship between them and the Emperor.

The modernising elements of the Constitution greatly developed those of 1931, to the extent that great care had to be taken in fitting them in with the imperial powers. This is clear in the treatment of all three branches of government, and provides interesting examples, at the theoretical level, of the difficulties of reconciling western constitutional concepts with the very different traditions and practices of Ethiopia.

This is most obvious with the judiciary, where the principle of judicial independence conflicted with the absence in the traditional system of any distinction between judicial and administrative powers. The problem was solved on paper by affirming the independence of the judiciary, while the Emperor received powers to pardon and to commute penalties, and to maintain justice through the courts. The balance has in practice been tipped towards the Emperor by the continuation of traditional practices, and by giving him power to appoint and remove judges subject to a special law which has yet to appear.

A similar reconciliation was required with the legislature, combining popular suffrage with the reluctance of the Emperor to resign all of the wide powers over legislation which he had previously held. The result is that the elected Chamber of Deputies is balanced by a Senate still directly appointed, while the Emperor and both chambers have the power of initiation and veto. Further, the Emperor can legislate by decree in cases of emergency arising during the recess, and he also retains the power of dissolution.

The Emperor's control of the executive government makes it necessary to exclude this from the parliamentary sphere, and the Emperor is therefore empowered to appoint all ministers and civil and military officials, and to legislate by order on matters concerning the organisation of the executive and the armed forces. Lines for future development are, however, provided by requiring parliamentary approval of the Budget, and by obliging ministers or their deputies to come to Parliament for questioning. Since the Emperor cannot subject himself to Parliament, moreover, it is in this field that the functions of the ministers are most clearly defined.

The chapter of the Constitution dealing with popular rights is the most indebted of all to western concepts; only the right to present petitions to the Emperor is firmly rooted in Ethiopian custom, though several Amhara values, including the insistence on justice, the respect for privacy, and the institution of private property, may help to provide a better basis for rights than exists in many African societies.[8] Many of the rights at present exist only on paper, though laws have been enacted to implement most of those on legal procedures, which for practical purposes are probably the most important of them. A number of rights commonly found in constitutions were considered and rejected when the Constitution was drawn up. These include guarantees of education and social security (which would be futile in view of the services which the government can at present provide) and the right to form political parties.

Other articles define the functions of the various parts of the government in greater detail than was previously thought necessary. The powers and procedures of Parliament, the arrangements for public finance, and conditions governing Regency and succession to the throne, are set out far more precisely than in 1931, and the Emperor is explicitly granted powers, such as the right to issue money, which he had earlier exercised as his prerogative.

Though the years since 1955 have seen the most striking political changes elsewhere in Africa, the Revised Constitution has yet to be amended, though a number of possible amendments have been canvassed. Members of the Chamber of Deputies have tried to improve their position by increasing their term of office from four years to six, and by extending parliamentary immunity to the recess; these efforts are unlikely to make much headway.

A more far-reaching attempt at amendment took place in 1961, when a Committee on Constitutional Revision was among the committees on possible reforms set up after the attempted *coup d'état* of the previous December. Its chairman was the Minister of Public Health, and the other six members were mostly of ministerial rank; it was assisted by the two foreign legal advisers, Sir Charles Mathew and Mr D. E. Paradis.

This committee was mostly concerned with the relations between the Emperor, the Prime Minister and ministers, the point at which the Revised Constitution is most vague and most open to further development. It recommended in its report that the Emperor should select the Prime Minister, who would then choose his own ministers, and present them to the Emperor for formal installation. It also proposed that the Council of Ministers should become an executive instead of an advisory body, and that the Prime Minister should exercise a number of executive powers in the name of the Emperor, thus realising the report's basic principle that the function and position of the Head of State should be separated from those of the Head of Government.[9]

Other suggested amendments provided for a special division of the Supreme Court to decide matters of constitutional interpretation, and tackled the problem of judicial independence by having judges appointed on the recommendation of a special committee, with security of tenure except in cases of proved incompetence or misbehaviour. Further revisions covered minor problems which had arisen in the application of the Constitution.

The Committee's report was completed in October 1961, and partly revised two months later after discussions with senior ministers. The most important of its recommendations, that the Prime Minister should select other ministers, was put into effect in March 1966, though the machinery of constitutional revision was not used for the purpose; but after six years there is still little sign that the remaining proposals will be implemented.

Any assessment of the effects of the Revised Constitution must take account of the continued powers of the Emperor. Not only does the Constitution itself leave him with vast powers, but it has been very difficult to implement parts of it, such as the guarantee of judicial independence, which would have limited them. The long delay in implementing any of the proposals for constitutional amendment underlines the point. The Constitution thus attempts no profound changes in the system of government, but restricts itself to the encouragement of a number of developments within the framework of the imperial supremacy.

Within its modest limits, however, the Constitution has had some effect, especially in instituting an elected Chamber of Deputies. This is the only point at which it has helped to create a new political force, and by far its most important results in changing the procedures of government have been in matters relating to Parliament. These matters have affected not only legislation, but also the executive government, as in the questioning of ministers and the bringing out of the Budget in advance, and it is only in the parliamentary field that the Constitution has effectively limited the powers of the Emperor.

More generally, constitutional provisions on such subjects as civil service regulations and the legalisation of trades unions have led to the enactment of implementing legislation; where such laws have not appeared, as over municipal councils and expropriation procedures, the constitutional guarantee is constantly used as a spur by critics of the government, especially in Parliament, and may eventually induce the government to take action. There has been no means, however, of enforcing the Constitution when the government has been unwilling to implement it, and several of the ideals which it proclaims have in this way remained dead letters.

One of the difficulties has been the lack of effective machinery for relating the Constitution to the work of the administration. The judiciary has for the most part been too weak to do this, though in the mid-1960s there was a marked increase in constitutional pleas before the courts, indicating a growing public awareness of the Constitution. Other efforts to interpret and enforce the Constitution have come from Parliament— the Chamber of Deputies in particular being ever ready to raise constitutional issues—and from the executive, where the legal department of the Prime Minister's office advises other departments on the constitutionality of suggested laws and actions, and in doing so has carried out some pioneering attempts at legal analysis of the Constitution.[10]

The Revised Constitution thus impinges at quite a number of points on the working of the government, and as often happens in Ethiopia, its effectiveness has gradually increased as people have grown more familiar with it; it was certainly far more important in 1967 than when it was promulgated twelve years earlier. But though it cannot be ignored, its effect has been very largely on the modern legal framework of the administration, which alone is susceptible to the sort of control which a constitution can provide. The central core of the executive government, by contrast, is hardly touched on in the Constitution, and even two years after the semi-constitutional changes of March 1966, it continues to operate along largely traditional lines through the personal relations between the Emperor and the senior officials. The more important areas of government thus continue to work through conventional practices to which the formal framework of government is at best only indirectly related.

The Formal Structure of the Central Executive

The Constitutions of 1931 and 1955 scarcely concern themselves with the internal structure of the executive government, or the distribution of powers between the Emperor and other officials, and this subject has been chiefly determined by imperial Orders, issued under the articles of both Constitutions which gave the Emperor power to decide the powers and organisation of government ministries and departments.

Since the powers of the executive have been vested both in theory and in practice in the Emperor, the other major institutions of the central government have effectively been able to operate only as his delegates and advisers. The Prime Minister, who heads the government beneath the Emperor, has had wide supervisory responsibilities over the rest of the administration, but until he was enabled to select ministers in 1966, he had no substantive powers of control. For almost all of the period since the office was established in 1943, he has therefore been a chief of staff to the Emperor in administrative matters.

The Prime Minister presides over the Council of Ministers, which consists of the heads of all of the departmental ministries and occasional ministers without portfolio. The Council has had a co-ordinating rather than a policy-making role, again because of the Emperor's supreme position, and until 1966 its powers were entirely advisory. It has now acquired the power to take decisions on legislative proposals and some other matters itself, but 'policy decisions' still have to be submitted to the Emperor for approval. No guidance is given on what constitutes a policy decision.

The departmental ministers have all been appointed by, and are directly responsible to, the Emperor; by the March 1966 changes, they are now 'proposed for appointment' by the Prime Minister before formal installation by the Emperor, and are 'directly responsible to Our Prime Minister and, above him, to Us (the Emperor) and the State'.[11] They were previously liable to be transferred or dismissed at will by the Emperor, and this power too has presumably been delegated to the Prime Minister, though the Order of March 1966 does not explicitly raise the point.

The powers of each ministry are formally vested in its minister, and both the ministries themselves and their specific powers have been varied by imperial Orders at various times since they were first formally established in January 1943. By the latest and most comprehensive reorganisation, of July 1966, there are now nineteen separate ministries:[12]

Agriculture
Commerce and Industry
Communications
Education and Fine Arts
Finance
Foreign Affairs
Imperial Court
Information and Tourism
Interior
Justice
Land Reform and Administration
Mines
National Community Development
National Defence
Pen
Planning and Development
Posts, Telegraphs and Telephones
Public Health
Public Works

Of these, the Ministries of Land Reform and of Planning were newly created in July 1966, when a number of responsibilities were also reshuffled between the existing departments. Two of the ministries, the Imperial Court and the Pen, are peculiar Ethiopian creations which reflect the closeness of the palace to the executive government. The Ministry of the Pen, as already indicated, is the traditional instrument of the imperial secretariat, and as such was especially important in the post-war decade; the Ministry of the Imperial Court handles largely ceremonial matters, but it is nevertheless thought appropriate that it should exist as a full ministry with representation in the Council of Ministers.

Below the immediate ministerial level, two further official ranks, of minister of state and vice-minister, have been recognised as 'political' rather than 'administrative' in the legislation dealing with government appointments. These are ranks rather than posts, in that they determine salary scales and official precedence, and it has been common for whole ministries to be run for long periods by ministers of state or even vice-ministers, who have been minister in all but name. It is also increasingly common for officials holding particular posts, such as Secretary-General of the Council of Ministers, to be assigned a rank, such as vice-minister, in order to fit them more clearly into the administrative hierarchy.

There is a formal distinction between this 'political' class, whose members are now all proposed for appointment by the Prime Minister, and lower officials—assistant minister, director-general, director—who are in theory recruited by the Central Personnel Agency. But there are no separate political and administrative hierarchies, for the political appointees are simply the highest officials in any given ministry.

Besides the ministries, there are government agencies of great number and variety, each dealing with a specific subject. The most important have been those dealing with communications and other public services, including the airline, roads, electricity and banking, but others have been set up whenever need has arisen, and include such diverse matters as coffee marketing, scrap iron, and tourism. Such agencies have usually been established by imperial charter, and have been run by a full-time general manager beneath the general supervision of a board of directors composed largely of ministers and other senior officials; political responsibility is channelled through the chairman of the board, who is usually the minister most closely concerned with the subject. There has been a recent tendency for some of the more administrative agencies, like the Planning Board and the Land Reform and Development Authority, to be incorporated in ordinary government ministries, and for some of the more commercial ones, such as Ethiopian Air Lines and commercial banking, to become government-owned enterprises under the ordinary company law.

Chapter 5
The Emperor

Haile-Selassie

Haile-Selassie I, Elect of God, King of the Kings of Ethiopia. The Lion of the Tribe of Judah has Conquered.* The ancient formula stands at the head of every imperial proclamation, conjuring up the developments of half a century of government in the name, and the continuity of a millennium of history in the titles. We must look at him closely. He is a very little great man, dapper and relaxed, his bearing upright, his handshake limp, and his skin rather darker than most photographs would lead one to suppose; only his face suggests that force of personality which has infused Ethiopia for over fifty years. The short neat beard and the sharp downward droop of the moustache, though grizzled by the passage of seventy-five years, still stamp his unmistakable features. His eyes are extraordinary; they stand out with a penetrating intensity which sometimes gives the impression that they are living an existence of their own, and looking at them, one can understand the feelings of those ministers who are said to tremble before him as a mouse before a cat.

It is with his ministers and courtiers that he should be seen, for the way in which the Emperor dominates the group, not physically but through the bonds of deference which draw the others to him, sums up the working of the central government. Haile-Selassie is the very centre of the political system, which radiates out from him to the concentric circles of personalities and institutions which surround the throne; and his domination of the last half-century shows that his delicate features and great personal charm conceal a politician of the greatest skill.

Many of his methods and qualities are illustrated by his upbringing and rise to power. He was born in 1892,† the son of Ras Makonnen, governor of Harär and cousin and confidant of the Emperor Menilek. He was raised in his father's fief and in the imperial court at Addis Ababa, and

* The less precise translation given in the English text of legislation is 'Emperor of Ethiopia, Conquering Lion of the Tribe of Judah', which presents as a title what is in fact a motto: the 'Lion of the Tribe of Judah' is Jesus Christ.
† His exact birthday is not recorded, and some estimates favour 1891, but his official birthday is observed as July 23rd, 1892.

had very little formal instruction, picking up his education instead by immersion, from his first years, in the deep waters of Ethiopian politics. As the son of a great nobleman, he was bred to authority, and by the age of twenty he had ruled the broad provinces of Sidamo and then Harär. This accustomed him to the exercise of great power, and to a traditional form of administration in which he was looked up to as the source of all authority and every benefit, in which he had to depend on himself alone, and in which he was not expected and was probably unwilling to delegate any of his power to others.[1] He was aided in this taxing position by a great capacity for hard work, an excellent memory, and a mastery of detail, three qualities which he still possesses. Equally, in his early experience of administration, his personal authority counted for everything, and there were no formal institutions, no definition of functions, and no separation of powers. The administrative habits which such rule involves have remained with him all his life.

At court, in the confused period which followed Menilek's decline, he was constantly surrounded by the intrigues endemic in Ethiopian political life; and that he not only survived them, but emerged at the head of the government, is evidence of his personal political skills. Secrecy and a penchant for subsurface activity were of course essential. Equally important was a capacity for manipulating other individuals, a gift which enabled Haile-Selassie to gain power in 1916, and which has served him equally well in retaining it. His management of the African Heads of State Conference of May 1963 shows that this skill has not deserted him, and can be applied even to those over whom he has no direct control. Small wonder, then, that he sometimes appears to be a master of marionettes, moving in a mysterious way to determine the actions of the lesser individuals who surround his throne.

The adroitness with which he moved into the Pan-African movement also illustrates his remarkable capacity for adapting himself to changing circumstances. The fifty years since his rise to power have seen far greater changes than any preceding era, and the political climate of 1916 or even of 1941 has quite vanished today. Yet Haile-Selassie has never been left behind by events, and throughout this time he has remained on top of the government, guiding change in some ways and adapting himself to it in others. That he should now, in his mid-seventies, sometimes seem out of touch with developments, is not nearly so astonishing as his domination of them for so long.

He has been able to adapt so successfully because he has always been accessible and open to persuasion, at least in matters which do not too closely touch his personal power, and because he has been concerned with the adjustment and authorisation of change, rather than with the active initiation of the changes themselves. He has thus tended to move with the times, and has been influenced by his surroundings as well as influencing them.

Another of Haile-Selassie's assets has been his adeptness at maintaining a cloak of ambiguity, keeping his exact position in doubt until the last possible moment. When a controversial matter arises in the government, for instance, he may make his views known indirectiy, but is careful not to commit himself beyond recall to any course of action. His freedom of manœuvre is thus maximised, while others remain in doubt, and he can always retreat and avoid responsibility should any of his plans go amiss.

A related trait has been his caution, which was particularly striking during the Regency. He was not the man to risk everything on a single bold throw, but contented himself with a very gradual consolidation of his position within the existing balance of power. Diplomatic reports are full of references to his unwillingness to take decisive action, a tendency due not so much to irresolution as to his making sure that the ground he occupied already was firm before taking any further step. Both in the central and in the provincial government, he waited for his opponents to attack him, and then gained power rapidly in the wake of their failure.

A similar caution is found in his approach to modernisation. He has been far more receptive than most of his generation to the advantages to Ethiopia of western innovations, in education, military organisation, and many other fields; but he has always taken great care to advance no faster than the general consensus would allow. Thus, he undertook to found the Tafari Makonnen School in 1922, but did not open its doors until three years later, by which time he had pacified the opposition of the conservatives.[2] Even after gaining complete control of the central government in 1928, he retained the same cautious approach, and was as likely to delay as to adopt the reforming measures suggested by educated Ethiopians and foreign advisers. It is characteristic of him that, both before and after the Occupation, he allowed the responsibility and the blame for his refusals to be taken by members of his entourage.

Some of this ambivalence may well have been due to a desire to retain some consensus in the face of very great changes; and it is only to be expected that Haile-Selassie should be wary of innovations which he does not fully understand. But much has also resulted from his appreciation of the dangers of modernisation to his own position, and the aspects of change most quickly grasped have been those which strengthened his centralised control. His ambiguity is best seen in his maintenance of a façade of modernisation, behind which many of the traditional modes have been continued. Such a façade may serve either as a substitute for development, or else to gain time while the necessarily slower genuine developments are taking place; both uses have appeared in Ethiopia, and this maintenance of a façade is itself a characteristic Ethiopian device.

49

The façade is also intended for foreign consumption, for the Emperor has long been interested in his 'image' abroad, and in related matters of prestige and foreign affairs. Examples during the Regency include the abolition of slavery and Ethiopia's entry into the League of Nations, and after the Italian invasion projected him on to the world stage. Since the war, the revival of his interest in personal diplomacy dates from 1954, when he made two long series of state visits to America and Europe, being away in all for four and a half months. This was the first time he had left Ethiopia since the Liberation, except for a short visit to Egypt in 1944.

Thereafter, his concern with foreign affairs increased, and he made foreign visits in 1956 and in every year since 1959, going as far afield as Japan and South America. He probably makes more state visits than any other head of state, and he clearly enjoys them for their own sake, even when they have no practical use. The rapid increase in number of small independent states, especially in Africa, has greatly enriched the field for Ethiopian diplomacy, and in particular for a head of state in Haile-Selassie's position. This opportunity to play the gratifying role of elder statesman on the international stage has coincided with difficulties and increased criticism in Ethiopia, and it is therefore not surprising that he has delegated more authority than previously in internal matters, especially to the Prime Minister, and has spent more of his time in a field where the personal rewards are far greater. The greatest effort in personal diplomacy which the Emperor has so far made was the African Heads of State Conference in Addis Ababa in May 1963, and it is therefore interesting that he took the planning of this into his own hands, even going to such lengths as personally looking for accommodation for President Nkrumah's bodyguard. In matters with which he is deeply concerned, his personal supervision thus remains as great as ever.

To a head of state in Haile-Selassie's position, diplomacy is inseparable from prestige, and matters which are likely to affect it receive his close attention. Impressive new buildings such as Africa Hall and the Addis Ababa Municipality have been erected with his encouragement, and at different times he has shown enthusiasm for the Imperial Navy, the legal Codes, and the Haile-Selassie I Prize Trust, all of which have had, in part, a similar justification. As he grows older, too, he has become concerned with his future place in history. The political process is affected when officials play upon this concern in order to gain favour and support. In 1964, for example, the President of the Senate had Parliament propose him (unsuccessfully) for the Nobel Peace Prize, and in 1961 the Prime Minister was able to argue that repression after the December revolt would forfeit his reputation as a liberal and magnanimous monarch.

The Emperor's hostility towards independent sources of authority has already been illustrated, and that this is based in his own personality, and

The Liberation, 1941. Resistance fighters display before the Emperor in front of the Gänät Le'ul Palace. Seated below the Emperor (l. to r.): Brigadier D. A. Sandford, Ras Kasa, Crown Prince Asfa-Wäsän, the Echegé (Patriarch Basiliyos) and Prince Makonnen, Duke of Harär.

The Anglo-Ethiopian Agreement of 1944. Earl de la Warr applies his seal, watched (l. to r.) by Tsähafé T'ezaz Wäldä-Giyorgis (Minister of the Pen), Bitwädäd Makonnen Endalkachäw (Prime Minister), Colonel Abiy Abäbä (Minister of War) and Ato Yelma Derésa (Minister of Finance).

The Federation with Eritrea, 1952. Tsähafé T'ezaz Wäldä-Giyorgis, Minister of the Pen, reads the Proclamation ratifying the Federal Act from the steps of the Menilek Palace.

not simply in political calculation, is most clearly shown by the nature of those with whom he chooses to surround himself. The individuals closest to him have been those most easily controlled, and those who retain some independence, through modern education or traditional prestige, have been kept at a distance. There has therefore developed a class of courtiers notable not for their ability, though there have been able men, nor even for their loyalty, for several collaborated with the Italians, but rather for their subservience to the Emperor. This is an oft-noted characteristic of royal entourages, but in a government so dominated by the court, it is certainly one which should be borne in mind.

The portrait of Haile-Selassie which emerges from these traits is one of a supreme politician in the traditional Ethiopian manner, with a mastery of the elements of political power which is perfectly adapted to his Ethiopian setting. This grasp of the means of government is far more evident than any guiding prospect of its ends, and he seems too much at home in the day-to-day details of political manipulation to have much concern for distant ideals. He naturally fails to appreciate much of what is most important to a moderniser, and though many of his actions are based on deliberate political calculation, this in turn is guided by a mind moulded—one might say imprisoned—in traditional forms. Criticisms of Haile-Selassie are therefore bound to involve judgements not simply of personality, but of the place of such traditional forms in a modernising Ethiopia.

Emperor and Government

Both Haile-Selassie's personal gifts and his long-established office have enabled him to act as a powerful and stable head of state. Unlike many African leaders, he has not had to struggle, once established in office, to prove his authority legitimate to his people, and he has not been cut off from them by the disturbing processes of modern education. He has now controlled the government for fifty years, and so has had time enough to identify himself with it, while every other politician has risen to power beneath him. The government is therefore very strikingly the Emperor's government. He has no rival at the centre of the stage, and he is constantly at work authorising government decisions, and supervising his subordinates through the balance and manipulation already outlined.

While Haile-Selassie has kept all his ministers dependent on him, he has at the same time succeeded to a remarkable extent in remaining quite distinct from them in the public eye. Many of the common people believe that while the ministers are grasping and corrupt, the Emperor himself is their champion; and foreign observers also often gain the impression that the Emperor is a man of selfless dedication, the unfortunate aspects of whose régime can be laid at the door of his self-seeking entourage. One explanation for this is that the Emperor in person redresses grievances, receives petitions, grants pardons, distributes largesse; he makes individual exceptions to the rules which his officials have to enforce. This is perfectly understandable. Politicians the world over try to gain the credit for popular actions, while avoiding the blame for unpopular ones, and Haile-Selassie is simply more successful than most. That the Emperor should never be in the wrong is an essential convention of the government, and it is given some verisimilitude by his readiness to disown the actions of his ministers whenever it is most convenient to do so. When something miscarries too badly to be ignored, a minister finds that the imperial support on which he relied has swiftly and silently vanished away. The Emperor is quite prepared to disown policies which he fully supports behind the scenes, but which he does not wish to appear to support for fear of antagonising those who lose by it. The ministers for their part take little of the credit and much of the blame, but they have to accept this as the price of office, secure in the knowledge that they will not actually fall far from favour unless they disturb the façade by seeking credit themselves. That it is indeed a façade is shown by the fact that ministers are not dismissed so long as they abide by the government's conventions. So no valid distinction can be made between the Emperor and the government of which he is so much part.

Daily contact between Emperor and government is maintained by constant visits of officials to the palace. Some of them may spend longer there than in their offices, and whenever the Emperor attends an official function, a bevy of ministers surrounds him. The Prime Minister and some others are at the palace daily, and on average ministers come three or four times a week, in addition to levees and other ceremonial occasions. Attendance varies greatly according to the individual and his relations with the Emperor, though for ministers it is partly formalised through the regular weekly appointments known as *Aqabé Sä'at*, which we will consider in the chapter on the imperial secretariat.

Many officials besides the ministers report directly to the Emperor. They include the heads of administrative agencies like the Municipality of Addis Ababa, senior officers of the armed forces, religious leaders, noblemen, wives of politicians, imperial informers, and so forth. Some ambassadors report straight to the Emperor instead of through the Minister of Foreign Affairs, and so do Governors-General and other provincial governors, depending on their personal standing. A few key officials have an entrée to the Emperor at any hour of day or night, including the Chief of Security and until 1960, Makonnen Habtä-Wäld (19) and the Commander of the Bodyguard; since then, the Prime Minister and the Minister of Defence have been in this select group.

The most powerful man in the government is the man at the Emperor's ear; and if the Emperor listens to them, even members of his personal household may gain influence exceeding that of a minister. Aba Hana Jema (10), Haile-Selassie's confessor and keeper of the privy purse, was often regarded as an *éminence grise* with an immense amount of backstairs influence, he was deep in the Emperor's confidence, and was custodian of the imprisoned ex-emperor Lej Iyasu before the war;[3] he died in the massacre of hostages in December 1960. His successor as keeper of the privy purse, Blata Admasu Räta, used to be a palace *valet de chambre*, and he too is said to be extremely influential. Such reports are impossible to confirm, but they point to an important element in a political system of this kind.

Officials come to the palace for many reasons. Often the Emperor calls them, at short notice, because something has cropped up for which he needs them; they may have to advise or inform him about some project, or answer complaints from a rival. A politician never knows when or why he will be called, and many of them hasten to the imperial presence in considerable trepidation. Many officials are there simply to show deference and be seen by the Emperor, and a minister may be reproached for not coming often enough. Older officials of the courtier class, such as Blaten-géta Mahtämä-Selassie (17), go as a matter of course; and a younger official out of favour, for instance because he had wavered during the 1960 revolt, might well go frequently to pay his respects to the Emperor as a mark of loyalty.

Access to the palace also serves more direct political ends. The Emperor is at the head of the government's channels of communication; his control over the working of the government requires a detailed knowledge of events within it, and the speed with which he gets to know of happenings in Addis Ababa is astonishing to anyone who is unaware of the size of the organisation which he uses for the purpose. He has at his disposal a vast number of informants, who are concerned not only to present their own actions in the best possible light, but also to report anything which might discredit their enemies. In this way, the system of balance between competing groups makes it very difficult to keep anything important hidden from him, and since he is at the head of a hierarchy of informers, many of whom report directly to him, he has a far greater range of information at hand than anyone else in the government. This is naturally of the greatest importance in maintaining his hold over the country.

In the first place, all the ministers report to him regularly on the state of their departments, and refer to him decisions which need his approval. This is done partly in writing and partly through interviews. They have to keep the Emperor informed of anything which he might want to know, since he will usually hear of it otherwise from someone else, probably in a light less flattering to the minister concerned. The minister would then be reprimanded for not telling him, and his position with the Emperor weakened. In addition, the Emperor often uses the claim of ignorance of some action by a minister as a preliminary to his blocking or disowning it, and disclaiming all responsibility for its results. This happens especially when something goes wrong for which the Emperor does not want to bear the blame, and by keeping him informed, a minister ensures himself to some extent against the possible consequences of his decisions.

Any other visitor to the palace provides information in the same way, and the Emperor also has informants placed wherever he may need them. In many ministries, there are officials who wield far more power than their formal position allows because they can go directly to the Emperor; in the Ministry of Justice, for instance, imperial desires are often transmitted through an assistant minister, Qäñazmach Ayänäw Adal. The information system which he thus commands runs all the way, without a break, from ordinary reports by appropriate officials to the activities of spies and paid informers. Some officials also run intelligence networks on his behalf, and naturally profit from their work themselves; the best known was that organised until 1960 by Makonnen Habtä-Wäld (19), who might serve as a model of the devious Ethiopian courtier in the traditional mould.

Questions of security are especially closely watched. The office of the Private Chief of Staff, the Emperor's adviser on military affairs, possesses all of the military codes, and has a decoding department which can decipher any message sent from one unit to another. Any radio communication may reach the Emperor in this way, and the latest reports are transmitted to him several times a day. This system was established by the Commanding Officer of the Bodyguard, Mulugéta Buli (26), a few years after the Liberation. More general matters of security come largely under the Public Security Department of the Ministry of the Interior, and under the Special Branch of the Private Cabinet, which was run for a few years until 1960 by Wärqenäh Gäbäyähu (34), who sided with the rebels in the 1960 revolt.

Plotting and intrigue are characteristics of Ethiopian politics, and while the sources of information at the Emperor's command seem extensive enough to keep him in touch with the least event, the possibility of their failure is shown by the mounting of a revolt led by the Commanding Officer of the Bodyguard and involving the chiefs of security and police. Many other plots, however, have been uncovered long before reaching the stage of the 1960 attempt, and even this one may have been lucky to get so far.[4]

One great bar to the efficiency of the system, valid throughout Ethiopian administration, is the apparent failure to organise and analyse the information coming in. Everything operates at a personal level, through rumours and accusations, and there is little room for calculated assessment. One result of this is that the wildest conjectures are sometimes taken seriously, while subtler plotters may creep through the net. But the chief weakness of the information system seems to lie less in a failure to follow intra-governmental machinations, than in the communication of general grievances and climates of opinion about Haile-Selassie's own régime. Informers cannot be expected to risk the Emperor's displeasure by telling him anything that he does not wish to hear; it seems never to have occurred to him, for example, that the 1960 rebels could have had any aim but their personal ambitions.

In practice, informing the Emperor cannot be distinguished from other political functions, and a minister who reports to the palace at the same time brings decisions for the Emperor's approval and suggests courses of action to him. Since the major interests are closely enmeshed with the government, moreover, this process also involves the articulation and aggregation of interests, a fact which indicates the multiplicity of the threads of government which come into the Emperor's hands. For the most part, officials come to the Emperor for his authority, in order to get his backing for their suggestions rather than to have him make the suggestions himself. The Emperor's authority is needed for any governmental action of the least importance, especially where any change is involved; and even when the course is clear and the minister can take the decision himself, he often needs the Emperor's consent both to protect his own position and to get the decision implemented.

One cannot assume, however, that the Emperor's approval has been obtained whenever his authority is invoked. The Ethiopian tendency to 're-interpret' orders from above has already been noted, and it is certainly possible for an official either to alter imperial orders in transmitting them to his inferiors, or even to pass off his own desires as the Emperor's. He would have to be very discreet and to understand what could safely be introduced, but since the inferior could not question what was ostensibly an imperial command and would be in no position to refer it back to the Emperor, an official with the Emperor's ear could exercise a fair degree of latitude. The extent to which such 're-interpretation' takes place is naturally impossible to discover, though some of the complexities of the chain of command from the Emperor are explored in the chapters on the imperial secretariat and on government expenditure.

In the decision-making process, the Emperor appears to be not so much a policy-maker as a policy-authoriser, though when there is controversy within the government, policy-making is automatically involved in the choice of which suggestion to approve. The Emperor certainly sometimes has ideas of his own, often in the field of prestige projects, but he shows few signs of an original mind, and he is even less in touch than most modern heads of state with the technical problems at the base of many decisions. The most common pattern is for a minister or other official to bring something to the Emperor's notice and try to interest him in it. In this way, the emperor is of vital importance as a catalyst, for the speed with which plans are carried out depends to a large extent on the interest which he takes in them. When his fancy is captured by a project, officials attend to it with great activity, and constantly report to the palace on the progress which it has made. But as the imperial attention turns elsewhere, the momentum declines, and junior officials find that ministers, who were previously ready to discuss the matter with them, are now busy with other things. The Emperor is thus concerned not so much with doing things himself, as with providing the personal authority and impetus required to get them done by others.

This rather passive nature of the Emperor's role is visible even in subjects like foreign affairs, in which he takes great personal interest. The Ethiopian entry into African politics was in large measure due to the activity of the younger foreign affairs officials in persuading the Emperor and others that this was the best course. Even in such a personal *tour de force* as the 1963 Addis Ababa Conference, the Emperor was backed by a great deal of advice and hard preparatory work, including important last-minute changes in his speech for which the Prime Minister was largely responsible. By the same token, the belligerent initial Ethiopian stand on the Rhodesian issue late in 1965 was due not to the Emperor's personal choice, but to the success of some of his advisers in persuading him that it was vital to the Ethiopian role in Africa.

The Minister of Foreign Affairs has virtually always been a man with easy personal access to the Emperor, and the Emperor's interest in the subject is confirmed by the presence since 1962 of a personal adviser on it, Menasé Haylé (24), who has also had an entrée to the palace. It forms an interesting contrast with Education, of which the Emperor was formally Minister for many years until 1966. This gave a symbolic emphasis to education, and the Emperor frequently visits schools and presides on educational occasions; but he did not show the particular interest in the Ministry which his position as Minister implied. This helps to support the view that the Emperor's advertised concern for education has largely been part of his modernising image.

Even for subjects without either personal interest or political importance, the Emperor is constantly needed just to keep the wheels of administration turning. Before 1960, his authorisation was needed for the spending of sums of as little as £7, though the usual minimum is now rather larger. His word is often needed to make one section of the government pay its debts to another, or to permit co-operation between different agencies; in view of the Emperor's concern for the 'image' of the country abroad, there may be more reason for his having to choose the best decoration scheme for the new Ethiopian Airlines jets in 1960. His activities range all the way from major policy questions to dealing with a stream of petitioners wanting the review of court judgements, pensions, and a host of other things. He sits, or in practice stands, regularly in his personal court, the *Chelot*, and he also spends much time in long church services and in a multitude of ceremonial duties. He is an indefatigable opener of conferences and layer of foundation stones, and he visits the provinces two or three times a year, most often Eritrea and Harär. It is therefore not surprising that he rises daily before five o'clock, or that he finds it necessary to take a rest each afternoon.

The role of the Emperor in day-to-day government has nevertheless altered since the revolt of 1960. Age affects even so active a man as Haile-Selassie; by the official reckoning he was seventy-six in 1968, and this has affected his hours of work, and also it seems his interest in minor government matters. It has also weakened his position by compelling politicians to take account of what may happen after his departure. The amount of work which he can do has been diminished by his increased concern for foreign affairs, which many interpret as a reaction to domestic failures, and there are also the pressures brought by gradual modernisation. The simple growth in scope of the government, shown by the rise in its Budget from £1,600,000 in 1942 to £65,000,000 in 1965, has diminished the closeness with which the Emperor can supervise it, and many technical matters arise for which he has no training.

But the relations of the Emperor with the government have been affected most of all by changes in the individuals who surround him, and changes of this sort chiefly distinguish the three main periods since 1941 which were outlined in a previous chapter. Though the same elements have been present throughout, first one and then another has predominated with changes in the imperial entourage. In the years before 1955, the greatest emphasis was on the Emperor's centralising mission, through the efficient machinery of the imperial secretariat directed by Wäldä-Giyorgis (33); between 1955 and 1960, when there was no outstanding figure, the Emperor's role as a balancer of groups was most in evidence; and since 1961, under the influence of civil servants like Aklilu Habtä-Wäld (3), the Emperor has been most clearly an authoriser and adjuster of policies presented to him, with a declining part in day-to-day administration. More generally, his position has been affected by the recruitment of younger officials, who are far less inclined than their seniors to look up to the Emperor, and more confident of their ability to work out the necessary solutions themselves. And while earlier in his reign, Haile-Selassie's centralising policy was aided by the traditional forms of

57

Ethiopian administration, more recently it has had to struggle against modernising forces which tend to assert their independence of him. In this way, general developments in the government since 1941 are reflected in the changing role of the Emperor.

To conclude, the Emperor's most important function has been to provide a single source of legitimate authority, for this alone ensures the stability which is needed for the exercise of the other functions of government. It is clear both from the nature of the imperial system, and from the Amhara social organisation which pervades it, that the structure of the government depends on a single authority figure, without whom it would be in danger of disintegration. The Emperor is not simply a chief executive; he carries out all of the functions of Hobbes' Leviathan, and many of those of the Constitution in Great Britain or the United States. The imperial authority thus provides a framework within which, however partially and inefficiently, decisions can be worked out. The maintenance of such a framework is no mean achievement in a country where traditional and westernising groups are so far apart as in Ethiopia; and much of Haile-Selassie's success has been due to his manner of balancing the different groups, listening to each and granting some of its aims, thus preserving a degree of consensus and preventing any group from openly challenging his régime.

Haile-Selassie has also done much to deserve his reputation as Ethiopia's moderniser. He has clearly taken over and expanded the Emperor's innovating role, which Téwodros and Menilek had developed before him. He has greatly increased education, extended the scope of the government, abolished abuses such as slavery, and initiated a great many changes in almost every field; whereas had he wished he could probably have maintained a far more conservative and, indeed, repressive régime. It is often pointed out that pressures for faster change have mostly been the result of the modernisation which he himself has fostered. But the imperial office used to carry out his reforms has, basically, retained its traditional form, despite the modifications forced on it by the great increase in central government functions. Its use as an instrument of modernisation has made it little more modern itself, for power has been exercised through it by the methods which Emperors have employed for generations, and while the administration has greatly expanded, it has done so about its traditional centre of the palace compound. Reforms which might have weakened the Emperor's position have been resisted, and in particular, the insistence on his authority for any important initiative has been maintained and even encouraged; and when one reads that the Emperor alone has taken the steps which have so changed Ethiopia in recent years, one must also remember that no one else has been in a position to do so.

The Imperial Family*

The rule of Haile-Selassie has been personal rather than dynastic. He has not appointed members of his immediate family to the high offices of state, and, indeed, princes eligible for the Crown are constitutionally disqualified from becoming ministers.[5] In this respect, Haile-Selassie has followed Ethiopian tradition, with its emphasis on the personal nature of the Crown, and its disregard of the imperial family except for succession and dynastic union.

The question of the succession has affected the government largely through the Emperor's unwillingness to allow any possible claimant to build up a position from which to challenge him. His tactics have resembled, though in less spectacular fashion, those of emperors who imprisoned potential rivals on inaccessible mountain tops, and his eldest son the Crown Prince, in particular, has not been allowed to gain much experience in governmental matters, or to establish an independent position in his province of Wälo. This has naturally given rise to rumours that he was to be displaced in the order of succession by some more favoured member of the Imperial family, such as his younger brother Makonnen, who died in 1957, or one of the Emperor's grandsons. Although no one has been groomed to take the Crown Prince's place, speculation over the succession has had an unsettling effect on the government, especially with Haile-Selassie's own advancing age.

The Emperor's policy of allying his own with other noble families is more easily detailed. His wife, the Empress Mänän, was a granddaughter of Negus Mika'él of the Wälo Galla, and a niece of the deposed Emperor Lej Iyasu. Four of their descendants have married into the aristocracy of Tegré, and four into Galla families from Wäläga; there has also been much intermarriage with the nobility of Shoa. The imperial family has in this way been allied with most of the great families of Christian Ethiopia, except those of Gojam, Lasta and Bägémdär; a projected alliance with the Gojam dynasty fell through after Ras Haylu's attempt to restore Lej Iyasu in 1932, and Bägémdär was likewise excluded until one of Haile-Selassie's granddaughters married a Colonel from Gondär in 1968. This poor representation of the central Amhara areas is echoed in the general regional composition of the government.

The Crown Prince

The Crown Prince Asfa-Wäsän was born in 1916, and named after a minor Shoan ruler. Through his mother, he is descended from the rulers of Wälo and was made its governor before the war. This attachment to a

* Refer to Figure 4 at the back of the book for this section.

59

territorial base which had opposed Haile-Selassie may help to explain the bad relations between the Crown Prince and his father, which were evident even before 1935,[6] and in these circumstances, in a court system, persistent rumours as to his paternity are only to be expected. He resumed his governorship of Wälo at the Liberation, but in 1947 he was recalled to Addis Ababa and since then has paid only token visits to his province. Most of his time has been spent in Addis Ababa, with frequent trips abroad.

As well as the governorship of Wälo, he holds a seat on committees such as the Crown Council and the National Defence Council, but these are all either purely formal or else advisory to the Emperor, and he could not exercise any greater power over them than his influence on his father gave him. The relationship between the two is one of the enigmas of the Ethiopian government. Certainly, Haile-Selassie has given the Crown Prince little chance to show his capacity, or to gain experience in governmental affairs, though on the other hand he has kept him close to the throne, and allowed him to figure on ceremonial occasions. The Crown Prince himself is extremely discreet, even with those who know him well, and it is impossible to say what informal influence he has with the Emperor. Certainly his views must differ from Haile-Selassie's, for he was a bitter enemy of Wäldä-Giyorgis (33), and he resented the presence in the government of several of the more devious politicians with whom his father has surrounded himself. His closest associates are mostly noblemen, and especially Shoans connected with his wife's family.

When Haile-Selassie is abroad, the Crown Prince acts in his stead, and only at such times is he directly concerned in the administration. He takes the Emperor's place in the regular weekly appointments with ministers known as *Aqabé Sä'at*. Routine business is conducted in the same way as when the Emperor is present, though the more important decisions are postponed until his return. The first time that the Emperor left the country for long was during his visit to the United States in the summer of 1954, when the Crown Prince took the *Aqabé Sä'at* in the presence of Ras Abäbä (1) and the Prime Minister. In his determination to make himself obeyed, he quarrelled with the Minister of Finance and offended a number of vested interests. He made a particularly good impression as judge in the Emperor's personal court, being noted for the discernment of his judgements and for the expedition of long drawn-out legal suits. He is also said to be quicker and more business-like than the Emperor.

While Haile-Selassie was abroad in December 1960, the Bodyguard revolt broke out, and the Crown Prince spoke on the wireless in favour of the rebels. There is little doubt that he was acting under duress, and no evidence that he actively supported the revolt, but the heir to the throne in a monarchy like Ethiopia is the automatic focus for opposition to the ruler, and in the unsettled conditions of the following year, the Emperor took the Crown Prince with him when he went abroad. Since then, however, he has continued to remain at home, and has been prepared to take fairly important decisions. In 1964, he dealt with complaints of favouritism in assessing taxes brought by some inhabitants of Bägémdär against the Governor-General, deciding in their favour, and was supported by the Emperor on his return.

He married the daughter of Ras Seyum of Tegré (28) in 1932, but they were divorced some twelve years later after she had borne him a daughter but no son. He then married a Shoan lady, niece of his sister's former husband Ras Dästa, and they have one son and several daughters.

By far the most important role of the Crown Prince is as a potential Emperor, and this has given him an established position uniquely aloof from ordinary political pressures; but he takes little part in day-to-day government, and is only rarely involved in the political machinery with which this study is concerned.

Other Members

Of the Empress Mänän, one heard surprisingly little, and she gave rise to few of the rumours or *bons mots* to be expected of anyone who had made an impact on the political scene. She was largely concerned with good works, and was inactive for several years before her death in 1962. Her traditional upbringing and devotion to the Orthodox Church suggest a conservative political outlook, but her influence was exercised in private with her husband, and is therefore impossible to assess. She is often said to have taken a large part in persuading the Emperor to go into exile in 1936, rather than retreating to Goré, but he may equally have been swayed by other reasons. The Empress was married to several other noblemen before Haile-Selassie, and her descendants by these have married into important families, though they are not regarded as members of the imperial family.

The Emperor's second son, Makonnen, was always his favourite, and was not only named after Haile-Selassie's own father, but was given the family fief of Harär rather than the enemy territory of Wälo. He enjoyed a privileged position with the Emperor, and was one of the best people to take requests for favours to him; these were likely to be granted, not only because of his father's attachment to him, but also because he sought in this way to make his son popular. This caused Makonnen to be tipped as a possible successor to the throne, though the likelihood of this may well have been exaggerated, since he was little interested in administration, and had practically nothing to do with governing his province. Indeed, he sometimes said that to become Emperor was the very last thing he wanted. His death in a car accident in 1957, like every sudden death in Ethiopia, gave rise to the predictable spate of rumours. His wife came from a well-established family in the south of Tegré, and their five sons have been constantly beside the Emperor; the eldest was born in 1947, and so far they have taken no part in government.

The youngest son, Sahlä-Selassie, had no bent for administration, and took no interest in his nominal governorship of the distant and unimportant province of Gämu-Gofa. He married into the nobility of Wäläga, and left a baby son at his death in 1962.

Two of the Emperor's three legitimate daughters, Zänäbä-Wärq and Tsähay, died young and left no descendants. The eldest daughter, Tänañä-Wärq, was married first to Ras Dästa, a Shoan nobleman who was killed by the Italians in 1936, and later to Andargé Mäsay (9). As with all members of the imperial family, her influence is very difficult to estimate, but it is said to be fairly considerable and in general conservative. Her only surviving son, Lej Eskender, is in charge of the small Ethiopian Navy, and has been suggested as a claimant to the throne, but although he has easy access to the Emperor, he has never been given the prominence of a potential heir, nor entrusted with any great responsibility.

None of Haile-Selassie's sons or grandsons has shown a sign of his own calibre, and certainly none could assume his commanding position in the government. They have been given little responsibility or chance to take an active role in politics, and all too often they have been sent abroad with nothing to do and a great deal to spend; this has cut them off from the Ethiopian roots which give Haile-Selassie his strength, and they command little respect from either traditionalist or modernising Ethiopians. The resulting decay of the younger generation, which only the Crown Prince and Lej Eskender seem to have escaped, has greatly sapped the vigour and future prospects of the imperial house.

Several of Haile-Selassie's daughters and granddaughters have married active politicians, who gain additional political influence from their connection with the imperial family. Shortly before her death, Princess Tsähay married Lieutenant-General Abiy Abäbä (2), a shy and courteous Shoan nobleman who has held many major posts and—a rarity among politicians—is universally respected; as the Emperor's Representative in Eritrea, he never wavered in his loyalty to Haile-Selassie during the 1960 revolt. Princess Tänañä-Wärq's husband, Ras Andargé (4), has like Abiy served as Minister of the Interior and as the Emperor's Representative in Eritrea, and also has extensive commercial interests; he has been an invalid since an accident in 1964. Two of Tänañä-Wärq's daughters by her earlier marriage to Ras Dästa are married to Ras Mängäsha of Tegré (21) and to Lej Kasa Wäldä-Maryam, the President of the University, and with their sisters have been active in a variety of social works;

another daughter, by Ato Abäbä Räta, the present Minister of Commerce, has married Ato Seyum Harägot (27), an Eritrean who is Minister of State in the Prime Minister's Office. Through such marriages, and through the ramifications of distant branches of the dynasty, the Emperor is in some way related to a great many members of his government;* this is evidence not simply of nepotism, but quite as much of the way in which the imperial family is integrated into the ruling classes of Ethiopia.

* See the chart of family connections facing page 211.

Chapter 6

Political Groupings

The Political Class

The Emperor is certainly the hub of the government, but he is far from being the whole of it; for to further his policy of centralisation, and to carry out the new and complex tasks involved by modernisation and administrative expansion, he has had to recruit a ruling class of administrators and politicians—aptly termed 'the new nobility'—on which much of the daily work of government has devolved. This political class consists largely of the holders of the major government posts, and of others who through their personal status or connections have enjoyed a place in the central political hierarchy. Its membership cannot be defined with any precision, since there have been no political parties to provide a distinctively political recruitment pattern, and until recently, political posts were not even formally distinguished from civil service ones; all have alike been subject to the Emperor's control. But there has emerged a core of leading officials, who move from one major post to another in much the same way as the front-benchers of an English political party.

Since 1961, the position of these leading officials has been supplemented by a formal division between the higher ranks of minister, minister of state and vice-minister, whose occupants enjoy the prestigious title of Excellency, and are now selected by the Prime Minister, and the lower 'civil service' posts theoretically filled through the Central Personnel Agency. There are between one and six members of this upper hierarchy in each ministry, and there were sixty-eight in the government altogether in November 1966; but its members have been recruited mostly from the lower ranks, and a junior official may always gain political status as a minister's *protégé*, through his family background, or through employment in a politically sensitive agency like the imperial secretariat. The 1966 changes in appointment procedures have not yet done much to sharpen the distinction between politicians and the rest, for the Prime Minister has not discriminated enough in his choice to make ministers distinctly his own appointees, or to lead to the formation of any 'opposition' of those not chosen.

This political class possesses a considerable homogeneity, due to its small size, its dependence on the Emperor, and the complex relationships between its members. The sheer genealogical aspect of this is most important, and illustrates not simply a tendency to choose high officials from members of established families, but also the way in which outsiders like Mulugéta Buli (26) or Däjazmach Keflé Ergätu (15), now Minister of the Interior, may, once they are established in office, be able to ally themselves with existing political dynasties. This homogeneity also reflects the distinctive position of the politicians as a 'transitional élite' produced by the fusion of the old-style imperial entourage with the small class of educated leaders common to the developing countries of Africa. The balance between these complementary sources of influence is central to the position of the new nobility, and we shall see that there has been a gradual fading in the importance of traditional traits, and some growth in the need for modern ones.

But despite these similarities, the tendency of Ethiopian politicians to split into competing factions riddles almost every government activity with their rivalries. The resulting groups are extraordinarily complicated; they are based on a wide variety of social, regional and other origins, on family connections, on personal friendships and enmities, and on the simple convenience of the moment. It is often quite impossible to predict how the government will divide on any given issue; but a general survey of the major divisions helps to bring out some important features of the government, and to illustrate some of the developments of the last twenty-five years.

The Nobility

In the Ethiopian political system, the Emperor is not the only source of legitimate authority. In the past, he has had to rule in concert both with the Church and with noblemen who themselves possess authority partly independent of his own. We have already seen how the power of the provincial nobility has been curbed by the centralisation of government since Téwodros, especially in the reign of Haile-Selassie himself. But noblemen have continued to be active in politics, and they form the most stable group within the central government.

The Ethiopian nobility, however, is not a distinct hereditary class. It is unusual to trace a powerful noble line, father to son, for more than three generations; different families and individuals rise and fall in a continually shifting pattern. One reason for this is that titles are not hereditary, but have to be earned by each individual holder, though the

65

son of a powerful father naturally starts with a big advantage. Another is the comparatively minor role of hereditary land-holding, as opposed to political and military office, in establishing a nobleman's power in the central government. A third reason is the bilateral kinship system which enables a nobleman to trace his descent equally through mother or father, and so tends to widen the class; Haile-Selassie himself derives his royal ancestry from his grandmother. It is also easy enough for a powerful politician to marry into the nobility, or to acquire the title and status which are the first step to becoming a nobleman himself.

This makes it very difficult to reach a satisfactory definition of the nobility. Often, the best criterion is simply whether a given politician is regarded by others and himself as a nobleman or not; for despite divergencies of outlook, noblemen are generally conscious of their own similarities of background and status, and of their differences from other members of the government. One aspect of this has been a tendency to despise upstart ministers whose lack of such personal status has forced them into complete and often servile dependence on the Emperor.

The leading noblemen have been descended from the major provincial dynasties, and from the great families which have surrounded the Shoan throne at least since the time of Menilek. Pride of place here goes to the family of Ras Kasa (13), whose genealogical claim to the throne was every bit as good as Haile-Selassie's. Ras Kasa himself, a great prince and devout churchman, typified much that was best in traditional Ethiopia, and provided a powerful support to the throne until his death in 1956. Three of his sons were murdered by the Italians in 1937. The youngest, Asratä (6), has served as provincial governor, President of the Senate, and since 1964 as the Emperor's Representative in Eritrea, where he combats Eritrean separatism with an iron hand. He helped to muster the forces which crushed the 1960 revolt, and he has a reputation as a determined conservative who might make a claim for the throne. He was given the title of *Ras* in 1966.

Second in precedence is the family of Ras Seyum (28), grandson of the Emperor Yohanes IV and ruler of Tegré, who was killed by the rebels in 1960. His son Mängäsha (21) also became a *Ras* in 1966, and since 1961 he has ruled in Tegré, where he takes an active part in development projects and appears to have built up a strong local power base. He governs by example and enthusiasm in the traditional Ethiopian manner, and is reluctant to co-operate with his equals or delegate to his inferiors. He and his nephew, Däjazmach Zäwdé Gäbrä-Selassie (36) who was Minister of Justice from 1961 to 1962, are the only leading noblemen to come from outside Shoa, though both are closely related by marriage with the imperial family.

Haile-Selassie's cousin Ras Imru (12) also ranks among the great lords.

He is a sincere and liberal man, reputed to be a socialist, though with many of the conservative traits natural to his traditional upbringing. He ruled as an enlightened provincial governor until the war, but since the Liberation he has been prevented from taking any active role in politics. For several years he was an ambassador in the United States and India, and recently he has stayed in Addis Ababa, as a rather pathetic figure in the Emperor's train. The 1960 rebels proclaimed him as a figurehead Prime Minister, in order to take advantage of his noble prestige and liberal reputation.

Other noblemen in the government have mostly come from the great families of Shoa, non-royal clans known as *Béza* and *Moja* which have roots in northern Shoa and have held high posts at court since Menilek's day and before. Lieutenant-General Abiy Abäbä (2) is the present leader of the *Béza*; a younger branch of the family, *Adisgé*, has risen to prominence in the last two generations, and includes Ras Bitwädäd Makonnen Endalkachäw (18), Prime Minister from 1943 to 1957, his son Endalkachäw Makonnen (7), Minister of Commerce from 1961 to 1966 and since then Ethiopia's representative on the Security Council, and several more. There has been only one *Moja* minister since the Liberation; the *Mojas* have a particular reputation for sticking together, and made a name for themselves in the 1960 revolt, when several of the leaders came from this clan.

Despite the participation of noblemen in the government, their prestige and independence have declined considerably with the Emperor's successful centralising policy, and Haile-Selassie has continued where the Italians left off in reducing them to dependence on the centre. One example of this is his very sparing use of the title of *Ras*, the highest below *Negus* or King, which has customarily been bestowed on the greatest leaders of the Empire. In the reign of Menilek there were some twenty Rasses at any given time, mostly the major provincial governors and the Emperor's chief supporters, and in 1930 four of the Rasses were the heads of the provincial dynasties of Shoa, Tegré, Gojam and Wälo. Haile-Selassie has created only eleven Rasses in the last twenty-five years. Two of them, Asratä (6) and Mängäsha (21), are major dynastic leaders in their own right; three more, Andargé (4), Mäsfen (23), and the late Makonnen Endalkachäw (18), are Shoan ministers and governors connected by marriage with the imperial family. Lastly, the title has been granted to several respected but politically impotent provincial noblemen in order to associate their provinces more closely with the centre; four of these have been leaders of old Eritrean families, reflecting Eritrea's special position, and to them may be added Ras Haylu Bäläw (11) who was elevated at the Liberation as the most amenable member of the dynasty of Gojam; the most recent creation, Ras Wubnäh, is an old resistance leader from

Bägémdär, and in 1967, the slightly lower title of *Bitwädäd* was given to four governors from Bägémdär, Gojam and Tegré.

In the central government, the nobility has fallen steadily in both numbers and prestige. Of a hundred and thirty-eight officials who have held high central government office since the Liberation, thirty would generally be regarded as belonging to it; but the proportion has dropped, with the expansion of the government and the replacement of traditional by more modern qualifications, from eight out of fifteen (53 per cent) in 1948 to nine out of sixty-eight (13 per cent) in 1966. It has always been, and remains, far higher in the provincial government, and as in many countries, noblemen have also tended to go into the armed forces. The status of the nobility has declined at the same time, and a present-day leader like Abiy Abäbä (2) commands nothing like the authority of an old feudal magnate like Ras Kasa (13); an educated nobleman of the younger generation has even less, and common educational backgrounds and the decline of the nobility's independence are gradually reducing the distinction between noblemen and other officials. Some caution is nevertheless required while Mängäsha (21) and Asratä (6) retain their present power in the north, for in the last few years they appear to have been allowed greater independence and political initiative than has been granted to any other provincial governor since the Liberation. It is too early to say whether this may form part of the historic pattern by which a weakening in central control as Haile-Selassie grows old is balanced by increased autonomy in the provinces.

Their traditional authority has been at the root of the noblemen's position: on the one hand, their functions within the government have been closely connected with it; and on the other, the fact that they are to some extent independent of the Emperor has led him to entrust less to them. Though some noblemen have certainly been very important, the positions of greatest influence have always been held by men whom the Emperor has raised to high office himself. One effect of this has been that the aristocracy has tended to form the opposition, though usually the loyal opposition, among the groups of courtiers who surround the throne. They have formed the chief opponents first of Wäldä-Giyorgis (33), later of Mulugéta Buli (26) and Makonnen Habtä-Wäld (19), and most recently of Aklilu Habtä-Wäld (3) and Yelma Derésa (35). It is they, after all, who have lost most through the Emperor's concentration of power in himself, and it is therefore not surprising that all of the revolts against Haile-Selassie, including that of 1960, have been led by noblemen.

Since members of the different noble families have intermarried a great deal, the group as a whole is linked by a network of family relationships, whose scope and complexity are by no means exhausted by the accompanying genealogical table.* This network has helped to maintain the stability of the group, and has provided each member of it with numbers of cousins and relatives by marriage on whom to call for political support. Some families of the high aristocracy, like Ras Imru's (12), have married outside it. In this way, the nobility merges into other groups and families which may work closely with their immediate noble relatives, but which would not be considered by noblemen as a whole as belonging to their class. Connections with other groups may also be maintained through the band of *protégés* and retainers by which most noblemen are surrounded. There are also many times when noblemen judge it best to co-operate with other groups, but it is most rare for members of the high nobility to subordinate themselves to men of lower status; one of the few exceptions was when Abiy Abäbä (2) worked closely with Wäldä-Giyorgis (33) before 1955, a connection which was greatly disapproved of by his fellow noblemen.

The posts which noblemen have filled in the central government have, by and large, been those which their traditional functions would lead one to expect. Until 1966 the Minister of Defence was always a nobleman, and so have been five of the eight Ministers of the Interior, since blue blood is an advantage in dealing with aristocratic provincial governors. Four noblemen have been Ministers of Justice, another subject of traditional importance, but it is curious that the Ministry of Public Works should have been for long periods under noble administration; a similar tenure of the Ministry of Posts might be explained by the need to find room for dignitaries too little used to ministerial administration to be entrusted with any more important department. Several court officials and one of the two Prime Ministers have also been from the nobility, but only a very few noblemen have held major posts in other ministries, and all of these have been educated abroad since the Liberation. They have scarcely been represented in the imperial secretariat, for many years the most important organ of government, or in the Ministry of Foreign Affairs, which is also closely controlled by the Emperor, and they have been markedly absent from most of the ministries dealing with finance or social and economic development.

Although the nobility has for the most part filled the more traditional posts, it is a mistake to regard it as a solidly conservative group. Several of the younger noblemen have combined their inherited self-confidence with a modern education to provide some of the most radical elements in the government, as is shown by their part in the 1960 revolt. Equally, when the Emperor reconstituted the administration to give it a more liberal flavour after the failure of that attempt, this was done largely by giving ministries to younger noblemen such as Endalkachäw Makonnen

* Refer to Figure 5 at the back of the book.

(7), Mika'él Imru (25), and Zäwdé Gäbrä-Selassie (36). To a large extent, this is a difference between generations, though between these three and Ras Asratä (6), who is undoubtedly a conservative, there is an age difference of only about ten years.

Closely connected with the nobility have been the Patriots, as the leaders of the wartime resistance are called. Many of them were noblemen, and others gained analogous prestige and independence through their wartime campaigns. It is not surprising that they should regard themselves as the true lovers of Ethiopia who had borne the heat and burden of the day, or that they should look down on the collaborators in the government still more than the noblemen look down on their social inferiors. At the time of the Liberation, they were an important political force, and several of them were taken into the government. Ras Abäbä Arägay (1), grandson of one of Menilek's generals, was the most important of them, and others who owed their positions largely to their Patriot records included the Galla Däjazmach Gäräsu Duki, and the Betwädäds Mängäsha Jämbäré and Nägash Bäzabeh of Gojam. Other Patriots, like Ras Mäsfen Seläshi (23), were already connected with important government families.

But while the Patriots were too important to be ignored, they were also too independent to be trusted. They had built up military followings whose first loyalty was to themselves, and they had gained great prestige by fighting their own battles for Ethiopia at a time when the Emperor had retired to the safety of Bath. Their sources of authority and of physical power were thus both independent of the Emperor, and some of them openly regarded themselves as his moral superiors. They were reduced to imperial control through the familiar means of divide and rule; many of them were brought to Addis Ababa and so cut off from their local bases of support, and the potentially dangerous were prevented from building up their strength by deft changes in appointments. Only Ras Abäbä (1)was given important posts, and even he, who was easier to handle than most, occasionally dabbled in conspiracy, and was kept for much of the time until 1947 in Sidamo or Tegré; thereafter, his position was gradually undermined through involvement in government intrigues and questionable financial transactions.

That Haile-Selassie's fears of the Patriots were well founded is shown by the number of revolts and conspiracies in which they took important parts, including the 1944 revolt in Gojam, a plot centred on the Crown Prince in 1947, and an attempt to assassinate the Emperor in 1951.[1] Perhaps the greatest of all the Patriot leaders, Afä Negus Takälä Wäldä-Hawariyat (32), has been in and out of jail for all the twenty-five years since the Liberation. But the importance of the Patriots has naturally declined over these twenty-five years, as many of them have died and a post-war generation has replaced them; and though there are still a number in active politics, and an event with wartime echoes like the proposed loan from Italy in 1964 still has the power to unite them, they no longer form a group distinct from the nobility.

The continued though declining presence of men of independent status in a government so dedicated to centralisation as that of Haile-Selassie also makes it necessary to ask whether they have any essential function to perform in the present-day administration. It seems that they are needed to maintain connections between the central government and the more traditional sectors of the state. One aspect of this was Ras Kasa's position as a spokesman for the Church; and their role is further illustrated by the employment of noblemen as Ministers of Defence and Interior, and also as Presidents of the Senate. In these fields, and even more in the provincial government, traditional sources of authority are still required, and Haile-Selassie would run a great risk were he to allow his government to get out of touch with them. While he could probably have dispensed with any particular nobleman since the Liberation, excepting always Ras Kasa (13), he could not have rid himself of the whole class without seriously weakening the political structure of Ethiopia. It is a vital though still unanswered question whether Haile-Selassie's policy towards the nobility has already undermined the cohesion and leadership which they might be able to provide in time of national crisis.

Non-Noble Groupings

As well as the nobility, almost every social group is represented in the government, with a higher proportion of those which have had the easiest access to education and patronage. This helps to explain the number of Churchmen, since until recently the only formal education has been that provided by the Church, and as in medieval Europe, this has been one of the main avenues to high office for the lowly born. Other officials have come from the squirearchy, which with the clergy forms almost the whole middle class of traditional Ethiopia, since trade has largely been carried out by alien groups, mostly of low social status. There are also sons of peasants and servants among the high officials, but they are naturally under-represented in proportion to their great numbers, having for the most part neither the inclination nor the opportunity to engage in government.

Middle-class groups of more recent origin have furnished other important officials. There has now been time for several families to emerge with a distinctly civil service background, including those of Blatengéta

Mahtämä-Selassie (17), former minister of many portfolios and son of a Minister of the Pen; and the Minister of Justice, Ato Mamo Tadäsä (20). Both of these were educated abroad, and naturally had no difficulty in introducing themselves into government circles. A few families have also been particularly exposed to foreign influence, often with long residence abroad, and many Eritreans have had the analogous experience of Italian rule.

But of all the social divisions of the government, the nobility is the only one which forms a recognisable political unit; the others do not comprise a single corresponding group, but rather provide the general mass of officials, much divided among themselves, against whom the nobility stand out. They share a number of characteristics, but these tend to divide rather than unite them, for as the noblemen are kept together by their semi-independent status and their network of family relations, so the others are distinguished by their lack of these sources of unity and support.

One result of this is that they are far more closely subject to the Emperor's control, for such authority as they possess must derive almost entirely from him, and most of them have reached high office simply because he has chosen to raise them to it; in doing so, he has naturally encouraged those who would be most dependent on himself. The differences which this makes was illustrated in 1955, when Wäldä-Giyorgis (33) was exiled to the governorship of Arusi; depending as he did on the Emperor, he was obliged to accept the appointment, and thereupon disappeared from political life. His noble supporter Abiy Abäbä (2), on the other hand, refused appointment to an equivalent post in Sidamo, and eventually accepted the embassy in Paris; as a nobleman with connections throughout the government, he could be sure of returning eventually to high office.

This dependence on the Emperor is particularly great among those who collaborated with the Italians during the occupation. To anyone used to the strictness with which collaborators have been excluded from high office in Europe, the ease with which they have maintained their position in Ethiopia comes as a surprise. Among the first appointments after Haile-Selassie's entry into Addis Ababa in May 1941 was that of a noted collaborator, Ayälä Gäbré, as Minister of Justice; two others, who later reached ministerial rank, retained their posts in the propaganda department, where under the Italians they had largely been employed in vilifying the Emperor. No fewer than six of the ministers early in 1967 had aided or acquiesced in the occupation, even though many of the collaborators, like the Patriots, have now died or retired. This certainly shows the Emperor's clemency and lack of resentment towards those who have deserted him; it may also reflect a less serious view of collaboration with the enemy than in Europe, stemming perhaps from the Amhara assumption of the worst in human nature, and acceptance of the tendency for followers to forsake a defeated leader. But there is also in this use of the collaborators a good deal of deliberate political calculation. The noblemen who collaborated, such as Ras Getachäw and Dajazmach Haile-Selassie Gugsa, were not readmitted to political life. The others were mostly employed in central government posts under the close supervision of the Emperor, on whom they were obliged to rely completely, and where they helped to balance the Patriots. Several former collaborators among the high officials have been noted for their inability to take decisions without reference to the Emperor. Asfeha Wäldä-Mika'él (5), a former interpreter for the Italians,[2] who as an Eritrean was in a rather different position from the other collaborators, moved into politics by attaching himself successively to the Crown Prince, Wäldä-Giyorgis (33) and Ras Andargé (4); this enabled him to become Chief Executive of Eritrea in 1955, and he took a leading part in dissolving the Ethio-Eritrean Federation. He was rewarded with the Ministry of Justice in 1963, moving to Public Health in the 1966 reshuffle, and provides the clearest example of a politician who has made his way up by deft changes in political allegiance.

Another group which has incurred the suspicion of the nobility and other traditional sources of authority are those high officials who have married foreigners, and thus aroused the long-standing Ethiopian distrust of undue foreign influence. The Prime Minister himself is married to a Frenchwoman, and Mamo Tadäsa (20) and Menasé Haylé (24), who are both among the most influential politicians of the younger generation, are married respectively to a Frenchwoman and an American Negress. This certainly refutes the charge, sometimes heard, that marriage to a foreigner will ruin an Ethiopian's political career, but it may well form part of the common pattern by which the Emperor has favoured those whose personal position is weak, in order to be the surer of his own supremacy. For while their dependence on the Emperor has in one way weakened the position of the non-noble politicians, it has had corresponding advantages, in that the Emperor has for this reason relied more upon them. He has delegated most to those whom he could most easily control; some of these have been from the lowest classes, some from the Church, and those, like Yelma Derésa (35), who have reached great influence from the minor nobility, have done so by waiving the claims to independent status which this might have given them.

This dependence, and the absence of the ties which bind the nobility, has also meant that connections between non-noble groups have for the most part lacked the stability of the aristocratic alliance. Family relations may unite politicians here and there, like the brothers Habtä-Wäld, but they do not extend to a whole class, and their groups have therefore for the most part been based on power relations. One aspect of this has been the informal alliances between major figures which have guided much of the general tenor of the government, and notably those between Wäldä-Giyorgis (33) and Makonnen Habtä-Wäld (19) before 1955, and between Yelma Derésa (35) and Aklilu Habtä-Wäld (3) since 1960. There have been many less important partnerships of convenience, and any influential figure attracts the support and co-operation of less forceful politicians who do not want to offend him. These all ultimately depend, however, on the support of the Emperor, as was shown when he detached Makonnen Habtä-Wäld from Wäldä-Giyorgis as a prelude to the latter's fall.

Another form of organisation has been the personal machine which many major politicians have built up; a network of *protégés*, skilfully placed in the most important parts of the government, makes sure that its leader's orders are carried out, and helps to frustrate the designs of his opponents. A characteristic device for achieving both of these ends is to place one's own supporters immediately beneath an opponent, so that they come to oneself for orders, instead of to their nominal chief, whose own instructions they are at the same time well placed for blocking. They also take part in intrigues in which the leader does not want to appear directly, they help to spread rumours, and in general they carry out the tasks of underlings in a party organisation. But it must be remembered that such a party is organised as a personal following, and is very different from the political parties of most other countries. It has no unifying aim or policy beyond the preservation of power, and it cannot survive the departure of the individual who built it up. These followings have been one of the most important instruments for wielding great power within the administration, though it has always been essential for a politician to enjoy the Emperor's confidence first, since it would otherwise be impossible to build up an effective following at all.

The heyday of such followings was before 1960, when the government was still largely controlled by men brought up in a traditional way. Wäldä-Giyorgis (33) and Makonnen Habtä-Wäld (19), in particular, headed large networks, and others had their more modest organisations. Since 1960, there has been no such vigorous exponent of traditional forms, and the most important political machine has been that of Yelma Derésa (35), which has operated in a less devious manner than those of earlier years. This is one instance of the trend away from traditional methods and towards more modern ones which has taken place since 1960, a trend also found in the decline of the imperial secretariat, the rise of the Prime Ministry, and the reform of the financial system.

While many of the most important politicians have acted through such alliances and personal machines, others have wielded influence in other ways. Mulugéta Buli (26), the former Bodyguard commander who was at his most powerful between 1955 and 1958, worked directly with the Emperor, and did not disguise his dislike for other politicians, though he was helped by a small personal following. The present Prime Minister, Aklilu Habtä-Wäld (3), has by contrast had virtually no machine at all, and though he too has worked closely with the Emperor, he has always been ready to co-operate with other groups and individuals. Other groupings have been guided by personal abilities and dislikes, such as Takälä Wäldä-Hawariyat's (32) capacity for intrigue and bitter hatred of Wäldä-Giyorgis (33), or by simple convenience, in the way that many politicians were content to support Wäldä-Giyorgis when he was in power, and transferred their allegiance when he fell.

Regional and Ethnic Groups

In the politics of modern Africa, it is scarcely necessary to emphasise the importance of regional groupings, or of the tribal or ethnic divisions to which they correspond. The same problems exist in this respect in Ethiopia as in the rest of Africa, but, as so often they are transformed by historical influences and by the peculiar palace politics through which the government is carried on.

The pre-eminence of the palace has meant, first, that regional differences have been raised less acutely than in many other parts of Africa, where such differences have often been institutionalised and encouraged by an initially democratic system which has led to the formation of political parties on ethnic lines. There are no parties in Ethiopia, and attempts to mobilise regional rivalries for political purposes have been discouraged, and at times severely repressed. Instead, regional differences have been expressed, at least in the central government, through the composition of the factions which surround the throne, and this has so far been an undoubted advantage to a country whose ethnic unity is fragile.

But second, historical developments and the position of the throne have led to a very uneven representation of the different areas in the government, and this disproportion has been very greatly to the advantage of the central province of Shoa. The present administration has developed in Shoa from the household of a Shoan Emperor and as part of a policy of centralisation on a Shoan base. The highest posts have therefore tended to go to Shoans, and on the outbreak of war in 1935, for instance, they occupied forty-three of the fifty-two most important positions in the central government.[3] This preponderence has been perpetuated by the

75

sources of patronage, by the concentration of schools and other facilities in Addis Ababa, and perhaps also by some tendency to favour Shoans on grounds of loyalty, since they naturally tend to be more committed to a basically Shoan régime. This is illustrated by the accompanying table, which shows the numbers of senior officials from different areas since 1941; except for the period immediately after the Liberation, the proportion of Shoans has never fallen below 60 per cent and has usually been about two-thirds, though there has been some decline from the peak of 77 per cent in 1959. Shoa has also provided the great majority of the most important politicians, and some preference is suggested by the fact that only just over half of the Ethiopian ambassadors abroad since the Liberation have been Shoan, whereas almost a quarter have been Eritrean, a distinctly lower proportion of the former and higher one of the latter than in the central government; the significance of this is that ambassadorships have been powerless posts, often given to officials in disgrace and others of whose loyalty the government has not been altogether confident.

Eritrea has nevertheless been by far the best represented of the provinces outside Shoa, and sharp rises in the numbers of Eritrean high officials in the central government have followed both the Federation in 1952, and its ending with the incorporation of Eritrea into the ordinary administrative system ten years later. This has been partly due to the higher degree of economic development in Eritrea than elsewhere in the Empire, with a consequently higher number of qualified Eritreans, and to the steady migration of Eritreans to Addis Ababa. But Eritrea has also been the most independent and most separatist of the provinces and the only one which it has so far been necessary to appease by appointment of its natives to central government positions.

Particularly striking, by contrast, has been the very small number of senior officials from the central Amhara provinces. Gojam, Bägémdär, Lasta and the surrounding areas form the heart of the Amhara country, and until the last quarter of the nineteenth century they also provided the core of the government. Yet today these areas are represented only by the smallest scattering of individuals. One reason for this may be the scarcity of men with a modern education, by comparison with the areas both to the north and to the south, but even more important is the absence of those historical and dynastic links which have given such advantages to the Shoans. The Gondaris and Gojamis have had far fewer ties with the present régime, and have therefore had less chance to establish themselves; several of their leaders have been consigned to the dignified impotence of the Senate, whilst their Shoan equivalents have been given executive positions.

The same has been true, but to a lesser extent, of the Tegreans, who come from the northern area towards the Eritrean border. They have been

Table 3

Numbers of Individuals from Different Regions holding high office in the Central Government, 1941–1966

Month & Year:	12/42	12/48	12/53	5/57	7/59	2/62	1/64	11/66	Total
Shoa	7	10	16	23	30	27	31	43	85
(%)	(54%)	(66%)	(66%)	(70%)	(77%)	(64%)	(60%)	(63%)	(62%)
Gojam	2	1	2	2	–	–	1	3	6
Bägémdär	–	1	–	–	1	2	2	2	5
Tegré	1	1	–	3	3	4	3	2	7
Eritrea	2	–	4	2	1	4	9	9	19
Wäläga	1	2	1	1	1	3	3	5	6
Sidamo	–	–	1	1	1	1	1	1	2
Ilubabor	–	–	–	–	–	–	–	1	2
Harari	–	–	–	1	1	–	–	1	2
Somali	–	–	–	–	1	1	1	1	2
Unknown	–	–	–	–	1	–	1	–	2
Total	13	15	24	33	39	42	52	68	138

This table covers officials with the ranks of minister, minister of state and vice-minister. The right-hand column brings together all such officials appointed between 1941 and the end of 1966.

helped by the possession of a strong local dynasty linked by marriage with that of Shoa, and the three Tegreans who have become ministers have all had very strong connections with the imperial family. They have also for many purposes formed a single group with the Eritreans, since they speak the same language and have much else in common, and they have thus been able to benefit from the combined sources of patronage.

The importance of local political leadership is further illustrated by the Wälägas from western Ethiopia, who form the only distinct group of Galla in the government. Their position is rather different from that of the great majority of the peoples absorbed into the Empire at the end of the nineteenth century; they were not so much conquered by the Amhara as allied with them, and remained under the government of local leaders who became Christian and married into the imperial family of Shoa. They have thus reached something approaching an equal footing with the peoples of traditional highland Ethiopia, and they have also shown a particular enthusiasm for modern education. Several Wälägas have occupied important government posts, the most notable being the Minister of Finance, Yelma Derésa (35).

They form an interesting contrast with the Galla of Wälo, who were brought into the political system in the 1870s, and were one of the most active forces in Ethiopian politics for over forty years before the death of their leader, Negus Mika'él, in 1918. They came close to controlling the throne under Lej Iyasu, and Haile-Selassie himself acknowledged their power by marrying Mika'él's granddaughter. He has nevertheless always regarded them, with some justice, as his enemies, and since the overthrow of Lej Iyasu they have played no part whatever in the central government.

The other provinces have been represented only by occasional individuals in the central government, and the only major politician to come from these areas, Mulugéta Buli (26), owed his position not to membership of any provincial group but rather, if anything, to his lack of membership of any of them. The peoples thus largely excluded from the government are mostly from the south of Ethiopia, including the provinces of Ilubabor, Käfa, Gämu Gofa, Sidamo, Arusi and Balé. They have never formed part of the central government, with which they lack religious, historical or dynastic ties, and it is therefore not in the least surprising that so very few of them should be found in important posts in Addis Ababa.

This pattern of provincial representation must be looked at in relation to the fact that the Shoan connections of a politician are likely to be the most important ones, and to the gradual emergence in Addis Ababa of a community of civil servants who tend to become assimilated to the Shoans. Thus, the father of General Mär'ed Mängäsha (22), Minister of Defence until his death in 1966, was from Gojam, but Mär'ed himself would generally be counted as a Shoan, because his major political connections were through his Shoan mother, and he acted as a member of the Shoan nobility. He was nevertheless the president of the Gojami regional association in Addis Ababa, and he was used in this way to help link the Gojamis with the administration.

Within the framework of the central government, provincial origins have had some influence, especially as a means of choosing protégés and building up personal followings. There has been a tendency to trust one's compatriots more than others, and help them in the government. A group recruited through provincial relations may try to gain benefits for its home area, especially in recent years, but such relations have also been used to establish connections through which to exercise power within the central government. One cannot talk of any systematic organisation, or even of concerted action, by politicians from a given area; but contacts between them are greatly encouraged by their common origin, and it is natural for an official to work to a certain extent through personal connections with others from his district. In this way, regional connections partly replace the family and status ties which help to unite the nobility, though the essential conditions of loyalty and dependence on the Emperor have ensured that such groups have had no overt separatist leanings. The Shoans have naturally tended to form the central mass of the government, from which other regions are distinguished, but even among them there have been a number of territorial subdivisions. Wäldä-Giyorgis (33) and Makonnen Habtä-Wäld (19) were both from the Bulga area of northern Shoa, and were said to favour their compatriots in choosing their *protégés*. Even more marked are the connections among those from the nearby district of Mänz, who are noted for the attachment which they retain for their homeland long after leaving it for Addis Ababa,[4] and who have their own particular regional association. The imperial family comes from the area, and this leads the Mänzis to regard themselves as a special élite. Another subdivision well represented in the government, and one which also has links with the imperial family, is that of the Amhara settlers and administrators who went to Harär with Ras Makonnen, Haile-Selassie's father, in the late nineteenth and early twentieth centuries.

The Tegreans and Eritreans have a particular reputation for clannishness, and in so far as this is justified, it may be due to a greater willingness to co-operate than is generally found among the Amhara; certainly, they are for the most part far more open and less secretive. They also tend to feel their position as a minority, with an intensity sometimes amounting almost to a persecution complex, and this further encourages them to combine. The result is seen in the tendency of Tegreans and Eritreans in high positions to move others of their kind into posts beneath them, and is to some extent evident in the ministries headed by northerners, where the proportion of Tegreans and Eritreans tends to be rather higher than in the rest of the government. They also illustrate the limitations of regional groups, however, for there are many cases of Tegrean or Eritrean subordinates at odds with ministers from the same area, and a few Eritreans, such as Asfeha Wäldä-Mika'él (5), seem to have tried deliberately to cut themselves off from their provincial origins.

The similar Galla tendency to combine is most clearly seen in the financial administration, where Yelma Derésa (35) has moved several of his fellow Wälägas into important posts, especially in the vital Budget Department of the Ministry of Finance; he has also employed Gallas in the Investment Bank and the provincial financial services, and he appears to have been trying to establish himself as a Galla leader. This sort of position can be precarious, since it runs the danger of rousing suspicions of local separatism, as was shown when a Galla breakaway movement late in 1966 proposed that Yelma himself become Prime Minister.

The unevenness of provincial representation in the central government, and its bias in favour of those who accept the imperial régime, may have helped to preserve the consensus on which the government has rested. But since this consensus has been achieved by suppressing some local interests, and under-representing others, it cannot be relied on to reflect with any accuracy feelings in the country at large, and its basis is therefore likely to be unstable. In particular, it provides little guide as to what might happen if serious upheavals on Haile-Selassie's departure brought ethnic divisions sharply into the open. The risk of division along ethnic or tribal lines is with little doubt the greatest danger that Ethiopia will have to face, and experience elsewhere in Africa has shown that latent differences of this kind can be brought very quickly to the surface once political conscious-ness has been aroused. And there are signs that such consciousness is slowly being aroused in Ethiopia today.

Any ethnic threat to the basic unity of the Empire would almost cer-tainly come from either of two sources: the Eritreans and Tigreans in the north, or the Gallas in the south. The Somalis in the south-east would probably take advantage of weaknesses elsewhere to break away to Somalia, but they could hardly succeed if the rest of Ethiopia held together. The other peripheral peoples are mostly small and divided, and in practical terms they have nowhere to go. The Amharas of the centre have no separatist inclinations, whatever the regional jealousies that from time to time divide them. They are the rulers and colonisers who have created the modern Empire, and they tend to look with suspicion and dis-quiet at attempts at self-assertion by the surrounding peoples; anyone of whatever group whose first loyalty was to national unity would in the last resort have to take their side, and any strong and united Ethiopia will have to continue to rely to a large extent upon them.

Of the possible sources of basic disunity, the Eritrean problem is most immediately pressing. There has been some Eritrean separatism since the time of Federation and before, though it has tended to fluctuate with the state of the harvest and other incidental factors; but since 1963 or 1964 an organised movement has developed, based on the western areas towards the Sudanese border, and apparently receiving intermittent arms and aid through the Sudan. Reports in March 1967 that its leaders were being trained in guerrilla warfare in Cuba and China may well have been instigated by the Ethiopians, who have been prone to raise the spectre of communism to ensure American support. Though the number of hard-core Eritrean resistance fighters is probably only a thousand or two, they have been able to hold down a Division of the Ethiopian army through classic guerrilla methods, maintaining themselves by a protection racket among local traders. In January 1967 the Emperor characteristi-cally took the problem into his own hands: he spent a month on a visit to almost every corner of the province, distributing largesse and trying to conciliate Moslems and other local groups. As a personal effort it was remarkable, but such methods are unlikely to do much to improve the basic situation. The Eritreans themselves are nevertheless divided, for a viable independence movement requires the support of the Christian highlands of the province, as well as of the Moslem plains. There have been some Christian converts to the separatist cause, including Däjazmach Tädla Bayru (30), a former leader of the party for union with Ethiopia and Chief Executive of Eritrea, but the highlanders have close connections with the Tegreans to the south, and though they are a proud people with considerable resentment of the privileged position of the Shoans, their two thousand-year links with the traditional Ethiopian state may prove the strongest in time of crisis.

In the long term, the greater danger to national unity is more likely to come from the Gallas, who probably compose a good half of the entire Ethiopian people. They were mostly brought into the Empire, by conquest, only seventy or eighty years ago, and in many areas they have just cause for resentment against their Amhara overlords. Much of their land, in particular, has been lost to Shoan settlers and absentee landlords, and local revolts are constantly breaking out and being suppressed in many of the southern provinces. This situation has existed for many years, but it has recently been reinforced by a growth of ethnic consciousness among educated Gallas. This trend is visible among university students, but it came closest to the surface towards the end of 1966, when a Shoan Galla general, Tadäsä Biru (29), and several associates tried to use a Galla regional self-help association as a means to arouse provincial Gallas to an awareness of their position, and press for political action. The government acted sharply against them, though it must be added that they commited several acts of needless violence as well as the political offences, and they were brought to trial before a special court in February 1967. This incident caused a great deal of interest, and certainly contributed to the growth of a Galla consciousness; but the Galla are a very diverse people, their position is very complicated, and it cannot be taken for granted that they will arise as a united political force in the near future, or at all. In accordance with its general policy of centralisation, the government has tried to assimilate the Galla to the Amhara, for instance through the spread of the Amharic language and intermarriage between Galla and Amhara families. The Imperial family, in fact, is now genealogically more Galla than Amhara, and there are few members of the Shoan nobility who have no Galla blood. At least in Shoa, where the process of assimilation has gone furthest, it is therefore impossible to make any clear division between the two groups, though the actual effectiveness of the process can only be gauged in time of crisis; Tadäsä Biru (29), for example, might have served as a model of an assimilated Shoan Galla until 1966, and many Ethiopians were before then unaware that he was a Galla at all.

Centrifugal tendencies may be counteracted both by the Amhara core, with its colonists and administrators throughout the Empire, and by the growth of national Ethiopian loyalties. Such loyalties have a far stronger base on which to build than in most African countries, and a sizeable proportion of Gallas, northerners and other groups certainly claim to place national unity above regional considerations. Should it come to a crisis after Haile-Selassie's departure, the deciding factor may well be the cohesion of the armed forces, in which all three of the main ethnic groups are well represented.

Church and Religion

The Ethiopian Church and state have long been linked in a very close alliance in which the state, or in practice the Emperor, has usually been the dominant partner. But the Church has retained an independent authority, derived from its links with the Patriarchate of Alexandria and its unquestioned spiritual supremacy, and Emperors themselves have gained much of their legitimacy from consecration by its archbishops; the withdrawal of Church support from Emperors who rejected its teaching, as we have seen, has usually been decisive in bringing their downfall.

The Church has therefore, like the nobility, incurred Haile-Selassie's long-standing wariness of sources of authority independent of himself, and a series of measures have been taken to reduce its effective political strength. This process started during the Occupation, for the Italians first attacked the Church as a centre of national resistance, and then divided it by inducing some of the senior clergy to support them, and to excommunicate those who opposed the Italian régime. But the Emperor took advantage of the situation on his return, and with the Regulations for the Administration of the Church of 1942, he took the first steps in centralising the Church under government supervision. This measure defined the different sorts of Church land and their liability to taxation, created a unified financial structure with a central Church treasury, abolished the temporal jurisdiction of the Church courts, and provided for high ecclesiastical appointments to be subject to the Emperor's approval.[5]

These changes were made, rather incongruously, under the authority of an article of the 1931 Constitution empowering the Emperor to organise administrative departments, and the Church was brought more explicitly under his control by the Revised Constitution of 1955. The Church was then proclaimed to be the Established Church of the Empire, a formula which presumably makes it possible for the secular authorities to regulate its position by legislation, and the Emperor was empowered to promulgate all Church regulations other than purely spiritual and monastic ones; he was also required to confirm appointments of the Archbishop and other bishops. This last power had only been possible since the Ethiopian Church gained autonomy from Alexandria by an agreement of 1948, a measure which satisfied Ethiopian nationalism and also cut off the Church from outside sources which the Emperor could not control. The centralisation of the Church has further been emphasised by the appointment of one bishop for each of the provinces, so that the diocesan organisation has duplicated the administrative one, though the Church is so firmly rooted in the Christian parts of the country as to make complete centralisation along the lines of the civil government virtually impossible.

This background of involvement and recent subordination is reflected in the Church's position in the central government. Certainly that position is still strong. The Emperor and the imperial family are constitutionally required to profess the Ethiopian Orthodox Faith, and Haile-Selassie is punctilious in his presence at Church occasions. This personal devotion to Orthodox Christianity is by no means incompatible with his policy of reducing the Church to his own supervision, and indeed helps to further it. Some attempt has been made to establish national unity by assimilating other areas to the essentially Orthodox Amhara, as is seen in the Civil Code of 1960 which recognises monogamous marriage as the only legal form and as a goal for the whole Empire, though there has also been some practical recognition that the requirements of Christianity cannot altogether be insisted on. The government's general support for the Church has been repaid in political allegiance, most clearly illustrated in the Archbishop's appeal for loyalty to the Emperor during the 1960 revolt, and there is little doubt that in time of crisis the Church would favour a 'traditionalist' government led by a ruling Emperor.

The relevance of religion to politics is further illustrated by the regional composition of the government, for both the Wälo and the Wäläga Galla were brought into the Ethiopian political system when their leaders were converted to Christianity, and otherwise their marriages with members of the Shoan royal family would have been impossible. Religious and family links, rather than ethnic identity in itself, have thus provided the chief criteria for admission to political life, and by the same token the southern provinces, from which so few high officials have come, are also the Moslem ones. There had been no Moslem minister until the Eritrean Salah Henit was appointed Minister of Posts in 1966, and of one hundred and thirty-eight senior central government officials since the war, only six have been Moslems; three of these have been Eritreans, two Somalis, and one Harari. This paucity of Moslems, in a land where they may account for as much as half of the population, is not simply the result of 'discrimination'; it reflects, rather, the way in which they have been largely left out of the whole sphere of government activity, in terms alike of education, recruitment, patronage and political groupings.

The influence of the Church is thus pervasive, but any more precise identification of its place in the central government must take account of the fact that it does not exist for this purpose as an identifiable institution, with more or less defined powers, functions and connections *vis-à-vis* the civil administration. Any Ethiopian 'institution' tends to crumble away on close approach, and the Church is no exception; it may best be defined, rather, in terms of the prevalence of certain attitudes and the influence of certain officials which are closely bound up with Orthodox Christianity.

One of these attitudes has been the preservation of Ethiopia's traditional insularity, for the Church, as custodian of much that is most distinct in Ethiopia's heritage, has been a primary object of foreign attack from the time of Grañ and the Portuguese Jesuits in the sixteenth century to that of the Italian Occupation. As a traditional influence itself, the Church has a tendency to support other established sources of authority, and to distrust foreigners whom it does not understand, and by whom it is little understood. This outlook may not be shared by those few clergy who have received a modern education at the Addis Ababa Theological College and abroad, and who can take their place with aplomb at ecumenical conferences the world over; but as yet these are far from typical of Ethiopian ecclesiastics, partaking as they do in a series of influences which have set Ethiopian insularity very much in retreat.

An attitude more clearly connected with the Church is the insistence that Orthodox Christianity should stand at the centre of modern Ethiopian nationalism, and should be an essential element in the securing of national unity. This is found in an emphasis on the connections, already considered, between Church and state, and in attempts to use the machinery of the state to foster Christian practices and assimilate the peoples of the outlying areas to the national religion. It may also gain strength from the religious aspects of the Ethio-Somali quarrel, and from appeal to the familiar picture of Ethiopia as a Christian island surrounded by potentially hostile neighbours.

But this attitude also is in retreat before a combination of government policy and political circumstance, seen first in the increasing secularism of the Ethiopian state. One aspect of this is the Pan-African foreign policy which has made it necessary for the government to play down Ethiopian peculiarities, and in particular its long-standing differences with Islam; joint communiqués these days are couched in terms of centuries of friendly co-operation. But far more important is the way in which development, as in Europe, is forcing the state to expand into fields where the Church simply cannot keep pace with it. Secular education has long overtaken the Church schools, and is pushing men to the fore for whom Church traditions no longer mean very much. The Church has had little to do with agricultural development or medical services, and to make much contribution it will have to change much of its own outlook and to adapt itself to a world in which the state is king. From being one of the twin columns of the established order, it will have to adapt its supporting role to that of a flying buttress.

The second reason for which a Church-centred nationalism is no longer adequate is the increasing need for an accommodation with Ethiopian Islam. It is clear that the dream of a wholly Christian Ethiopia cannot be realised, at least within the country's present boundaries, and that the achievement of national unity will require some Moslem participation in the state. The Emperor has often spoken publicly for religious toleration, and he regularly receives Moslem leaders at the end of Ramadan and confers titles on Moslem notables in Harär and Eritrea. There have been signs of a more active conciliation since 1966, with the appointment of Salah Henit to the Council of Ministers, the Emperor's gifts for Moslem education and similar purposes during his January 1967 tour of Eritrea, and an increasing number of imperial state visits to Moslem countries. Protests by Churchmen against such activities have reportedly been rebuffed.

It has also been the Emperor's policy to bring non-Orthodox Christians into the government, where they could balance the Orthodox Churchmen. One of these has been Amanu'él Abraham, a devout Lutheran who encouraged the establishment of foreign mission schools during his three-year tenure of the Ministry of Education in the mid-1940s, especially in his native province of Wäläga; his dismissal was generally ascribed to clerical influence, but he has since held many other senior posts and is now the Minister of Communications. Catholics have also been used, and despite strong protest, Churchmen failed to prevent the opening of diplomatic relations with the Vatican, or the employment of Jesuits in the University College of Addis Ababa. In this case, the Emperor adopted a characteristic compromise by appointing a devoted Orthodox Churchman, Blata Marsé-Hazen, as Chairman of the College Governors, so that anything of which the Church disapproved could be taken to the palace. Haile-Selassie has appointed several Catholics to ministerial rank, some of them colleagues from his own brief education by Catholic priests in Harär, and Catholics at present in the Council of Ministers include Mamo Tadäsä (20) at Justice and Asfeha Wäldä-Mika'él (5) at Public Health. But there has been no evidence of any political groupings based on these affiliations, which tend to be sources of political weakness.

As the attitudes characteristic of the Church have declined in the government, so also has the representation of Churchmen. For Church influence has depended especially on men with Church connections, and at a time when Church schools provided the country's only formal education, there were naturally quite a number of them in court positions. There has been a particular place for the *debteras*, who are not priests but custodians of the Church's fund of learning, and who have a reputation as subtle, not to say sneaky, politicians; like most Churchmen they tend to work close to the court, and one of the more important of them was Gäbrä-Wäld Engeda-Wärq (8), Vice-Minister of the Pen and secretary of the Crown Council until his death in the 1960 revolt. A priest killed at the same time was Aba Hana Jima (10), Haile-Selassie's private confessor, who had been his confidant for over forty years. Beyond this palace clique the senior ecclesiastics have easy access to the Emperor; they include the old Patriarch Basiliyos, who as deputy head of the Church took a leading part in the reorganisation of the 1940s, but has now lapsed into senility, and the acting Patriarch Theofilos, Bishop of Harär, who is often tipped as the Emperor's favourite Churchman. Ras Kasa (13), as a great and devout nobleman, also wielded great influence on behalf of the Church, and several senior politicians, like the Habtä-Wäld brothers and Blatengeta Mahtämä-Selassie (17), are the products of Church families.

Through such individuals the influence of the Church has been exercised and its attitudes expressed, but it would be a mistake to talk of any distinct Church 'party'. Churchmen have worked through personal connections with the Emperor and the different groupings, and there has been nothing much to unite them beyond their shared attitudes towards religious affairs. Over the last dozen years, moreover, the number of influential Churchmen has sharply declined. As so often, this reflects the death or retirement of old leaders and their replacement by men who do not share their upbringing, methods or ideals. There is still of course an ecclesiastical presence in the government, partly channelled through the Ecclesiastical Affairs Department of the Emperor's Private Cabinet; but there is no Churchman with the power wielded, in their different ways, by a Ras Kasa (13) or an Aba Hana (10). The change is illustrated by the present Prime Minister who, though from a Church family, was educated abroad and has nothing like the interest in Church affairs of his late brother, Makonnen Habtä-Wäld (19), who was brought up in a monastery. Religion remains in the last analysis one of the foundations of the imperial government, and the Church may well have a crucial influence on the succession, but it is now hard to trace clerical influence on major government decisions; the relationship between Church and state in the central government has thus already sunk a great deal from its former closeness, and is likely to decay still further with changes in recruitment and administrative methods.

The Influence of Education

Education has in Africa been the watchword of development, the universally acclaimed precipitant of the new age; for modernisation has been very largely a process of importing and adapting new skills and attitudes from the developed countries to the north, and western secular education has been the means through which these are acquired. Even in Ethiopia, where education has not come as an accompaniment to European colonisation, this connection has long been recognised, and early this century the Emperor Menilek founded in Addis Ababa the school which bears his name. Further schools were established by Haile-Selassie during the Regency and the first part of his reign, and young men were systematically sent to complete their education abroad. There were two hundred and fifty or more of these students at foreign centres of learning, most of whom survived the war and occupation, and many of them have held important positions in the post-war government.* Since the war, education has markedly expanded, though it is still low by the standards of many other African countries, and the number of graduates educated abroad now runs into thousands; they have been supplemented by the graduates of the University College of Addis Ababa, which was opened in 1951 and merged ten years later into the new Haile Sellassie I University, and by secondary school leavers. The majority of these graduates, both of the pre-war and of the post-war generations, have automatically joined the government, and their influence has been felt both in the decline of traditional élites, and in the slow process of administrative modernisation.

Ethiopian graduates have differed from those of other African countries in their need to displace such traditional élites before taking over the major posts; and the first fifteen years after the Liberation were dominated by divisions between largely traditional forces, notably the nobility on the one hand, and the personal *protégés* of the Emperor on the other. The position of these *protégés* was scarcely less 'traditional' than that of the noblemen whom they opposed, since Emperors have constantly used men dependent on themselves to offset those with independent authority, and the most important of Haile-Selassie's followers at that time were strongly influenced by traditional modes and values. This was especially true of Wäldä-Giyorgis (33) and Makonnen Habtä-Wäld (19), neither of whom had any modern training, and both of whom depended on long-established techniques and large personal followings. Educated politicians, even when like Aklilu Habtä-Wäld (3) and Yelma Derésa (35) they held high offices, had to adapt themselves to this situation, and at best could only guide the efficiency of their own departments.

* See Table on page 20.

The position gradually altered as the importance of the old divisions declined, and as politicians educated abroad before 1936 worked their way up in the government. Most of these had joined the government soon after the Liberation, but it was some time before they gained an appreciable number of important posts. This process is illustrated quantitatively by Table 4, which shows the changing numbers of educated men in senior positions. The sharpest increase took place between 1948 and 1953, but the educated only started to dominate the administration between 1955 and 1960, as the most important of the others died or retired. Among the Emperor's personal *protégés*, Wäldä-Giyorgis (33) was dismissed in 1955, and Makonnen Habtä-Wäld (19) and Mulugéta Buli (26) were killed in 1960; of the more important noblemen, Rasa Kasa (13) died in 1956 and Ras Abäbä (1) in 1960, while Bitwädäd Makonnen Endalkachäw (18) retired to the Senate in 1957.

Since 1961, as a result, most of the important ministers have been men

Table 4

Education of Senior Central Government Officials, 1941–1966

Year		42	48	53	57	59	62	64	66	Total 41–66
Not educated abroad	Ministers	8	7	8	10	8	6	5	7	81
	Vice-Min.	–	4	5	10	16	15	15	19	
Educated abroad before 1936	Ministers	2	–	3	6	6	7	11	11	29
	Vice-Min.	3	4	8	5	5	5	8	7	
Educated abroad after 1941	Ministers	–	–	–	–	–	3	2	5	26
	Vice-Min.	–	–	–	2	4	6	10	19	
Unknown	Vice-Min.	–	–	–	–	–	–	1	–	2
% educated abroad	Ministers	20	–	27	37	43	63	72	70	40%
	Vice-Min.	100	50	62	41	36	43	53	58	
Total	Ministers	10	7	11	16	14	16	18	23	138
	Vice-Min.	3	8	13	17	15	26	34	45	

The same officials are covered as in Table 3; ministers of state are included with ministers, where they have executive control of a ministry, otherwise with vice-ministers.

with advanced education, the chief exceptions being the two leading noblemen, Abiy Abäbä (2) and the late Mär'ed Mängäsha (22); several minor ministers also lacked foreign education. The number of vice-ministers in this category remains surprisingly high, but in 1966 several of these were on the fringes of the administration, while no fewer than eleven were in the Ministries of Defence, Interior and Palace, where more traditional tendencies still prevail. Their position therefore does not in general offset the preponderance of educated officials, and of the major posts, only those of President of the Senate, and Minister of Defence have not yet been held by graduates. The first graduate, Afä Negus (Chief Justice), was appointed late in 1967.

Many of the present senior officials were educated before the war, and had joined the government in some capacity by 1942. The first of the post-war generation of graduates did not do so until nearly ten years later, and most of them are still in the process of working their way up through the government. Before 1960, very few of them were yet in major posts, and though the number has increased sharply since 1961, and they are especially strong in foreign affairs, the government is still dominated by men of the older generation. The younger officials are far more numerous in the ranks of assistant minister and below, where they have had a considerable effect in improving the general quality of the administration.

The differences between these generations, and between educated and uneducated officials as a whole, are marked enough to make their separation more than a matter of convenience. Most striking is the contrast between the administrative methods of the graduates and the others, seen particularly when the techniques of a minister like Makonnen Habtä-Wäld (19) are compared with those either of his brother Aklilu (3), or his successor as Minister of Finance, Yelma Derésa (35).* While some of these differences may be due to personal traits, and educated officials retain traditional characteristics to a varying degree, the general tendency is clear. In addition to their greater administrative competence, the educated officials have enjoyed a relationship with the Emperor rather different from that of their predecessors, for they have tended to act rather more as career politicians and administrators responsible to him, and rather less as courtiers and personal servants. This tendency is difficult both to generalise and to define, and it is not true of all ministers, but it is found in a degree of technical expertise, a greater readiness to delegate and accept delegation, and some diminution in attendance at the palace. This changed relationship is bound to accompany an increased institutionalisation of the administration.

While the educated politicians of the older generation have been distinguished from the uneducated by their more modern methods, they

* These techniques are examined in Chapters 9 and 11.

have differed from the younger officials in their generally greater readiness to work as technicians within the framework laid down by the Emperor. Like the Emperor himself, they have been able to adapt themselves to changes which have not interfered with their powers or tenure of office, and many of them have expressed very liberal or even radical opinions; but most of them have nevertheless lacked firmly held principles of policy, either conservative or reforming, and while they have suggested courses of action, they have not been prepared to persist in them in the face of imperial disapproval. They have thus tended to abide by the conventions discussed elsewhere. This tendency may be applied not only to Aklilu Habtä-Wäld (3), the leader of this group, but also to many of its other members.

The contrast is not complete, for some of the post-war generation, and especially those closest to the Emperor, have so adapted themselves to the imperial régime that they are quite as subservient as their elders; and many more lapse into traditional administrative habits, of which the most annoying is a persistent obstructiveness inadequately concealed beneath a front of superficial charm. But among the younger officials there nevertheless tends to be a far greater restlessness with the existing framework, sometimes accompanied by a positive belief in the ends to be accomplished. Part of the reason for this may be an enthusiasm which will decline with age, or to the lack of the habits imbued in the older politicians by a quarter-century of deference; the younger officials, too, have to think of a future in which too great a commitment to the old régime may be a disadvantage. But more is due to the possession of technical skills beside which the old methods of management are outdated, to a belief in radical ideals to which the atmosphere is far more conducive than it was twenty-five years ago, and to a consequently greater reluctance to follow a line laid down by the Emperor.

This does not mean that there is any cohesive young men's party in the government, for like other officials they are divided by their origins, personal likes and dislikes, degrees of radicalism and in other ways; nor is it possible to distinguish systematic divisions based on different countries or subjects of education, though many little groups and personal ties date from undergraduate times. One can only point to education as one of the many factors which go to make up the complexity of Ethiopian political groupings.

What, then, of the overall effect of education and the educated élite on the government and its development since the war? In the first place, it has certainly been the major influence, directly or indirectly, in bringing about such modernisation and development as has occurred. The improved administrative standards of the government are one example of this, the extension of its functions another. The institutional changes which we shall consider later are very largely the product of the replacement of traditional groups of various sorts, educated along native Ethiopian lines if at all, by western-educated graduates; and this has made it possible for government agencies to provide services which could previously be performed only by foreigners. A second result has been the acceptance by the government, formally at least, of the goals of development for which the graduates have pressed, including the Five Year Plans and as yet imprecisely defined hints of 'land reform'; in foreign affairs, the policy of pan-Africanism has been a connected and rather more successful change, pressed on the Emperor by a number of post-war graduates. But the graduates have notably failed to make the sort of impact on the government which is needed for the effective implementation of the reforms which most of them support. They have not scaled the 'commanding heights' of the political system, which are still held by a man who, whatever his claims to be a moderniser, is very far from them in outlook; and they have not so far provided that driving force which is what the government most obviously lacks. Though active and sometimes successful in their own restricted spheres, they have not seriously affected the foundations of the imperial system of government, and still less therefore have they established the bases of any system which could replace it.

Chapter 7
The High Officials

The Way to Power

The active politicians in the government have been distinguished largely by their connections with the Emperor and with groups within the government, and it is naturally through such connections that they have mostly been recruited. This is true both of the old guard who have surrounded the throne for the last twenty-five years, and of the younger officials who have only risen to prominence in the late 1950s and the 1960s. In this respect, the earlier period is the more important, for almost all of the major politicians of the last quarter-century joined the government either before the war or immediately after it. At that time, a young man had simply to bring himself to the Emperor's notice in order to gain a government post; thereafter he could work his way up through diligence, loyalty, and adaptation to the features of the political system described later in this chapter. Most of the really influential individuals had in any case strong personal links with the Emperor: some were brought up in the palace, while others joined his entourage before 1936, or during his wartime exile in England.

Most of the rest scaled the ladder of patronage through family connections at court. A nobleman, especially a Shoan, would have relatives who presented him to the Emperor, and the sons of existing officials were brought up in the close circle round the throne; other politicians found posts for their younger brothers and cousins. Any of the political groups discussed in the previous chapter could serve as a channel of recruitment, and in this way different political forces have come to be represented in the government. The effectiveness of each particular group is naturally reflected in the changing numbers of its members in high office. The influence of status groups has thus very significantly declined, both in their falling representation in the central government, and in the diminution of the independence and distinctness of noblemen. There has been no similar decline, however, in the importance of regional groups, and the recent growth of local and ethnic consciousness may well increase their effectiveness as channels of recruitment.

Two further paths to office in the Liberation period were more closely connected with modernising tendencies, the first being through the small standing army established before 1936. Mulugéta Buli (26) rose to great power in this way, using his military training as the first step in attaching himself to the Emperor, and others profited similarly from training in Ethiopia or France. Second, some patronage was open to those educated abroad, who could obtain a post on graduation, and then work their way into the political class as they came to the Emperor's attention. This form of recruitment is most clearly seen with Eritreans who emigrated to Ethiopia before 1936, and, having no personal connections, had to make their way through their own abilities. But both of these more modern channels were connected with traditional ones, for the Emperor took an active part in sending students abroad, and many officials used their influence to procure advanced education or military rank for their relations. Aklilu Habtä-Wäld (3) is a clear example of a politician who has risen on the twin foundations of his foreign education and the patronage of his elder and more powerful brother.

When the government was reconstructed after the Liberation, officials were recruited from all these traditional and modern sources, preference naturally being given to those who had already held office before the war. The claims of resistance leaders also had to be considered, though even at that early date several former collaborators were admitted to office. By contrast, recruitment was negligible between 1943 and the return of the first of the post-war graduates nearly ten years later, and no one who has yet become a minister joined the government during this period. This gap was due primarily to the lack of advanced education during and immediately after the Occupation, and has resulted in a marked division between pre-war and post-war generations.

Recruitment of high officials since 1950 has only slightly differed from the earlier period. Greater weight has been given to university education, and the employment of new entrants has been less haphazard than in Liberation days; an individual's starting rank and salary may indeed be determined solely by the nature of his degree. A university degree has been an almost essential qualification for members of the younger generation reaching high office, and academic qualifications enjoy a high prestige within the government. They seem in fact to have a rather higher status than their value for actual performance in political office warrants, and even senior politicians often retain a hankering for academic *kudos*. But only a few of the new graduates have been picked out for high political office, and these have often held posts with political implications from the start of their careers; several have risen through the imperial secretariat. Personal connections have still formed the chief criterion in their selection, and for almost every member of the post-war generation who has reached ministerial rank, a strong source of influence can be found, the most common being family connections in the government; this is true both of noblemen and of other politicians. Regional links and the patronage of existing high officials have also sometimes been important. The armed forces have for the most part remained distinct from the processes of political recruitment, but several officers have risen to power within the central civilian government; some of these have been influential generals with easy access to the palace, while others have risen through the security services.

Meanwhile, the technicians among the younger educated élite have been working their way up through slower channels of promotion, and especially since 1966 they have been appointed as vice-ministers in many of the more technical departments. Since they lack the personal commitment to the present régime which marks the political appointees, they may be able to provide the basis for a competent bureaucratic administration if for any reason the present politicians are forced out of office.

While origins have been important in selecting members of the political élite, by no means everyone with birth or connections, or even ability, has risen to a powerful position. The reasons for this are to be looked for in the machinery of appointments, for as in any political system, appointments are a vital weapon for controlling officials at every level. Since 1941, every major post has been in the Emperor's hands,* and a stroke of the pen can at any moment raise an individual to unlooked-for heights or send him into virtual exile, besides determining his pay and the whole pattern of his life. The system of appointments has therefore been very carefully manipulated to secure the loyalty and obedience of officials, providing both the carrot for good behaviour and the stick for bad. Rumours of impending government reshuffles constantly circulate in Addis Ababa, and each new list of appointments is greeted with great interest and much discussion. The promoted hold celebratory parties.

One reason for this is the great prestige attached to senior government jobs, and to the indications of imperial favour which appointment to them gives; for in so small a community every eye is on the palace, and there are few if any alternative channels of power and status through which to advance one's career. Government posts also provide scope for influence, and often for self-enrichment, and they provide a major field for competition between political groups, each of which tries to move its members into the most important positions. Ethiopians discussing appointments

* A Central Personnel Agency was established in 1961 to handle appointments up to the rank of assistant minister; it did not appear to limit the Emperor's freedom of action in making such appointments when he wished to, though promotion at this level is now increasingly determined within the ministry concerned, usually by the minister. The changes of March 1966 gave much of the initiative in selecting senior officials to the Prime Minister, and clearly increased his influence, but they have not in practice removed the Emperor's interest and final say in the making of such appointments.

are quick to note whether one politician has gained promotion for his followers, or whether another has succeeded in having a rival dismissed to a diplomatic post, a distant provincial governorship, or the Senate. The bald announcements in the *Negarit Gazeta* gain importance as political indicators from the fact that virtually no other events bearing directly on machinations within the government are officially proclaimed and immediately verifiable; most other political information travels secretively and by word of mouth, and the appointment lists form the only direct contemporary evidence even for so momentous an event as the fall of Wäldä-Giyorgis (33) in 1955.

Appointments are decided in secret. The final decision is presumably the Emperor's, but one can infer that changes are often made with the advice or at the instigation of important officials, who compete with one another to get their views accepted. The ability to influence the Emperor's choice of appointments serves as a measure of a politician's importance, and it is an essential element in the power of a Wäldä-Giyorgis or of a present-day major minister like Yelma Derésa (35) that his support or disapproval may make all the difference to one's chances of promotion or disgrace. The hand of the Prime Minister may be detected in many of the major appointments and dismissals in the five years before the increase in his powers in March 1966, and individual ministers have gained greater control over the filling of positions beneath them; this was formalised in 1966 by requiring the Prime Minister to consult the other minister concerned about appointments of ministers of state and vice-ministers to his department. One person who seems never to have been consulted, at least until 1966, was the appointee himself, and on receiving a summons to the palace he had no means of telling if he was to be made a minister, or banished to diplomatic exile; however, the ministerial appointments of April 1966 were discussed in advance between the Prime Minister and the prospective appointee. There have also been a few cases in recent years of officials refusing to accept the posts to which they were appointed.

The Emperor himself takes an active part in appointments, for they are one of the most important means for changing or maintaining the balance of forces in the government, and for keeping officials dependent on him. Sometimes he gives one a startling promotion, to ensure his loyalty; others are raised, transferred and played off against each other, with a strong tendency for those most dependent on him to hold the most stable positions. The instability of the senior posts has nevertheless been exaggerated, and it is by no means true that 'officials no sooner get acquainted with one post than they are transferred to another'.[1] The turnover of ministers and acting ministers has been less in Ethiopia even than in the United Kingdom within periods of single party government. The most important posts, including the Ministry of the Pen, the Prime

Ministry and the Ministry of Finance, have changed hands least often, being reserved for men very close to the Emperor; but even in the highly political ministries held largely by noblemen—Justice, Interior and Defence—continuous tenures of six years have not been uncommon. By contrast, the minister most often changed since 1941 has been that of Posts.

The stability of ministerial posts has also depended on the balance between factions. During the long ascendancy of Wäldä-Giyorgis (1941–55), a minister or acting minister stayed in one post for an average of four and a half years; this tenure was precisely halved between 1955 and 1961, when the balance of power within the government was far more delicate, and there was no predominating group or individual. In the five years after the reshuffle of early 1961, which marked the rise of Aklilu Habtä-Wäld (3) and Yelma Derésa (35), there were only eight changes in the eighteen ministries. Haile-Selassie does not therefore constantly move his officials around to prevent them from establishing independent positions, though this may account for the appointment of Ras Abäbä (1) to Tegré in 1943 and as Minister of the Interior in 1949. Few ministers have been independent enough to make it worth changing them for such a reason, but even the Commander of the Bodyguard has changed only twice since 1941, though Mulugéta Buli (26) was frequently rumoured to be about to stage a *coup d'état*, and Mängestu Neway actually did so.

This striking fact makes it necessary to examine the oft-repeated assumption that personal loyalty to the Emperor is the first and great requirement for appointment to high office. Such loyalty has certainly been important, in such very different characters as Abiy Abäbä (2) and Makonnen Habtä-Wäld (19). But against this must be set the fact that the 1960 attempt was led by the chiefs of the Bodyguard, the police, and the Emperor's personal security service—three posts in which one would have supposed loyalty to be the very first consideration. Again, Brigadier General Tadäsä Biru (29), who as commander of the police flying column helped to swing the balance in Haile-Selassie's favour in 1960, was in 1966 the leader of a Galla movement against him. On such occasions the Emperor is apt to grieve, more in sorrow than in anger, that men who owe everything to him should show such ingratitude. Two elements should here be borne in mind. First, the secret heart of an Ethiopian may be so far beneath the surface as to be completely unpredictable until he chooses to declare himself; and this reserve may conceal a freedom of action which appears only at time of crisis. Second, the Ethiopian tendency to follow a leader only so long as he is successful has already been noted, and it was illustrated both in 1936 and in a certain amount of wavering by high officials in 1960. The relationship between Haile-Selassie and his officials is chiefly one of power rather than personal feeling, and in this author's judgement a completely powerless Haile-Selassie would be attended only by a few of his present entourage, many of them too deeply compromised to be acceptable to a successor régime.

The reasons for which ministers have actually been demoted or dismissed, on the other hand, provide some guide to the conventions which govern their behaviour. Most spectacular of dismissals was that of Wäldä-Giyorgis (33) in 1955, which is considered at length in a later chapter; but it is worth remarking here that his fall came at the moment when he tried to assert himself as a powerful leader in his own right, rather than as a servant and assistant of the Emperor. The fortunes of some of the ministers appointed in 1961 to give the government a more liberal flavour after the December revolt are more generally relevant. The first to go was Ras Imru's son Mika'él (25), who claimed a greater independence at the Ministry of Foreign Affairs than the Emperor or the Prime Minister were prepared to give him, and was sent as Ambassador to Moscow. At the Ministry of Education, Hadis Alämayähu (9) lost his job after revealing that Ethiopia was educationally well behind most other African countries, a revelation which greatly weakened the Emperor's carefully built up image as the keen supporter of educational advance; he became Ambassador in London, where he stayed until brought back to the government as Minister of Planning in 1966. Miliyon Näqneq, who then took charge of the Ministry in the absence of any senior official, tried to improve the position with ambitious schemes for expansion, but was shifted in a couple of months to a minor post in the Ministry of Foreign Affairs, and thence to Tokyo, where he spent the next five years. Most ambitious of all were the plans of the new Minister of Justice, Däjazmach Zäwdé Gäbrä-Selassie (36) to ensure the independence of the judiciary and reform the structure of the congested court system. The laws designed to do this were blocked and delayed by a variety of devices, and Däjazmach Zäwdé was dismissed in 1962.

These and other officials were demoted not simply because they advocated changes; the Prime Minister and others have done so without losing imperial favour, and several high officials with fairly liberal views have retained their positions in the government. Nor is it only that the reforms in themselves would have weakened the Emperor's power, though certainly he was not prepared to release his hold over the judiciary, as Zäwdé's proposals would have required. The vital element was the method which the reforming ministers used, openly taking the initiative and making themselves directly responsible for changes, instead of contenting themselves with suggestions to the Emperor behind the scenes, and accepting the amount of change which he was prepared to grant. Had ministers been allowed to take such initiatives, it would greatly have weakened the Emperor's control over the government, involving an important break in the centralised form of the Emperor's leadership, and opening up channels of authority which he did not dominate. Further, these ministers upset the façade behind which the government has been carried on. It has already been shown that the Emperor has taken care to present himself as the sole protector of his people, and the only person really concerned with their interests; all the credit for improvements has had to be his, and the officials have been regarded, often correctly, as self-seeking and corrupt. Hadis (9) showed the flaws in the Emperor's image as the benevolent father of Ethiopian education; Zäwdé took the process a step further by claiming the credit for his proposals himself, venturing on to a field reserved for the Emperor, and demonstrating that officials were afraid to take initiatives and responsibility because the Emperor himself obliged them to be so.

While ministers have held fairly stable positions, they have thus been able to do so only so long as they have accepted the conventions laid down by the Emperor; and this acceptance of a master/servant relationship, rather than loyalty in itself, has been the key element in their success. They have had to work within the system of checks and balances, allowing themselves to be used as scapegoats when anything goes wrong; they have had to confine their initiatives to making suggestions to the Emperor, rather than taking independent action; they have had to use his authority rather than their own as the basis for their activities; and they have had to take care to avoid any action which might weaken their position in the palace. The process of appointments has favoured those who can adapt themselves to these conventions, and officials showing undesirable amounts of independence have found promotion blocked, and have been moved to unimportant posts. By dint of their upbringing and experience, however, most senior officials have been quite content to work beneath the guidance of the Emperor, and the exceptions have mostly been younger educated Ethiopians, trained in other methods.

The Ministers

The ministers stand at the peak of the central government hierarchy, and provide the chief link between the Emperor and the nineteen executive ministries; they together make up the Council of Ministers, and they perform much the same administrative functions as their equivalents anywhere in the world. Their political freedom of action is, however, greatly limited by the supreme position of the Emperor, and it follows from the last section that they have no power to carry through sweeping changes in government policy or organisation; most of them indeed have no desire to do so. Their effective power is also restricted by the inade-quacies of the administrative machinery at their disposal, and by the pressure on their time of committee meetings and other routine functions, including attendance on the Emperor.

It must also be remembered that Ethiopian ministers do not command the political activities of the government in the same way, for instance, as the members of the British Cabinet. There is not only the position of the Emperor to be considered, but also the presence of other political struc-tures which largely stand outside the ministers' field of activity. A pro-vincial governor-general is roughtly equivalent to a minister, and though provincial government is under the nominal control of the Minister of the Interior, the more important governors-general pay little heed to the Ministry and deal directly with the Emperor, especially when the minister is not a powerful politician in his own right. The armed forces tend to be more firmly under the Minister of Defence, but nevertheless stand apart from the central administration which the ministers control. Diplomatic posts and the Senate are similarly distinct, but serve largely as places of retirement for the aged or out of favour. The men who head these different hierarchies all form part of the new nobility, and it is common for them to be switched from one type of job to another: Lieutenant-General Abiy Abäbä (2), for instance, has held posts as minister, provincial governor-general, ambassador and senator; but the power of ministers as such extends only to the central government and to subjects such as foreign affairs which are closely directed from the centre, and it cannot be assumed that they control government activities outside this sphere.

The political weight of ministers varies very greatly according to their characters and their relations with the Emperor. Some, like Täfärä-Wärq (31) and Blatengéta Mahtämä-Selassie (17), have been content to act as his devoted servants, with little ambition or activity; some are interested above all in the material comforts of office, and their first concern is to do nothing which might jeopardise them. Some, as the last section showed, have come to grief in trying to force through programmes whose realisation was beyond their power; others, more modest in their ambitions, have confined themselves to lesser projects suited to the nature of their influence.

But ministers who work skilfully within the conventions of the govern-ment, combining ambition and ability with the confidence of the Emperor, exercise very great political power. The Emperor provides the authority for government decisions, but the initiative comes mostly from those around him, among whom the ministers are especially important; and since the Emperor is always open to persuasion, the advice of a major minister carries a great deal of weight, particularly if there is no rival politician urging the opposite view. The ability to influence the Emperor in private carries with it authority in dealing with the rest of the government; for through the threat of going to the Emperor, a minister can wield power outside the palace to the extent that he has influence within. In this way, the senior ministers act through the Emperor, using his authority to get what they want, and sheltering behind it in case of opposition. Personal connections are thus highly important in determining a minister's power, especially over decisions for which the Emperor's authority is needed, and his influence will be all the greater if he can combine imperial backing with the use of friends and *protégés* scattered through the administration.

As in most countries, the key political ministries have been those of Defence, Finance, Foreign Affairs, Interior and Justice, though the peculiarly Ethiopian Ministry of the Pen was the most important of them all until 1955. Owing to the Emperor's interest in personal diplomacy, the Ministry of Foreign Affairs has consistently been held by officials who work closely with him, but are at the same time modern enough in education and outlook to rub shoulders with the foreign diplomats with whom they have to deal. Finance has required a rather different set of qualities, and owing to its importance and complexity, has been controlled by influential imperial *protégés* strong enough to resist undue demands for funds and yet remain beneath the Emperor's supervision. The Ministers of Defence, Interior and Justice have needed traditional status in order to retain control of their subjects, and have therefore often been noblemen; the influence of the Ministry of the Interior in particular has depended on the personal standing of its minister.

But these tendencies have not been constant, for the nature of ministerial positions has changed considerably over the last twenty-five years, as the major ministers have gradually ceased to be the competing heads of rival political factions, and have emerged increasingly as administrative heads of departments. Personal stature has been replaced by official position as the major source of political power, and this change has to some extent been accompanied by the replacement of traditional by more administrative methods of government.

We can illustrate this process by looking at the major ministers of 1953, and comparing them with their equivalents in 1967. In 1953, the Prime Minister and five of his nine colleagues were noblemen, descendants of the old ruling families of Shoa with the addition of Ras Abäbä Arägay (1), who by his exploits as a resistance leader earned himself a personal stature scarcely matched in the Empire; between them they held the ministries of Interior, Justice and War. Of the remaining ministers, Wäldä-Giyorgis (33) at the Ministry of the Pen and Makonnen Habtä-Wäld (19) at Finance wielded even greater power than the noblemen, and through the trust which the Emperor had in them and their astonishing gifts for subsurface manipulation in the traditional manner, they made themselves feared and respected throughout the government. Only the two other ministers, who included Aklilu Habtä-Wäld (3) at Foreign Affairs, owed anything to a university education.

Fifteen years later, only Aklilu still holds ministerial office, and of the others only Abiy Abäbä (2) remains in active politics. The noblemen have disappeared: there are none among the twenty ministers today. But more surprisingly, the old-style imperial *protégés* like Wäldä-Giyorgis and Makonnen Habtä-Wäld have vanished with them. What do we find instead? First, almost every minister has a university education, quite a number of them since the war; but what is immediately striking is that only Yelma Derésa (35) at Finance, and perhaps Käbädä Gäbré, the newly appointed Minister of Defence, have any noteworthy personal stature, against the half-dozen or more 'big men' who held office in 1953. Even Aklilu as Prime Minister depends as much on his official rank as on his personal position, and any of the remaining seventeen ministers could be changed without making much difference to the power structure of the government, so long as the regional and educational distribution of ministers was maintained. Ministries which used to be headed by major politicians, like Justice, Interior and Foreign Affairs, are now in the hands of political lightweights; and present-day imperial *protégés* like Mänasé Haylé (24) or Mamo Tadäsä (20), though they have easy access to the palace, have nothing like the personal impact of a Mulugéta Buli (26) or Makonnen Habtä-Wäld (19).

This is an important change, and it demands investigation. For a start, what was the 'stature' which modern ministers have lost? For the noblemen, it was the respect and authority which came from their place in the traditional hierarchy, and their ability to live up to expectations of the role of a aristocratic leader. For a self-made man like Wäldä-Giyorgis, it was the intensity of his grasp of power, the skill with which he maintained an army of his own supporters and manœuvred within the palace system, and the active support which he received from the Emperor. The present-day ministers, except perhaps for Yelma Derésa (35), possess none of these qualities. They are for the most part men who have made their way up by staying out of serious trouble; they have no standing in the traditional order of things which is now disappearing; they are not particularly ambitious, and are certainly not prepared to risk very much in the search for further power; and they lack the borrowed impetus which the Emperor's greater political activity provided in the earlier period. Those who are prepared to pursue personal initiatives have been removed from the higher ranks, or prevented from reaching them, through the pressures discussed in the last section. And the result is the power vacuum which can be sensed throughout the central government.

What, then, have the new ministers gained which their predecessors did not possess? There has certainly been a very great improvement in the efficiency of administration, however surprising this may seem to those who have to put up with the inefficiency which remains. Some of this can be ascribed to the ministers' education, and the presence of a growing cadre of educated and qualified officials below them. Another aspect of the process has been the increasing power of ministers within their own departments, resulting from the decline of intra-departmental rivalries and from the minister's growing control over appointments in his ministry. There is now little of the open competition between minister and vice-minister which afflicted the government before 1960, and the personal machines through which a politician like Makonnen Habtä-Wäld (19) could by-pass another minister have disappeared. Control over his ministry enables a minister to dominate its field in the government as a whole, for he submits problems on the subject to the Emperor, and decides which questions from his ministry are to go to the Emperor or the Council of Ministers. He can initiate and veto legislation in his field, and other proposals need his backing because he has to persuade the Emperor and Council to accept them. If he has a pet project of his own, it is unlikely that anyone else will stand in its way.

Ministers' power has also gained from the increasing independence of their ministries. The centralised control provided by the imperial secretariat until 1955 has vanished, and the personal rivalries which compelled ministers to take decisions to the Emperor before 1960 have weakened. Ministers are still very sensitive to any hint from the palace, but its activity has declined; and though they still rely on the imperial authority, this dependence has become less personal and direct, a tendency which is likely to increase with the selection of ministers by the Prime Minister, which places an additional step between them and the throne. The growing influence of the Prime Minister has scarcely offset the relaxation of imperial control, since he has been careful not to impose himself on other departments; and the reforming ministers in 1961 were given wide initiative in proposing policies in their fields, even though they had not the authority to implement them. Individual ministers are thus in some measure the gainers from the general decline in co-ordinated central direction in the government; but this trend cuts in two directions, for in this as in other fields, administrative modernisation is offset by the apparent failure to develop new political foundations and sources of initiative to replace the vanishing old ones.

Foreigners in the Government

Modernisation in Ethiopia is largely a matter of importing and adapting foreign ideas, and foreign help has therefore been needed in a great many fields, especially technical ones for which few skilled Ethiopians have been available. Foreigners have therefore taken an important part in the modernising sectors of the government ever since the Ethiopian Empire, under Téwodros, started to look for guidance to the techniques and achievements of the developed countries of Europe, and foreign advisers have been fairly systematically distributed through government departments since the early reign of Haile-Selassie. Their position has been a very interesting one, both because they stand at a crucial point in the process of development, and because Ethiopia has been very differently placed in this respect from the other countries of Africa. In the absence of colonial administrators both to run the westernised machinery of government and to hand it over, step by step, to Africans, the foreigners have always had to work beneath the political control of Ethiopians; they have had to guide from below.

Ethiopia has a long reputation for xenophobia, matched by an equally ancient tradition of hospitality to strangers, and these conflicting attitudes strongly affect the work which advisers can do. On the one hand, some individuals have been widely accepted and have taken an important part in measures of modernisation; among them are Plowden and Bell, the two English friends of Téwodros, Alfred Ilg, the Swiss who helped Menilek in many of his contacts with Europeans, and others in more recent times. Other foreigners, on the other hand, have been treated with great suspicion. The guiding principle has generally been that foreigners have been treated on their merits as individuals, and freely used where they have been useful, so long as they possessed the patience and discretion essential for them to fit into the Ethiopian system; but any undue influence on Ethiopian affairs, especially by organised groups of a particular nationality, has immediately aroused hostility. Ethiopians have been jealous of their independence, and have welcomed foreigners only so long as they stayed in what has been regarded as their proper place. Between three and four hundred years ago, the Portuguese were at first greeted as welcome allies, but later expelled or killed when they tried to convert the emperors and the whole country to Roman Catholicism. Most strikingly, the Italian occupation of 1936–41 was deeply resented, but individual Italians have since the Liberation been able to live untroubled throughout the Empire. At present, the Americans come under much suspicion as the dominant foreign influence, and there is general distrust of Greek and Armenian traders who are often regarded as parasites on the Ethiopian community.

For the first three years after the Liberation, Ethiopia agreed to appoint only British advisers, except after consultation with the British government, and suspicion of British motives was then naturally at its height. But since 1944, as before the war, foreign help has been obtained from many sources. British experts have worked mostly in education, though some have helped in the administration of justice and elsewhere; Swedes have administered telecommunications; Yugoslavs have provided expertise for the Planning Board; and Poles, Greeks and others have been recruited for jobs in a variety of government departments. Most important has been the United States, understandably in view of the amount of money which it has provided; Americans have managed the highways, the airline and other agencies, and have included the most important general advisers and legal draughtsmen.

Foreigners have worked in two main ways: with executive powers in special government agencies, or else as advisers without such powers attached to ordinary ministries. It has been very rare for them to be given responsibility within the ministries, though there have been foreign judges and a foreign attorney-general.

Government agencies have been used for public services including roads, banking and electricity, and have provided a means by which foreign managers could handle technical matters beneath the supervision of an Ethiopian board of directors; they have also been used to channel foreign development funds. Initially most of them were foreign operated, but Ethiopians have now largely taken over, especially since the early 1960s, and Ethiopian Air Lines is the only remaining agency with a foreign management. Many others continue to employ foreigners in technical positions.

Such corporations have not given foreigners much scope for political influence, and the only one to gain much political importance through them was the American Victor Harrell, General Manager of Ethiopian Air Lines from 1952 to 1962, who had easy access to the Emperor in the early part of this period. This was mostly because the Emperor was personally interested in the airline and there was no one else capable of advising him on it, but over the last ten years the position has changed. Ethiopians have been quick to resent any attempt by foreign managers to gain political influence, especially by going to the Emperor; George Rea, who was Governor of the State Bank from 1956 to 1959, twice took differences with the board of directors to the Emperor, and the resentment which this caused was one of the reasons for replacing him by an Ethiopian.

The second main way in which foreigners have been employed has been as advisers, and they have worked in some advisory capacity in almost every ministry. Most of them are attached to ministries for indefinite periods, and some have spent many years in Ethiopia; others have been specially called in to advise on particular matters like pensions and trades union legislation. Like foreign officials in government corporations, they may come from any country, but their recruitment and general position are rather more personal than those of agency officials. They work mostly with Ethiopians at the vice-ministerial or assistant ministerial level, but any senior adviser has fairly easy access to his minister.

One of the major functions of advisers has simply been to apply their expertise to tasks for which no qualified Ethiopian has been available, and many advisers have been entirely concerned with this purely technical work. They have until recently been responsible for all legislative drafting, and in the financial field they have drawn up taxation regulations, devised accounting procedures, and prepared the detailed comparisons of income and expenditure on which the annual Budget is based. Of a similar nature has been the drafting by advisers of many of the Emperor's speeches, a tedious task which involves a mastery of high-flown platitude, but which has brought with it no influence over government policy. They may also carry out any odd job required of them, including contacts with the foreign community in Addis Ababa, and the negotiation of industrial concessions. In this way, they have played an essential part in maintaining the modernised superstructure of the government, and though they are gradually being replaced by Ethiopians, it will be long before they can entirely be dispensed with.

The second function of advisers has been, naturally, to give advice, a task which largely consists in trying to persuade Ethiopian officials to accept measures for the modernisation or reform of the government's programmes and methods. In this respect, as Perham has pointed out,[2] the position of an adviser is a very difficult one. He has no executive powers, and whether his advice is accepted depends very largely on his personal relations with the Ethiopians with whom he works. No adviser has ever been able to enforce his advice on the government, and very frequently it is ignored. Much of their time has been spent working on plans and projects which their employers have no serious intention of putting into effect, for advisers have often been the unwilling victims of the assumption that a committee or an expert's report is an effective substitute for action in the field concerned. Advisers have also been discouraged from working closely with one another, for this has tended to arouse suspicions of improper influence.

Further difficulties have resulted from the adviser's function of encouraging western methods through influence on officials who work along very different lines, and it is not surprising that much of the advice has been presented in terms which the Ethiopians in question have been unable to appreciate. It has therefore been necessary for advisers to adapt themselves in some measure to Ethiopian methods, while not losing sight of the fact that they are there to change them. This has required not only rare personal qualities, but also great experience of Ethiopia, and the most influential advisers have spent at least several years there.

The influence of advisers has had to be exercised mostly behind the scenes, since self-assertiveness on their part has tended to raise suspicion, especially, as with agency officials, when they have tried to work with the Emperor. Dr Leon Gershkowitz, a very able Yugoslav who helped to found the Emperor's Private Cabinet in 1959, aroused opposition in this way, and left after only two years in Ethiopia. In the 1940s and early 1950s, when the government was far smaller and worked in a still more personal way, major advisers would be called for by the Emperor about once or twice a month, but by the 1960s they saw him far less frequently than this. At that time, the Emperor sometimes asked advisers for recommendations on particular policy problems, such as Ethiopian policy towards the Korean War, often requesting memoranda in advance. The last such case of which I am aware was early in 1961, when he called for reports on basic matters of government policy and organisation from several senior advisers, in the wake of the attempted *coup d'état* of the previous December. It has been impossible to discover whether these reports, which seem to have been unanimously in favour of more rapid modernisation, had any effect.

Because of the conditions under which they work, the influence of advisers is very difficult to assess. They have been involved, as technicians or persuaders, in almost all of the modernising measures which the government has taken, but they have never been able to take the decisions involved, and much of their work and many of their recommendations have had no effect whatever. This is even true of the two advisers, both of them Americans, who have been especially influential. The first, John Spencer, first worked for the government during the Italo-Ethiopian crisis, and his return was specially requested in 1943, when he gained from the prevailing suspicion of the other advisers, all of whom were English. He worked particularly with Wäldä-Giyorgis (33), though at that time he could also gain easier access to the Emperor himself than has since been possible, and he was notable among advisers for his ability to adapt himself to Ethiopian political methods. He lost influence after the fall of Wäldä-Giyorgis in 1955, partly because of changing political conditions, and partly also because some Ethiopians considered that he had presumed on his position. He left in 1960, and like several other advisers, he had lost effective influence for some time before his departure. His successor, Donald Paradis, worked mostly with the Prime Minister, though he also had wide connections with other politicians, and in addition to the general run of miscellaneous matter which comes an adviser's way, he was especially concerned with questions of governmental reorganisation. He left Ethiopia in mid-1968.

The position of the advisers illustrates both the very personal way in which the government works, and its gradual modernisation. But the lesson which most strikingly emerges from their successes and failures is the way in which the instruments of modernisation have had to assimilate themselves to traditional techniques in order to have their greatest effect. Results have been achieved, in so far as they have been achieved at all, not by straightforward initiatives or sweeping schemes for reform, but rather by slower and more modest proposals in keeping with the nature of the present political system. According to one's political viewpoint, this fact may be regarded either as a tribute to the system, or else as a condemnation of it.

Chapter 8
The Imperial Secretariat and its Decline

Imperial Orders and the *Aqabé Sä at*

In the constant traffic between palace and government offices which marks a court administration, the imperial secretariat has a place of its own, and one of great potential importance. History is full of the examples of mayors of the palace who by controlling the source of authority have effectively wielded power themselves, and the great English offices of Chancellor, Privy Seal, and Secretary of State witness that the ostensibly secretarial functions of writing and registering royal orders can grow in the hands of able and ambitious men to very much more than that.

Ethiopia is no exception. The Emperor's secretary, the *Tsähafé T'ezaz*, has long been one of the most important officers of state, and as in Europe, his position has often been held by clerics and other lowly-born *protégés* of the monarch, to provide a balance to the pretensions of the nobility. Since the reign of Menilek, the *Tsähafé T'ezaz* has received the modern title of Minister of the Pen, and a small department closely attached to the palace has grown up around him. The writing and despatch of imperial orders is of course his most important function, and an official of the Ministry is always at the palace to note down the Emperor's wishes and issue orders based upon them; the imperial secretaries, who hold the rank of vice-minister or assistant minister in the Ministry of the Pen, may even be sent for at dead of night if something slips into the Emperor's mind. The Minister of the Pen received several other functions by the Ministers (Definition of Powers) Order of 1943, including general supervisory powers transferred to the Prime Minister when that office was created later in the year. He also gained control of the *Negarit Gazeta*, in which all laws are published, and it was laid down that 'the Minister of the Pen may communicate directly with all officials in Our service'.[1]

Officials may be at the palace at any hour of day, and the Emperor likewise may give orders whenever there is need for them; but the process has to some extent been institutionalised through the regular weekly appointments between individual ministers and the Emperor which are known as *Aqabé Sä'at*, roughly translatable as 'appointment'. This system has never been formally established, but it has existed at least since the Liberation, and the Emperor referred to it when he told high officials in 1961 that[2]

We shall reserve for each of you a certain period each week when We shall ask you to report on the progress you have made in your programmes and on the difficulties which you have encountered.

Every minister has an appointment on a given day each week, and so do some of the heads of other agencies; Ras Kasa (13), until his death in 1956, had an *Aqabé Sä'at* on Friday afternoons simply by virtue of his personal position. The procedure is institutionalised to the extent that the Crown Prince takes his father's place when the Emperor is away, and the senior official in a ministry deputises when necessary for the minister. An imperial secretary takes notes on the discussions and prepares orders from what the Emperor says; until 1958 an official from the Prime Minister's Office was also present, and compared notes with the secretary, but this lapsed when Aklilu Habtä-Wäld (3) combined the offices of deputy Prime Minister and Minister of the Pen. The appointments vary between fifteen minutes and an hour, depending on the importance of the official and the amount to be discussed.

In *Aqabé Sä'at* each minister reports the activities of his department to the Emperor; he gets clearance of decisions needing imperial approval; he requests additional funds or orders to the Ministry of Finance to release those which have already formally been granted; he suggests new projects and seeks imperial support for them, and in general raises any of the matters which a minister has to bring to the Emperor. In the Emperor's absence, the Crown Prince deals with routine decisions but defers the more important ones. The exact nature of the subjects arising depends on the minister concerned, for some bring minor details while others have more of political importance to discuss; but *Aqabé Sä'at* is largely concerned with administrative matters, since really important or controversial decisions are discussed further behind the scenes.

Changes in *Aqabé Sä'at* would provide a sensitive indicator of the Emperor's changing role in day-to-day government, were it not that information on the subject is scanty. There is general agreement that the amount of trivial detail going to it has declined since 1960, and the times allotted to it were reduced after the government changes of March 1966, though rumours that it was to be abolished altogether were not realised. It has also been weakened by the Emperor's frequent absence and the growth of other institutions, for the Prime Minister now has his own *Aqabé Sä'at* with several of the ministers, and the Council of Ministers has taken over much of the detailed financial work which earlier went to the Emperor. But ministers continue to use *Aqabé Sä'at* for matters in which the Emperor is personally interested.

Overall, the *Aqabé Sä'at* has been one of the most important regular decision-making mechanisms in the government since the war. Its effect has been to emphasise the personal responsibility of each minister to the Emperor, and thus to hamper attempts at collective responsibility under the supervision of the Council or the Prime Minister. It has provided each minister with a court of appeal where he could argue his side of a question before the highest authority, and at the same time it has given the Emperor a channel for direct intervention in the affairs of each ministry. Its effects on the financial system have been especially great, and are considered in a later chapter. It is thus an example of the traditional methods by which the government has been centred on the Emperor, and its diminishing importance provides some evidence of their decline.

The Supremacy of the Secretariat, 1941–1955

The immense power wielded through the imperial secretariat for the first fourteen years after the Liberation, and the virtual disappearance of that power in the years since 1955, provide one of the most spectacular contrasts in Haile-Selassie's government since the war. This in itself makes it worth pausing to examine in some detail the power of the secretariat and the way in which it operated during those post-war years; but even beyond that, a description of the Ministry of the Pen in the days of its greatness provides a far better commentary than any generalisations could do on the working of a traditional palace administration of a type that has already largely vanished.

Because of the immense importance of imperial orders throughout the government, the Ministry of the Pen, rather than the Prime Minister's office or the Council of Ministers, is the natural focus for co-ordination under the Emperor. For through its connection with the Emperor, the Ministry is more closely concerned with the running of the whole administration than any other institution, and the power in the hands of the Minister is therefore potentially very great.

The Minister of the Pen from 1941 until 1955, *Tsähafé T'ezaz* Wäldä-Giyorgis Wäldä-Yohannes (33), exploited this potential to the full. Born into a humble Shoan Amhara family, he began his career as an interpreter before the war; in 1934, he joined the Ministry of the Pen as a director-general, and then started the close working relationship with the Emperor which was to last for over twenty years. His great influence at the time of the Italian invasion has already been noted. When the Emperor went into exile in 1936, Wäldä-Giyorgis went too, returning with him in 1941.

His personal gifts suited him for a position of power. Like the Emperor, he was very hard-working, and adept at handling the intricacies of the government machine; he had the ruthlessness and ambition with which to fight his way to the top from the lowest beginnings; he was completely discreet; and he had the ability, very rare in Ethiopians of his background, to take responsibility without referring every detail to his superior. By 1941, he had also acquired an intimate knowledge of the Emperor's moods and mental processes.

This knowledge was extremely important, since Wäldä-Giyorgis' power depended entirely on the Emperor's confidence. He had no independent source of strength whatever. As a mere cobbler's son, he had neither the supporting network of friends and relations which noblemen possessed, nor the standing derived from a position in the traditional hierarchy. Once he was in office, he could attract both associates and subordinates, but since these were drawn to him by fear and respect for the power which the Emperor's confidence gave him, they could neither replace that confidence nor survive its withdrawal. This entire dependence was at the same time a source of strength, since the Emperor would not have entrusted nearly so much to anyone who did not rely completely on him. Only someone like Wäldä-Giyorgis could be relied upon to follow the interests of his employer.

Wäldä-Giyorgis certainly received a far greater measure of imperial confidence than any other politician of Haile-Selassie's long reign. The Emperor even appears to have supported a proposal, shortly after the Liberation, that he should marry his eldest daughter, Princess Tänañä-Wärq; this met strong opposition from the Empress and the nobility under Ras Kasa (13), and the Princess married the future Ras Andargé Mäsay (4). Far more, moreover, was delegated to Wäldä-Giyorgis than to any other politician, and though he could never remove his opponents entirely from the scene, he was allowed to build up a personal supremacy which has never yet been equalled.

Once this imperial trust had been gained, it could be used in many ways, one of the most important of which was naturally the sending out of the Emperor's orders. The Emperor, for instance, would often given an order only in general terms; or Wäldä-Giyorgis might have to infer what he wanted from vague indications or assumptions, since there would be times when he really meant what he said, and other times when he had to appear to comply with a request in order to please a petitioner, or to give the impression that he supported some scheme for which in fact he had little inclination. Wäldä-Giyorgis then had to translate these indications into detailed orders to the departments concerned, an operation which gave great scope for turning things to his own advantage. Further, the Emperor never signs his orders himself nor even checks them before despatch, and it was widely said that Wäldä-Giyorgis sent out orders without any word from the Emperor at all.

The advantage was increased by the fact that such orders went out in the name of the Emperor, whether it was he or his Minister of the Pen who had decided a particular matter. An imperial order could not be questioned, at least openly, for that would be to question the authority of the Emperor, and so the very closeness of Wäldä-Giyorgis to the Emperor protected him to some extent against attacks from other officials. This system suited both him and the Emperor: to one it gave the exercise of power, to the other the avoidance of responsibility. Should something go wrong, the Emperor could always blame Wäldä-Giyorgis for the mistake, and thus preserve the essential façade of imperial infallibility.

The Ministry of the Pen could also be used to hamper Wäldä-Giyorgis' enemies and to help his friends, by manipulating the flow of orders to them. He himself coupled the Ministry of the Pen with the Ministry of the Interior from 1943 until 1949, and with the Ministry of Justice thereafter; here the speed with which he could get imperial orders, and the latitude delegated to him, made him a most efficient administrator. He could do nothing to change or delay orders which the Emperor particularly wanted to be sent, but years of experience would tell him which these were. Others might be kept back 'for study', or Wäldä-Giyorgis might take them back to the Emperor and suggest that they be changed, or get the Emperor to issue an order effectively countermanding an earlier one.

There were great advantages for Wäldä-Giyorgis in being at the centre of the government machine. He was always present, making his views heard with the Emperor at the most propitious moment. There was no one between him and the Emperor, while other officials had to deal with the Emperor to some extent through him. In any committee to which he belonged, Wäldä-Giyorgis would handle those matters, naturally the most important ones, which had to go to the Emperor, and in this way, he took the leading part in co-ordinating Ethiopian policy for the return of Eritrea.

His presence at the centre also gave him an unrivalled listening-post, and a point of vantage from which to survey the whole governmental scene. In so hierarchical a system, such a point could only be found at the very apex, and Wäldä-Giyorgis therefore had a far more effective information service than any of his rivals. Even when he could do nothing to prevent an order from going out, he knew exactly what orders had been sent to whom; he knew what the Emperor was doing, who had seen him, and most of what had been decided; and he had large numbers of informers to tell him what was going on in every part of the administration. Such reliable information is especially valuable in a country where horizontal communications are extremely bad, and the processes of government are marked by secrecy, complexity and continual intrigue.

Both to provide information and to help Wäldä-Giyorgis in other ways, a well-organised network of *protégés* and supporters was necessary, and his followers were many and well placed. One of the most important was Keflé Ergätu (15), who from 1942 until 1955, with one short break, was in charge of public security. Another, Makonnen Dänäqä, was second in command of the Imperial Bodyguard at the Liberation, and became deputy Commissioner of Police in 1945, and Aide-de-Camp to the Emperor two years later. It was Wäldä-Giyorgis' policy to have as many of his men surrounding the Emperor as possible, since that was where power ultimately lay, and at the same time to control the important areas of police and security. He also had many *protégés* in the Army, though in the Imperial Bodyguard his hold was weaker. Others were spread through every level of the administration, including the provincial government, over which he established control during his six years as Minister of the Interior. In general, most of the career politicians in the government, especially those of humble background, were his supporters.

He was more loosely allied with other important figures, such as the Habtä-Wäld brothers, a closely knit family of great importance from the Liberation to the present day. The eldest brother, Makonnen (19), formed a close alliance with Wäldä-Giyorgis before the war, and this continued after the Liberation, when Makonnen was Minister of Commerce. The two other brothers, Akalä-Wärq and Aklilu (3), were several years younger than Makonnen; Akalä-Wärq was at one time Wäldä-Giyorgis' personal assistant, before taking charge of the Ministry of Education; Aklilu worked very closely with Wäldä-Giyorgis during his long tenure of the Ministry of Foreign Affairs, especially over negotiations of the British Agreements of 1942 and 1944, and over the recovery of Eritrea. Wäldä-Giyorgis was also very careful to cultivate the alliance of the resistance leaders at the Liberation, and many of them became his supporters, though others opposed him.

The chief group of Wäldä-Giyorgis' opponents consisted loosely of the Shoan aristocracy, who regarded themselves as the Emperor's rightful assistants in ruling the country, and therefore resented Wäldä-Giyorgis' position. These included his matrimonial rival Andargé Mäsay (4), Bitwädäd Makonnen Endalkachäw (18), and Ras Kasa (13), whose *protégé* Gäbrä-Wäld Engeda-Wärq (8) was second in charge of the Ministry of the Pen, and so partly checked Wäldä-Giyorgis on his home ground. The resistance leader Ras Abäbä (1) was attached to this group, but at times judged it wiser to make common cause with Wäldä-Giyorgis. This section of the nobility was closely connected by marriage with the imperial family, most of which—and especially the Crown Prince—opposed Wäldä-Giyorgis.

Wäldä-Giyorgis could never destroy these opponents, since their place in the traditional hierarchy was too secure, but he could usually scotch them, and whenever possible, he kept them away from the Emperor. Thus, Andargé was made Governor-General of Bägémdär in 1946, and was moved to Eritrea as the Emperor's Representative on the Federation in 1952. Ras Abäbä was kept in Tegré from 1943 until 1947, when he made his peace with Wäldä-Giyorgis and returned to Addis Ababa. Similar tactics were used against personal opponents like Takälä Wäldä-Hawari-yat (32), a first-class intriguer who was made governor of distant Boräna in 1946 and imprisoned the following year, and Tadäsä Nägash, who spent most of the period between 1941 and 1955 in provincial posts. Bitwädäd Makonnen received the then insignificant post of Prime Minister, where in any case he had neither the energy nor the ability to become a serious rival to Wäldä-Giyorgis.

In a different position was Mulugéta Buli (26), Commander of the Bodyguard, who maintained far greater independence. His control of the Bodyguard helped to balance Wäldä-Giyorgis' influence in the Army; he ran his own competing intelligence service; he alone was able to obtain financial appropriations without going through the Ministry of the Pen; and he retained a control over appointments beneath him which Wäldä-Giyorgis could rarely upset. But while he was in a position to co-exist with Wäldä-Giyorgis, he was not strong enough to challenge him. His dependence on the Emperor was quite as great as that of Wäldä-Giyorgis, his parentage was quite as undistinguished, and as a Galla his social status was even lower. He opposed the aristocratic group quite as bitterly as he opposed the Minister of the Pen, and he remained without allies, a figure apart from other high officials. While he maintained control of his own field, he was therefore unable to venture outside it.

The last group of opponents, the intellectual liberals, were very weak in the period before 1955, since the post-war graduates did not begin to make themselves heard in the administration until the mid-1950s. The leader of the liberals after the Liberation was Lorénzo T'ezaz (16), an Eritrean who had been prominent in the pre-war government. He became Ambassador in Moscow in November 1943, a post equivalent to exile, and paid only short visits to Ethiopia before his death in 1947. Another member was Agäñähu Engeda, one of the best-known of Ethiopian artists, who died in the same year. During the 1940s the acting Minister of Finance, Yelma Derésa (35), was also generally regarded as a liberal, but he did not openly oppose Wäldä-Giyorgis, and gradually dropped his radical ideas.

Supported by so many allies, and faced by such a diverse band of opponents, Wäldä-Giyorgis maintained his position of supremacy for a dozen years after the Liberation. He reached his peak in 1949, when a government reshuffle increased the power of his allies and reduced that of some of his opponents. Ras Abäbä (1), who had been establishing his position at the Ministry of War since his return from the governorship of Tegré in 1947, was removed to the Ministry of the Interior, and replaced by Abiy Abäbä (2), one of the very few Shoan noblemen with whom Wäldä-Giyorgis remained consistently on good terms. Wäldä-Giyorgis himself vacated the Ministry of the Interior for that of Justice, but in the previous six years he had established so many nominees there that he could continue to control it through them, as was emphasised by the appointment of his supporter Keflé Ergätu (15) as vice-minister. The Habtä-Wäld clan, allies of Wäldä-Giyorgis, also moved up, Akalä-Wärq and Aklilu being confirmed in charge of the Ministries of Education and Foreign Affairs, but with higher ranks, while Makonnen (19) left Commerce for the Ministry of Finance, a position which he had long coveted. Yelma Derésa (35) moved from Finance to Commerce, and was sent to Washington in 1953 after a quarrel with Wäldä-Giyorgis.

Wäldä-Giyorgis' position started to decline in about 1953. The first sign of this was that rather less was delegated to him by the Emperor, and rather more was carried out without his knowledge. In 1954, his great enemy Takälä Wäldä-Hawariyat (32) was released from prison, and Muligéta Buli (26) had one of his *protégés*, Ato Täfäri Sharäw, appointed to a post in the Haile-Selassie I Foundation without Wäldä-Giyorgis being informed, a manœuvre which greatly angered him. The turning-point came in late 1953 and early 1954, with the end of the alliance between Wäldä-Giyorgis and Makonnen Habtä-Wäld (19) which had lasted for over twenty years. The ostensible cause of this was a quarrel between a supporter of each of them over whether Makonnen could levy a tax on a market near his property at Nazrét, south of Addis Ababa; but it is unlikely that this trivial matter could have caused a break without some deeper reason, and in particular it is very probable that the Emperor was somehow concerned with it. Makonnen was not the man to take such an important step without imperial backing, and in any case he would not have taken the risk unless the Emperor's confidence in Wäldä-Giyorgis had declined.

Once this split had been made, all of the enemies of the Minister of the Pen discovered that they had at last a chance of ousting him, and united behind Makonnen. They did all they could to weaken Wäldä-Giyorgis' position with the Emperor, even going so far as to assert that he was planning to set up a republic; they could use the very size and efficiency of his machine against him, by presenting it as a dangerously powerful potential rival to the Emperor himself. It nevertheless came as a surprise to Wäldä-Giyorgis when in April 1955 he was banished to the governorship of Arusi: Bruce had described just such a dismissal two centuries before in words which show how timeless are the ups and downs of Ethiopian politics:

It is true he was removed by what, in other times would have been called preferment; but things had now changed their qualities, and places were not estimated, as formerly, by the consequence they gave in the Empire, but by the opportunities they afforded of constant access to the king, and occasion of joining in councils with him, and defeating those of their enemies.[3]

With the appointment of Wälda-Giyorgis to Arusi, his machine immediately collapsed. Many of his former allies had prepared beforehand to leave the sinking ship, including Täfärä-Wärq (31), the Emperor's Private Secretary, who became the new Minister of the Pen. Of his supporters, Abiy Abäbä (2) was sent as Ambassador to Paris, and Keflé Ergätu (15) was moved from the Ministry of the Interior to Härär, though both have returned to high office in the 1960s. Enemies filled the posts they had vacated. The new Minister of the Interior, Mäsfen Seläshi (23), was one of these, and the two vice-ministers were Takälä Wälda-Hawariyat (32) and Tadäsä Nägash, both long noted for their hatred of Wälda-Giyorgis. In their new positions, they frustrated him as much as possible, and sent down to Arusi men who already had reason to dislike him. Ras Abäbä (1) moved back to the Ministry of Defence, and Mulugéta Buli (26) became Chief of Staff.

One reason for Wälda-Giyorgis' dismissal was undoubtedly that he had acquired an exaggerated view of his own importance and indispensability, forgetting how completely his basic position depended on the Emperor. Many stories are told of his vanity at this time, in taking precedence over members of the Imperial Family and claiming that the real power in Ethiopia was not the Emperor but himself; and it is true of Wälda-Giyorgis as of other officials that he fell when he tried to replace the Emperor's authority by his own.

His fall may also be correlated with general developments in the government at that time. The process of centralisation under the Emperor was virtually complete, and there was no longer much need for the machinery through which it had been achieved. The traditional structure of the government was being modified after the reunion with Eritrea, and a new generation was entering it with the return of graduates from abroad. There were few signs of genuine liberalisation, but the appearance of reform was in the air, and Wälda-Giyorgis could be left as a scapegoat for the inactivity of earlier years. Many people gained the impression that this contributed to his dismissal, and though causal connections are difficult to establish, the events certainly fall into a common pattern.

It is said that Takälä Wälda-Häwariyat (32) once told Wälda-Giyorgis that while the fortunes of others might rise and fall with the political tide, Wälda-Giyorgis, once he fell, would fall for ever. While the story is apocryphal, it shows an accurate understanding of Wäldä-Giyorgis' position. This depended on a degree of imperial confidence which, once lost, would be very difficult to regain, and without this trust it would be impossible to reassemble the large political machine which was necessary for the exercise of such great power. Perhaps most important of all, the very fall of such a man creates strong interests against his return; those who overthrew him are terrified of his reappointment, for they have much to lose by it, and they can therefore be relied upon to make sure that both his personal machine and his standing with the Emperor are completely destroyed. Wäldä-Giyorgis' lack of personal authority and of family connections meant that there was no one to support him and keep his name before the Emperor during his disgrace. His family depended on him quite as much as he depended on the Emperor, and after his fall his brother, Makonnen Wäldä-Yohanes, was convicted on a charge of embezzling about £150,000.[4] Nor would former *protégés* have reason to work for his return, since they were attracted to him by the power which he no longer enjoyed, and would be anxious to disown him for fear of running foul of the men who gained office by his fall.

This was illustrated when Wäldä-Giyorgis returned to Addis Ababa in the late spring of 1960. It was wildly rumoured that he was going to be put in charge of the newly formed Private Cabinet, and reinstated to his old pre-eminence. All of his former enemies, however, including such opponents as Makonnen Habtä-Wäld (19), Ras Abäbä (1) and Tadäsä Nägash, united to dissuade the Emperor from such a step, and in June 1960 he was appointed Governor-General of the still more distant province of Gämu Gofa. The massacre of the hostages at the end of the 1960 revolt removed many of his bitterest enemies, including the three mentioned above, and during 1961 Takälä Wäldä-Hawariyat (32) was again imprisoned and Ras Andargé (4) became Governor-General of Sidamo. There was therefore little opposition when Wäldä-Giyorgis returned to Addis Ababa in 1961, but he has since remained in complete retirement, preserving his discretion about the past, and has done little beyond preparing a few materials for the Emperor's projected autobiography.

The Secretariat in Decline, 1955–1968

Ato Täfärä-Wärq (31), the Emperor's Private Secretary, who became Minister of the Pen on the dismissal of Wäldä-Giyorgis (33), was, like his predecessor, a Shoan of unimportant family who had started his career as an interpreter; but there the resemblance ends, for he had neither the energy nor the capacity to become a major political figure, and both the

Emperor and the ministers were naturally chary of replacing Wäldä-Giyorgis by anyone of the same calibre. The Ministry of the Pen therefore subsided into little more than a secretarial agency, a striking example of the way in which the power of Ethiopian institutions, especially those close to the Emperor, has been determined by the personal positions of the individuals in them. In 1957, Täfärä-Wärq became Minister of the Imperial Court, responsible for supervising the ceremonial aspects of the palace. It had no control over the rest of the administration, though any agency so close to the Emperor may be used by him for political errands such as summoning officials to see him; the offices of the other court officials may be used in the same way.

In May 1958, Aklilu Habtä-Wäld (3) became Minister of the Pen, and still holds the post in 1968. He was already deputy Prime Minister, with no full Prime Minister over him, and he has steadily improved his position since then, and especially since the revolt of 1960. This improvement has, however, been carried out through the Prime Minister's office rather than through the Ministry of the Pen, and is therefore considered in the next chapter. In particular, Aklilu has not used the characteristic function of the Ministry of the Pen, that of sending out imperial orders. His position as Minister has nevertheless helped him, notably as a source of information on orders sent out by the Emperor, and he has also made some use of the Ministry's supervision of the *Negarit Gazeta*. In 1958, for instance, a decree increasing the powers of his brother Makonnen (19) was published in it, to the complete surprise of the other ministers concerned, instead of going through the Council of Ministers.

The work of the Ministry of the Pen has since 1958 been carried out largely by the Emperor's Private Secretary. The character of this post has changed considerably since Täfärä-Wärq (31) ceased to hold it. Täfärä-Wärq continues to exercise, as Minister of the Imperial Court, a number of functions, such as interpreting for the Emperor, which he previously carried out as Private Secretary; and the Private Secretary's Office has become a department of the Ministry of the Pen. The process started when Täfärä-Wärq held the two offices, though they had separate budgets and organisations until 1958. In May 1958, Kätäma Yefru (14) became both Private Secretary and Assistant Minister in the Ministry of the Pen, and by the Budget of 1959/1960 the Private Secretary's Office had ceased to be a separate entity under the Civil List, and had become part of the Ministry. The transformation was completed after the death in the 1960 revolt of Ato Gäbrä-Wäld Engeda-Wärq (8), who had carried out most of the routine functions of the Ministry, since these then fell to the Private Secretary. He has therefore been responsible for noting down imperial requests and issuing them as orders, though the more important ones are still signed by the Minister himself.

There have been three Private Secretaries since 1958, of varying political importance. Kätäma Yefru (14) held the office until August 1961, when he became acting Minister of Foreign Affairs. He is said to have taken an active part in the *Aqabé Sä'at*, and in particular to have suggested frequently that ministers should take decisions themselves, instead of bringing them to the Emperor. Lej Kasa Wäldä-Maryam, a member of the Galla nobility of Wäläga who had previously been Kätäma's deputy, then held the post until he became President of the University in 1962. His marriage to a granddaughter of the Emperor and a certain amount of imperial confidence helped to strengthen his position, and he is said to have enjoyed some freedom in the drafting of orders, with the result that ministers would clear requests with him before taking them to the Emperor. His successor, Ato Yohanes Kidanä-Maryam, has shown very little independence, and has restricted himself to the simple role of a secretary. Even the more influential private secretaries have been fairly junior politicians, and have had nothing even remotely approaching the importance of a Wäldä-Giyorgis (33).

The decline of the Imperial Secretariat since 1955 has thus been very marked, and a number of reasons for this can be suggested. Some of them are implicit in the fall of Wäldä-Giyorgis, including the completion of the centralising process, and the dangers of having a single able and ambitious man in control of vital channels of communication with the Emperor. The Emperor has not given any other official the confidence which he gave to Wäldä-Giyorgis, and other ministers would naturally do all they could to prevent such an official from establishing himself.

This decline also reflects other changes in the methods of government, such as the diminution of imperial control of the details through which much of the power of the Ministry of the Pen was exercised. The highly personal methods which the use of the Secretariat involved have also become obsolete with the disappearance of personal political machines and the gradual establishment of administrative procedures, for instance for financial appropriations. The growth of an important modernising group would also be difficult to reconcile with the tight central control which a powerful Secretariat provided, for the relaxation of this control is to some extent the price for keeping reforming elements within the political framework. All of these are aspects of the gradual modernisation which, though it still has far to go, has accompanied the rise of educated officials to most of the senior posts.

His Imperial Majesty's Private Cabinet

In any modern executive dominated by a single man, there is room for expert advisers to keep the leader informed of the technical aspects of decisions, and to appraise suggestions coming from the regular departments of state. The use of presidential advisers in the United States is the most obvious case of such a system, and the Private Cabinet was an attempt to introduce it to Ethiopia. It was never formally established, but the first appointments were made to it in December 1959.

The impetus for its foundation came from two soldiers closely attached to the Emperor, who were determined enemies of most of the ministers: Mulugéta Buli (26), then the Emperor's Private Chief of Staff, and Colonel Wärqenäh Gäbäyähu (34), the Chief of Security. Mulugéta had for many years assessed ministerial suggestions for the Emperor as part of the intelligence system described in Chapter 5, and his contempt for the civil administration ensured that the resulting advice was independent if not impartial.

The Private Cabinet was intended to extend and systematise this service. In its original conception, it was exceedingly grandiose, and was to include fourteen departments covering the whole scope of government. No appointments were made to three of these, and several of the others, including the Imperial Chronicles Department, the Office of the Private Chief of Staff, and the Special Branch for intelligence, were simply existing agencies brought into the new organisation. The Press and Information Department has been entirely concerned with examining the foreign press, providing the Emperor with the background to world events, and the public with suitably laudatory cuttings on Ethiopia from foreign periodicals.

The remaining departments each covered the affairs of several ministries, and were intended to serve as a clearing house for information, and to assess plans submitted to the Emperor by the ministers. This would not only serve the Emperor's love of balancing groups within the government, but would offset his ignorance of technical matters, and give him direct access to sources of expertise which would otherwise be blocked. In particular, the Private Cabinet was intended to represent the views of young Ethiopians recently returned from intensive education abroad. It also had international implications, in that Mulugéta (26) was closely connected with the Yugoslavs in Ethiopia, and a Yugoslav adviser, Dr Gershkowitz, helped him in setting up the Cabinet.

The Private Cabinet was founded at a time when Aklilu Habtä-Wäld (3), was trying to build up the Prime Minister's office, and it may also have been meant to balance this. In any case, he and other ministers could not be expected to approve of a body which came into the vital field of their access to the Emperor, and many ministers, usually of different factions, combined against it, including both Aklilu, and Ras Abäbä (1), who was Chairman of the Council of Ministers. Mulugéta's influence was then declining, and on the day the Private Cabinet started work in December 1959, he was moved to the less important post of Minister of National Community Development; the chief supporter of the scheme was thereafter Wärqenäh Gäbäyähu (34). Its opponents retaliated by influencing appointments to the organisation, and in particular two followers of Makonnen Habtä-Wäld (19), took charge of Economic Planning and Social Affairs.

The Private Cabinet undertook a variety of assignments. It summarised information sent to the Emperor and sought out further information itself, and it reported on projects passed to it by the Emperor, especially when he wished to delay them, or when he was inclined to reject them and wanted both to be provided with reasons for doing so and to find someone who would be blamed for their failure by their supporters. In this way, the Private Cabinet served to some extent as a protective buffer to the Emperor, in much the same way as Wäldä-Giyorgis (33) had done. Its balancing function was increased by the absence of any consultation between the Cabinet and the agency which had originated the project which it was studying. This made its recommendations more independent, but naturally led to criticisms that the Cabinet was out of touch with the practical difficulties of administration.

It also made recommendations of its own, and investigated any problem which the Emperor desired. Thus, it reported on long-term Ethiopian policy towards Somalia and Ogaden shortly after Somalian independence in 1960, and recommended educational propaganda and other measures among Ethiopian Somalis. This report was shelved until March 1964, when the border crisis in Ogaden caused it to be re-examined. The Private Cabinet was more successful in its recommendation of a Central Personnel Agency. It was concerned only with fairly long-range plans and particular projects such as this one, and took no part in day-to-day administration. It had no concern, for instance, with the authorisation of financial appropriations, or even with drawing up the Budget.

The struggle between the ministers and the Private Cabinet continued until Wärqenäh Gäbäyähu (34) was killed fighting for the rebels in the revolt of December 1960. Not only did his death remove the leader of the Private Cabinet's supporters, but the manner of it placed a powerful argument in the hands of the surviving ministers. As a result, the institution swiftly declined. The Special Branch, the Office of the Chief of Staff, and the Chronicles, Judicial and Ecclesiastical Departments continue to function on their own, but have little connection with one another or with the central departments. Of the eight director-generals and above in the central departments, seven ceased to work there regularly during 1961 and 1962, though most retained formal posts in the Private Cabinet, and only Mäba'a-Selassie Alämu of the Press and Information Department remained. The officials who had effectively left the Cabinet continued to use their formal positions there as a means for obtaining access to the Emperor.

An attempt was made to revive the moribund institution when Dr Menasé Haylé (24) was appointed Chief of Political Affairs in May 1962. He had recently returned from fourteen years in the United States, and was qualified and interested entirely in foreign affairs. Since the Press and Information Department also dealt with foreign events, the Private Cabinet thereafter worked almost exclusively in this field. That the Emperor should retain such personal advisers only in foreign affairs illustrates his increased specialisation in the subject, and his leaving more of the detail of home affairs to the Prime Minister and other ministers. Examples of the effectiveness of the Private Cabinet are hard to find, since its advice is given and discussed behind the scenes. Reports of friction between Menasé (24) and Kätäma Yefru (14), the Minister of Foreign Affairs, suggest that it has made itself felt, but this is quite inseparable from the personal relations between the two officials and the Emperor. Menasé accompanied the Emperor on most of his foreign tours between mid-1962 and mid-1966, and was especially in evidence during the state visit to the United States in 1963. He took charge of the Ministry of Information early in 1965, but retained his position in the Private Cabinet, and continued to spend much of his time in attendance on the Emperor. He was appointed ambassador to Washington in July 1968.

In addition to their formal functions, members of the Private Cabinet had some importance simply because of their easy access to the Emperor. They could make their views heard at the right time and place, and could suggest things to the Emperor even when they had not been officially consulted. But this did not involve any of the systematic appraisal of ministerial policies for which the Private Cabinet was originally designed.

The experiment of the Private Cabinet, and its failure, illuminate a vital section of the government. The Cabinet lay in the highly important field of access to the Emperor, which it threatened to control by placing a systematic institutional barrier between the ministers and the source of authority. Such a barrier would have cut at the roots of ministerial influence, by subjecting ministerial requests to independent and probably hostile scrutiny, and it is therefore not surprising that a combination of very powerful interests arose against it. The ministers had the advantage of being experienced politicians long known to the Emperor, and they had had time to build up their own positions. It would therefore have required a very able individual completely trusted by the Emperor to carry the day against them, and the Private Cabinet never possessed anyone of this stature. The nearest approach was provided by Colonel Wärqenäh (34), but he was unable even to control it completely, let alone turn it into a powerful agency, as is shown by the infiltration of the Cabinet by *protégés* of his enemy Makonnen Habtä-Wäld (19). The consequent decay of the Private Cabinet thus further underlines the lessons implicit in the fall of Wäldä-Giyorgis (33).

The Crown Council

The Crown Council advises the Emperor on matters of state, and does not form part of the imperial secretariat; but the two have a certain amount in common as traditionally-based bodies closely attached to the Emperor. The decline of the Crown Council since 1941 therefore confirms the fading importance of traditional institutions already noted with the Ministry of the Pen.

In the Revised Constitution of 1955, the Council was charged with several functions too closely connected with the Throne to be entrusted to the Council of Ministers, including the certifying of incapacity in the Emperor or the Crown Prince, and recommending action to the Emperor on the activities of members of the Imperial Family. It was to consist of the Archbishop, the President of the Senate, and other dignitaries appointed by the Emperor.[5] But this Council was not established by the Constitution, and seems to have existed at least since the Liberation, serving for informal consultations between the Empcror and the major nobles. Perham referred to it in 1948 as 'an informal policy-making body and as such the central focus of power under the Emperor'.[6] Its chief members at that time were the senior cleric who later became Archbishop, Ras Kasa (13), Ras Seyum of Tegré (28), and Bitwädäd Makonnen Endalkachäw (18), though other councillors attended according to the subject discussed. These members still attended in 1954, with Ras Abäbä Arägay (1), Ras Haylu Bäläw (11) of Gojam, and an aged warrior, Ras Adäfresäw. Another member, from 1943 until his death in 1953, was Däjazmach Amdä-Mika'él, head of the Shoan clan of the *Moja*. The Crown Prince and the Duke of Harär, though not the Emperor's third son, are included in a list of May 1957; Ras Kasa had died the previous year, and Ras Seyum and Ras Haylu Bäläw are left out. The members were the same in 1959, except that the Duke of Harär had died.[7] The Council had a secretariat, under Ato Gäbrä-Wäld Engeda-Wärq (8) of the Ministry of the Pen, a *protégé* of Ras Kasa, and an office in the Menilek Palace, close to that of the Council of Ministers.

The Council was thus strikingly composed of members of the aristocracy, with a high proportion of Rasses. The more recently created Rasses, Mäsfen (23) and Andargé (4), were not included, and nor were important politicians of humbler origin such as Wäldä-Giyorgis (33) or Makonnen Habtä-Wäld (19). An interesting omission was Ras Imru (12), most liberal and most closely related to the Emperor of all the Rasses, who was abroad as an ambassador for much but not all of the period.

There has been no reported case of the Council carrying out the specific duties assigned to it by the Constitution, but it has had other functions which to some extent follow from its membership. Clearly such a body would not take much part in day-to-day administration, which is dealt with by quite a different set of officials. Its importance lies in the fact that it included most of the figures commanding great respect by virtue of their place in the traditional political hierarchy. The Archbishop and Ras Kasa carried great weight in Church affairs; Kasa (13), Seyum (28) and Haylu Bäläw (11) were the heads of the royal lines of Shoa, Tegré and Gojam; Adäfresäw and Bitwädäd Makonnen (18) were members of the Shoan nobility, and Ras Abäbä gained great prestige as leader of the Patriot forces during the occupation. In the hierarchical society of Ethiopia, such men are greatly looked up to, and even the Emperor could not afford to ignore them.

It may therefore be inferred that one of the main functions of the Council was to represent the traditional élite in decisions for which consensus was necessary, thus maintaining national unity in a period of change. Haile-Selassie's preference for working by consensus adds weight to reports that he would consult the Council over any important step. The Council's consideration of the Revised Constitution provides an example of such consultation in the interests of consensus; other examples have been hard to find, since the Council works directly with the Emperor. and is not involved in the machinery of government. Meetings have been irregular, but the secretariat and the stability of the membership have ensured some continuity.

The Council is more likely to have taken a fairly passive role than to have played any active part in policy-making. Such a traditionally-based body would be better suited to the evaluation of suggestions than to making them itself, and it is unlikely that one so devoted as the Emperor to weakening the power of the nobility would have given a council of noblemen any greater share in the decision-making process than the needs of consensus demanded. Further, though the members of the Council were all of high prestige in the country at large, few of them were of a calibre to stand up to the Emperor within the government. Ras Haylu Bäläw (11) has never been of any political weight; Ras Abäbä was noted for his humble demeanour, even towards inferiors; Ras Adäfresäw and

Bitwädäd Makonnen (18) had long been attached to the Emperor, and were consequently dependent on him; and the Archbishop had also risen to his high position under the Emperor's wing. Of Ras Seyum's (28) status as a great independent lord there is no doubt, but his power was largely wielded in his province of Tegré, and he remained aloof from the central government. There remains Ras Kasa (13), unquestionably the most important member, and much of the weight of the Council will have depended on the extent to which he exercised his great influence through it.

But Ras Kasa died in 1956, and over the next few years the Council as he knew it virtually disappeared. The Duke of Harär was killed in a car crash in 1957, and Ras Seyum, Ras Abäbä and the secretary, Ato Gäbrä-Wäld (8), were all shot dead in the massacre of hostages at the close of the 1960 revolt. Ras Adäfresäw died in 1961 and Betwädäd Makonnen two years later, and since the Archbishop has long been in very bad health, this left the Crown Prince and Ras Haylu as the only effective survivors. This list of obituaries reflects the fact that practically none of the traditional leaders remains, and there is certainly no longer any such group of men whose opinion the Emperor would have to consult. So successful has his policy of centralisation been that his prestige now easily overshadows that of every other leader in the country, and the Crown Council thus died away with those whom it was its function to represent.

Recently, however, the Council seems to have taken on a new lease of life, since four appointments to it were announced in 1966, all of distinguished ex-officials of whom only one had much claim to nobility. Among them were Blatengéta Mahtämä-Selassie (17), and a provincial governor from the *Moja* clan who unlike several of his relatives had stayed loyal to Haile-Selassie in 1960. Ras Imru (12), Ras Haylu Bäläw the Prime Minister and the acting Patriarch also attend, and Lieutenant-General Abiy Abäbä (2) has a place *ex-officio* as President of the Senate. This body clearly lacks the prestige of its predecessor, despite the presence of Imru and Abiy, and it may have been re-created to provide a place of dignified retirement for senior politicians; but it holds occasional meetings, and it is said that the Emperor submits major policy decisions for its advice.

Chapter 9

The Growth of Central Institutions

The Council of Ministers

The Council of Ministers is one of the distinctively modern institutions of the government. It has very little basis in traditional administration, and though various official councils have existed since 1908, they have not been important, and the Council in its present form dates only from 1943. It is therefore not surprising that it has not formed the hub of the executive government. Its powers have been only advisory,* and the Emperor is not a member: he has never attended regularly, and does so only on special occasions to add weight and sometimes publicity to the Council's deliberations.[1]

The establishing Order made all ministers and vice-ministers members of the Council, but it is not clear whether vice-ministers ever attended regularly when the responsible minister was also present. At least since 1955, the general rule has been for all ministers to attend, but for vice-ministers to do so only in the absence of the minister. However, some ministers have refused to attend, because of their relations with other ministers or to emphasise their dependence on the Emperor alone, and some vice-ministers have come with their ministers, to give help or to spread responsibility. The Minister of State in the Prime Minister's office attends as assistant to the Prime Minister. There have been at least two ministers without portfolio, and other officials are fairly often called in to give details of proposed legislation or other subjects which particularly concern them. The usual attendance is between fifteen and twenty.

The Minister of the Pen was at first Chairman, but this function was soon afterwards transferred to the Prime Minister, and Bitwädäd Makonnen (18) therefore presided from 1943 until 1957. Ras Abäbä (1) was then appointed Chairman, there being no full Prime Minister, and Aklilu Habtä-Wäld (3), Prime Minister since 1961, has presided since Ras Abäbä's death in December 1960. The Chairman sits at the head of an oval table, with other ministers ranged down the sides in order of seniority. Decisions are usually reached by consensus.

* In March 1966, it obtained the power to take decisions, but those on 'matters of policy' still have to be submitted to the Emperor.

Perham refers to twice-weekly meetings, with daily ones in time of pressure, and this frequency has been maintained. The Council meets on Tuesdays and usually on Fridays, and more often when there is a deadline to be met. The agenda is circulated in advance, with relevant documents such as drafts of legislation, and detailed minutes are taken and made available to the Emperor. The Council secretariat handles the agenda and minutes, and also prepares orders and authorisations on the basis of decisions in Council. The first publicly-announced appointment of a secretary was in October 1955, but at least two men had previously held the post. A set of rules of procedure was adopted in 1961, but there were procedural rules of some sort before that.

Each minister informs the secretariat of matters concerning his department which need discussion, and except for urgent business these are supposed to come before the Council in order of submission. In practice, matters which ministers prefer to block without openly opposing may spend a long time before reaching the Council, and several measures proposed in the aftermath of the 1960 revolt, including laws on the press and on the appointment of judges, have been so long before the Council as to have lapsed into oblivion.

The Council has several regular committees, which tend to cover specific administrative chores, such as the annual budget and other financial appropriations, rather than broad areas of policy. *Ad hoc* committees are frequently set up, and major legislative proposals usually go to a committee before consideration by the whole Council. Much of the Council's time is taken up with draft laws, and even subsidiary legislation, which is issued on the authority of the competent minister, usually goes before it. The amount which the Council alters drafts varies very much from one occasion to another, though many proposals have been informally but effectively cleared before they come before it at all. Sometimes a draft is referred to the Prime Minister's office for revision, and other proposals have undergone varying amounts of change.

Appropriations also occupy much of the Council's attention, and in this field its scope has markedly increased in the 1960s; the annual Budget, which deals entirely with allocations rather than taxation, is examined in detail, and the Council has taken over from the Emperor much of the authorisation of additional spending. Beyond this, the Council serves as a general clearing house for approval of proposed loans and concessions, and of a wide variety of development projects. In 1960, for instance, the Council approved the purchase of jet aircraft by Ethiopian Air Lines, an important decision which involved the whole future of the airline, the building of a new airport in Addis Ababa to take the jets, and the raising of a large loan in the United States. It is very probable, however, that the ministers made sure of the Emperor's support before committing themselves, and the Emperor in any case approved the decision at some point in the proceedings.

This question of the relations between the ministers and the Emperor is central to the position of the Council. It must be remembered that collective responsibility has no place in the traditional system, and that ministers are both divided among themselves and individually dependent on the Emperor. Very few of them would oppose anything which he definitely wanted, though there is some room for covert opposition through the traditional forms already noted; and many decisions which would be the concern of a Council of Ministers elsewhere do not come before it in Ethiopia, since the head of the executive is not a member of the Council, and takes decisions outside it with the help of only a few ministers. Foreign affairs and defence, for example, are unlikely to be greatly affected by anything that happens in Council, and in other matters a minister often prefers to take problems to the Emperor, whose decision is both more authoritative and easier to obtain.

The Council is therefore little more than a formality over something which the Emperor supports, and even if some ministers at first oppose it, they change their opinion when confronted by the Emperor in person. Although the Emperor's methods incline him to take notice of advice from the Council, he is not obliged to accept it, and many ministers in any case give him the advice which they think he wants to hear. The Council may also serve as a block to things which the Emperor opposes. When a minister brings some decision to him, he approves it directly if he supports it, and may pass it to the Council for further study if he opposes it, but yet does not want to reject it openly. This explains the delays which some proposals suffer in the Council, while others pass through with little difficulty.

But there are also occasions when the Emperor wants the decision of the Council on subjects which he has not finally decided himself, and on others with which he is not greatly concerned. These include the Budget, some cases of arbitration between ministries, and much legislation, especially the more technical proposals and those, like the institution of the Central Personnel Agency, whose general principles have been cleared with him in advance. Over these, the Council naturally has a great deal more scope. It also serves as a meeting ground between the different factions in the government, where compromises may be worked out, or where one group may try to block the proposals of another. In the time of Wäldä-Giyorgis (33), for instance, the Council was one of the few parts of the government dominated by his opponents, and they could use it to delay some of the things which Wäldä-Giyorgis wanted. Since 1961, its most important members have been the Prime Minister and the Minister of Finance.

The Council therefore appears to have a useful function in the co-ordination and consideration of legislation and some other executive activities. Its value is increased by the comparative lack of co-ordinating machinery below the ministerial level. But despite its administrative usefulness, there is no evidence to suggest that the Council takes a more active role in government. It is far from being a leading policy-making body, for this function is still largely carried out between the Emperor and individual ministers, and when the Council appears to make an important decision, it often only reflects the dispositions which the Emperor has already made behind the scenes. Nor does the Council provide any impetus for the effective implementation of government policies. The co-ordination which it supplies is limited to the resolution of clashes and difficulties, and does not extend to active and unified direction of the country's affairs.

Formal decisions of government policy are sometimes announced through another council, which consists of the major figures of the realm meeting in the presence of the Emperor. The Crown Prince, the Crown Council and the Council of Ministers provide the nucleus of its member-ship, though bishops, governors-general and other important officials may attend. It meets very irregularly, one or two times a year in the mid-1950s but markedly more often in the months after the 1960 revolt.[2] It has no constitutional existence nor formal powers, nor even a name, and it can scarcely be classed as an established institution. The chief function of this council is to express a consensus already arrived at, giving publicity and solemnity to important decisions, including one in 1946 to press for the 'return' to Ethiopia of Eritrea and ex-Italian Somaliland. The Planning Board, whose only function is to promulgate the Five Year Plan already drawn up by experts, has a similar membership and purpose. The council sometimes holds discussions, on subjects which have included Ethio-Somali relations, without announcing any decision. Such meetings may have some effect in enabling the Emperor to sound out the opinions of members of the government, to clarify his own ideas, or to seek a consensus; a great deal depends on whether his mind is already made up, and on the extent to which the result is already a foregone conclusion.

The Prime Minister's Office, 1943-1957

To modernise and systematise the higher administration, there is clearly a need for a head of government who can co-ordinate activities and gradu-ally assume from the Emperor the direction of affairs. The Minister of the Pen might perhaps have evolved into such an official, like his equivalent in England, but it has already been seen that he operated in too personal a way, too close to the Emperor, for this to happen. These functions have therefore fallen to a new official, the Prime Minister, whose office was created in 1943 with broad supervisory powers over the rest of the government.[3]

It was nevertheless many years before the Prime Minister even started to exercise such powers, since at first he stood completely outside the main structure of the government. He had no place in the traditional system, in which the administration was still directed by imperial orders passed through the imperial secretariat, and until the secretariat declined there was therefore no machinery through which his theoretical powers could be exercised. Nor was the first Prime Minister, Bitwädäd Makonnen Endal-kachäw (18), the man to exercise them. As a high nobleman, he commanded great respect, but though 'noted for his magnificent presence, his delightful manners, and his unquestionable devotion to the Emperor'[4], he was not a forceful politician, and in most of his activities he served largely as a dignified figurehead. He was probably appointed Prime Minister at least partly so as to give him a position of impressive impotence while his opponent Wäldä-Giyorgis took over the real powers of his previous post as Minister of the Interior.

The administrative responsibilities of the Prime Minister's office were at that time few. The presence of its representative at the *Aqäbé Sä'at* provided information but no control over the transmission of imperial orders. It supervised the Administrative Court, which heard disputes within the civil service now dealt with by the Central Personnel Agency, and for a time it was responsible for the Auditor General's office, but these gave little scope for influence. It was responsible for relations between the executive and Parliament, but Parliament also was then unimportant. It had no other active functions, and its few officials often found themselves with practically nothing to do. In November 1957, Bitwädäd Makonnen was appointed President of the Senate, and at the same time all of the officials in the Prime Minister's office left for other posts, a fact which indicates the personal nature of the position, and the lack of continuity between its two holders.

The Development of the Prime Ministry since 1958

Bitwädäd Makonnen's successor was the Minister of Foreign Affairs, Aklilu Habtä-Wäld (3), who took over as acting Prime Minister, and was appointed full Prime Minister in 1961. His ten years in office have seen the gradual growth of an institutional premiership which has owed com-

The Emperor and his Ministers. The inaugural meeting of the reconstituted Council of Ministers, April 1966. On the Emperor's right: Crown Prince Asfa-Wäsän, Aklilu Habtä-Wäld (Prime Minister), Yelma Derésa (Finance) and other ministers. On the Emperor's left: Ras Imru, Ras Mäsfen Seläshi (Deputy Governor of Shoa), Abäbä Räta (Commerce), Akalä-Wärq Habtä-Wäld (Education), Amanu'él Abraham (Communications).

Tsähafé T'ezaz Aklilu Habtä-Wäld, Prime Minister.

Ato Yelma Derésa, Minister of Finance.

Ato Mamo Tadäsä, Minister of Justice.

Dr. Menasé Haylé, Minister of Information.

paratively little to traditional organisation and techniques. This has been possible first because Aklilu is a very different man from his predecessor: whereas Bitwädäd Makonnen was a noble figurehead, Aklilu is the type of the career civil servant. He came from a Church family, and reached high office under the protection of his elder and more powerful brother, Makonnen Habtä-Wäld (19). But his background was very different from Makonnen's, for he was educated in France and is married to a French-woman, and as a result he is regarded by some as more French than Ethiopian; certainly his administrative methods are rather more European than those of most of his contemporaries. He has a few supporters and assistants, but no machine of organised followers and informers such as his brother built up, and he has a great aversion to the crowds of hangers-on in which Makonnen delighted.

His European methods naturally suited him for the Ministry of Foreign Affairs which he directed continuously from October 1943 until April 1958. He took the leading part in all of the more important diplomatic negotiations, including the British Agreement of 1944 and the Federation with Eritrea, and was also on a great many government boards and commissions. This long concern with foreign affairs brought him much into contact with the Emperor, but he tried to remain aloof from intrigues and factions within the government, and he is said to have been an irregu-lar attender at the Council of Ministers during his years at Foreign Affairs.

Like all those who have wielded the greatest influence, he is entirely dependent on the Emperor. His foreign connections are a source of suspicion to many, and his social background provides no traditional base for authority. Nor has he ever been inclined to challenge the important figures of the day, as is indicated by the unusual lack of ups and downs in his career. He worked fairly closely with Wäldä-Giyorgis (33) without being one of his ardent supporters, and after his fall he remained in alliance with his eldest brother, but without doing much to antagonise the opposing faction. Least of all has he been inclined to argue against the wishes of the Emperor.

He is thus a competent but unassertive administrator, content to improve his position little by little, without trying to upset the balance of power within the government. He is not corrupt, but he enjoys the comforts of office, and has taken no rash step which might jeopardise them. Taking warning from the fate of Wäldä-Giyorgis (33), he has not tried to make himself supreme, and he has no firm policy commitments. During the 1940s he was regarded as a liberal, but this gave rise to no break with his conservative brother, and he has now left any hint of radicalism behind him. There is some difference of opinion over what rate of modernisation he actually favours, and some of his supporters say that he presses a more liberal line with the Emperor than he allows to appear in public; but in general, he seems to encourage a modest pace of change without suggesting anything controversial.

In the ten years since his appointment, Aklilu's position has steadily improved. In 1957, he was not even the first among equals, and it is only since the revolt of December 1960 that he has become the major figure of the government. With the death as hostages of several important politicians, Aklilu then emerged as the Emperor's chief adviser, and it has since become usual for important policy matters to be discussed in advance between them. He has also profited from the general decline since 1960 in traditional methods and factional intrigue, since his European training and lack of a personal machine suit him to a more modern form of government.

This change is reflected in the gradual rise in the power of the Prime Minister's office, and in an increasing influence over the all-important subject of appointments. But even since 1961, Akilu has had to share his position with other politicians, notably the Ministers of Finance and Defence, and he has not been able to limit the access of officials to the Emperor. Though increases in his formal powers had been canvassed ever since the failure of the December revolt, it was not until March 1966 that these were implemented, and the Prime Minister received the power to select other ministers. These changes have had no dramatic results, but they marked the emergence of Aklilu as second in authority only to the Emperor; less definite but perhaps more significant is the increased influence with which rumour has endowed him.

The growth in Aklilu's position since 1960 can be seen in a number of ways. One of the most striking is the manner in which he takes over much of the general co-ordination of government affairs during the increasingly frequent absences abroad of the Emperor, and visitors to the Prime Ministry include important officials, such as the Minister of Defence, who would never have been seen there before 1960. A good deal of co-ordinating work goes to the Prime Minister even when the Emperor is at home, and he has adjudicated disputes between the Ministry of Finance and others over appropriations, and between ministries over what should be included in programmes for foreign aid. He has gained further co-ordinating functions through his chairmanship of the Council of Ministers, and his feeling for consensus and his lack of self-assertion have suited him for such work as this.

It goes without saying that he works closely with the Emperor, and he is at the palace daily. He has naturally both consulted and been consulted by the Emperor over important questions such as appointments, and he has also taken over from the Emperor some supervision of administrative detail. Since 1966, for instance, most ministers have had regular appointments with the Prime Minister to report on the work of their departments, in addition to their *Aqabé Sä'at* with the Emperor.

But the Prime Minister's office has not simply been a one-man department; it has contained a cluster of senior officials who have helped Aklilu to extend the office's influence over much of the internal working of the government. One of the clearest examples of this is in the legislative process, every stage of which is now supervised by the Prime Ministry or some connected agency. Its legal department provides a general drafting centre for the government, and legislative proposals which it has not itself drawn up are usually reviewed there, either by the legal adviser, Mr Paradis, or by the vice-minister. The Council of Ministers is presided over by the Prime Minister, and some official from the Prime Ministry usually sits on its more important committees. The Prime Minister also has constitutional responsibility for supervising relations between the executive and Parliament, a function whose importance has greatly increased with the adult suffrage since 1957, and a minister of state or vice-minister has been specially charged with parliamentary affairs, and shepherding legislation through the Chambers. Finally, the Prime Minister as Minister of the Pen is responsible for publication of all laws in the *Negarit Gazeta*.

Beneath the Prime Minister, there have been one or two ministers of state, and as many as four vice-ministers. Several of them have been concerned with Parliament, legislation, and the special department set up in 1965 to co-ordinate different approaches to the Somali problem; but others have had wider responsibilities ranging over central government affairs, and these have tended to be officials with some stature of their own, and with personal access to the Emperor. The most important of them, Mamo Tadäsä (20), was deputy to Aklilu from 1958 until he became Minister of Justice in 1966; he had a permanent seat on the Council of Ministers, often taking over as acting minister of Foreign Affairs during the absence abroad of the Minister, and he sat on a multitude of government boards, committees and commissions, as well as being Head of the Central Personnel Agency; the Emperor often uses him for personal commissions, though as a Catholic with a French education and a French wife, he arouses even greater suspicion of undue foreign influence than the Prime Minister. Since 1966, his place has been taken by Seyum Harägot (27), an Eritrean married to a granddaughter of the Emperor, who had been Mamo's understudy since 1958, and performs broadly similar functions.

Not surprisingly, the personal connections of the officials of the Prime Ministry have been rather more effective than its formal powers, and it has not been able to gain any systematic control over the rest of the government. Attempts to set up departments for the general co-ordination of the activities of the ministries have been hampered by the reluctance of ministers to submit themselves to the officials of lower rank who ran these departments. Any initiative therefore had to come from the Prime Minister himself, with the result that junior officials could function effectively only as advisers to him. The Prime Ministry was also niminally responsible for several agencies such as the Planning Board and the Institute of Public Administration, but it never asserted control over them, and in the reorganisation of 1966 they were transferred elsewhere.

Overall, the Prime Minister's office has thus developed into a useful supervisory agency, with some influence throughout the central government. It has taken over some of the functions left not only by the Ministry of the Pen, but also by the more general slow withdrawal of the Emperor from the field of day-to-day government, and it has gained from the increasing importance of modern subjects, such as legislation, with which the Emperor has never been particularly concerned. This does represent a growing process of institutionalisation; and one result of Aklilu's peculiarly untraditional administrative methods, and of his reluctance to assert himself, has been that his supervision has taken a less personal form than might have been expected of almost any other politician. He has also been a major stabilising influence, as is illustrated by the cautious and well-balanced Cabinet which he selected in April 1966, after gaining the power to nominate his own ministers.

But this limited success only serves to emphasise what the Prime Minister does not do. He provides no unified executive direction of the government, whether by enforcing general policy initiatives or by commanding the obedience of other high officials; and it must also be remembered that he has had very little to do with the vital areas of provincial administration and the armed forces. This is certainly no English premiership, though it has some affinity with the French Prime Ministry under General de Gaulle. The Emperor remains the direct source of political authority; and the importance of the Prime Minister lies in his position as an imperial delegate and adviser, whose power holds only within the limits set by the Emperor's pleasure.

The position of the Prime Ministry is thus a direct consequence of the nature of the political system as a whole. It may be urged that a more active and forceful politician than Aklilu could at least have held the government more closely together, and infused it with some guidance and impetus within the imperial system, and this is probably true; but it may be answered that this is not the sort of politician who would receive the necessary imperial support. And if this is so, then one can scarcely look to the Prime Ministry for an alternative executive to tide over the hiatus which is likely to follow the Emperor's departure.

Chapter 10
Parliament and Legislation

The Legislative Process

The constitutional distribution of powers outlined in Chapter 4 provides Ethiopia with quite a variety of legislative forms. The different types of law are the same in the Constitutions of 1931 and 1955, though far more precisely defined in the latter, and excluding constitutional amendments, they fall into two and a half primary forms: Proclamation and Decree, and Order. A Proclamation is the usual form for major legislation, and has to receive the approval of both chambers of Parliament, and the Emperor, before going into effect.[1] Proclamations may cover any subject except those reserved to other legislative forms, and they are also used for parliamentary approval of treaties. In cases of emergency arising during the parliamentary recess, the Emperor may promulgate Decrees, which have the force of Proclamations and cover the same subjects, except that certain matters, including treaties, the Budget, and loan authorisations, must be dealt with by Proclamation.[2] Decrees have to be submitted to Parliament when it reconvenes, for approval or disapproval, and continue in force unless disapproved by both chambers. The indiscriminate use of Decrees, in cases which can by no stretch of the imagination be called emergencies, has been one of the main bones of contention between the executive and Parliament. Before 1955, the term 'Decree' was used for minor enactments by the Emperor over medals and administrative regulations, which would now be called Orders; laws now termed Decrees were published as Proclamations, but without reference to parliamentary consideration.

Certain fields, notably the organisation of the government and the armed forces, are reserved to the Emperor by the Constitution. Enactments on these are regulated by Orders, requiring neither prior nor subsequent parliamentary action.[3] The distinction between the fields of Order and Proclamation is most clearly seen in legislation setting up new government departments, where financial and other provisions needing parliamentary consent are detached from the Order, and published by Proclamation or Decree.[4] In practice, however, the distinction has not yet been fully established, and a number of powers have been granted by the Emperor for which parliamentary authority should be needed.[5]

Other legislative forms include Legal Notices, which contain subsidiary legislation; and more through legislative confusion than anything else, some charters of governmental organisations have been published not by Order but by Notice or General Notice which are usually reserved for matters of information only. Some legislative functions have also been carried out by unpublished administrative acts, especially Ministerial Circulars; the machinery of economic planning was set up by Circular of the Ministry of the Pen,[6] and the Courts Proclamation of 1962 was suspended by Circular of the Ministry of Justice, an action which was clearly *ultra vires*, pending the passage of a confirming Proclamation. The consistent use of legislative forms has greatly improved over the last ten years, due especially to the co-ordinating activities of the Prime Minister's Office, but the process is not yet complete.

The primary legislative forms differ only in their consideration by Parliament, and within the executive they follow the same procedure. The initiative in producing important general legislation, such as the establishment of the Central Personnel Agency, has since 1958 come usually from the Prime Minister's Office, which may also draw the attention of other ministries to laws needed in their fields. Most other laws are proposed by the ministry or agency chiefly concerned, and though the initial impetus may come from the minister himself, an adviser, or a senior official, the approval of the minister is the essential factor. This is one of the ways in which the increased influence of ministers has been felt.

The Emperor is little concerned in this process, except as an important catalyst. Few of the matters in which he is particularly interested require legislation, and the initiative for an important law rarely comes from him. On the other hand, major proposals require his approval, and the speed with which they are enacted, if they become law at all, is greatly affected by his attitude. Laws which he favours escape the delays and blockages to which other proposals are subject, while if he disapproves of a proposed law, without wishing openly to reject it, it will find its way blocked at some point along the legislative channel.

The actual drafting is usually carried out by foreign advisers, usually in consultation with the Ethiopian officials concerned. Much of the work has been done by the adviser in the relevant ministry; and civil service laws have sometimes gone to the Institute of Public Administration, an advisory agency which was set up under the auspices of the United Nations. Since 1958 there has been an increasing tendency for drafts to be drawn up by the legal department of the Prime Minister's office, which has served as a general drafting department, working in co-operation with any other ministry or agency. So far, there have been few Ethiopians qualified to undertake legal drafting, and those available have usually been used for political posts, rather than for this technical work.

Drafts go through varying amounts of review within the government. Often they are discussed with ministries closely concerned, or sent either to special committees or to semi-permanent bodies like the Committee for Administrative Reform; they may also be considered with greater or lesser degrees of formality elsewhere in the administration. In the post-Liberation period, drafts were sent to the Consultative Committee for Legislation, set up in 1942 to certify that laws were not 'repugnant to natural justice and humanity', and could be applied to foreigners and Ethiopians alike.[7] Although appointments were made to it as late as 1952, it does not seem to have been of any importance, and laws were simply sent to its members for signature.

General review of legislation has been taken over by the Prime Minister's office, a function which has developed from the tendency of the Council of Ministers to refer legal matters to the vice-minister of the office's legal department. Proposals which the office has not itself drafted are usually looked over either by the vice-minister or by the legal adviser. At this point, the skill with which the law has been drafted, and its consistency with the Constitution and existing legislation, are taken into account, while changes are suggested to the Prime Minister for inclusion either directly or in the Council of Ministers. This forms part of the general extension of Prime Ministerial control over this field which has already been noted.

The draft is then sent or returned to the Council of Ministers, which considers virtually all Proclamations, Decrees and Orders, and many of the Legal Notices. If passed, the draft Proclamations go to Parliament, Orders and Decrees to the Emperor for his formal assent, and Legal Notices directly for publication. No changes are made by the executive after the Council of Ministers stage, and if the Emperor has views on the subject he will already have made them known; some bills, however, have been so altered in Parliament that the executive has refused to accept them, and they have either been sent back to Parliament, or quietly 'pocket-vetoed'. If accepted, laws of all kinds are published in the official gazette, or *Negarit Gazeta*, in which all legal enactments have appeared, in Amharic and English, since 1942.

The legislative process proceeds at the leisurely pace characteristic of Ethiopian administration, and it usually takes a draft several years to reach the *Negarit Gazeta*. The group of laws on banking, referred to as long-pending in 1958 and finalised in July 1960, was published in July 1963,[8] while the Civil Aviation Decree and Order took twenty-five months between final drafting in July 1960 and publication, as emergency legislation, in August 1962. Such periods are not exceptional, and laws to which less importance is attached, such as the Antiquities Proclamation, have taken even longer. Urgent legislation, on the other hand, is dealt with at the speed of which Ethiopians are capable in, and only in, emergencies. The Order ending the Federal status of Eritrea in 1962 and that declaring a state of emergency on the Somali border in 1964 went through every stage from initiation to publication within forty-eight hours, and did not go to the Council of Ministers.

Two kinds of law have been dealt with through a special procedure: the Budget, which is considered in the next chapter, and the legal codes. The idea of codification was seized upon by the Emperor, doubtless with the Code Napoléon in mind, as the 'supreme accomplishment of Our life, as a monument for the generations waiting impatiently on the threshold of existence'.[9] The drafts were prepared by Swiss and French lawyers, except for the procedural Codes which were largely of English inspiration, and submitted to a special Codification Commission, established in 1954. This was composed of Ethiopian officials and foreigners with experience of Ethiopian law, and was responsible for amending the draft and supervising its translation into Amharic.[10] The Commission did a great deal of work, though its more important decisions, such as the omission from the Civil Code of the detailed provisions relating to Moslems, must have been sanctioned by the Emperor. The drafts apparently received little attention in the Council of Ministers, since the Commission had already studied them, and were then presented to Parliament. The Penal Code appeared in 1957, the Maritime, Civil and Commercial Codes in 1960, the Criminal Procedure Code in 1961, and the Civil Procedure Code in 1965.

The process of codification illustrates several general characteristics of Ethiopian government. First, the operation was carried out with a secrecy and lack of public discussion found in few other countries. Whereas the custom elsewhere is for the draft code to be made public, and to form the basis for suggestions by affected groups and individuals, the Ethiopian drafts were never made public at all, and merchants, for example, were given no opportunity to comment on the application of the Commercial Code to Ethiopian trading conditions. Second, the practical usefulness of the Codes was sacrificed to their prestige value. One aspect of this was the choice of sophisticated model codes, based on the most modern social and legal theories, rather than more simple guides adapted to the lack of legal qualifications of those who would have to apply them. Another aspect was the haste with which the Codes were put into effect, due to the Emperor's concern for the project; thus, the Commission did not have time to study the section of the draft Civil Code on the application of the laws, and therefore left it out.[11] Both of these characteristics of the codification naturally reduced the effectiveness of the Codes once they came into force.

The machinery for considering draft laws within the government is, however, for the most part adequate. Conspicuously lacking, by contrast, is any central co-ordination for *initiating* laws; there is nothing which could possibly be termed a government legislative programme. This reflects the general lack of a coherent policy or united impetus in the government, since such a policy would call for implementing legislation, and one result of its absence is the huge number of proposals which never become law. Some of these are drafted by advisers in the vain hope of getting their ministers to accept them; some are promoted by individual officials, and gather dust when they are moved to other posts; still more fall by the wayside, through deliberate blockage or simple inertia, and join the discarded reports and recommendations which clog the archives of Ethiopian ministries.

This lack of a legislative programme also draws attention to the fact that written law has a smaller place in Ethiopia than it has either in European countries or in those African states which are rather more purposefully committed to change. On the one hand, legislation is not one of the principal means of implementing government decisions, and on the other, there can be few parts of the world where the daily life of most of the people is so little affected by written law. The effective field for it is small in a country poor in communications, unaccustomed to enforcing the details of proclamations and without adequate machinery for doing so. The situation has certainly changed since 1941, and especially since 1961, but it still cannot be assumed that a law on marriage or commercial transactions, let alone on cruelty to animals, will be enforced outside Addis Ababa.

The importance of legislation is nevertheless increasing, especially in subjects touched by recent changes, where custom is no longer adequate; and it is in these fields, including trades unions, banking, and taxation, that laws are most effective and most easily enforceable. The scope for legislation is bound to grow, moreover, both with the increasing complexity of such affairs, and the expansion of written law into fields, including many of those formally covered by the Codes, in which traditional practices still prevail. This will only become possible with an increased appreciation and understanding of written law, but there is evidence, at least within the government, that this is taking place. It is shown by a growing concern for legality and for legislation, which in turn is expressed through a growing interest in those institutions, such as the legal department of the Prime Minister's office and the Law School of the University, which are chiefly concerned with modern forms of law.

The Infancy of Parliament, 1931-1957

The Parliament of Ethiopia has developed under very different conditions from those of other countries, in Africa and elsewhere, and these differences must constantly be remembered in assessing its position, its functions, and its development. While in other African countries, Parliament has been used to provide a basis of legitimate indigenous authority to replace the departing colonial régime, in Ethiopia this basis was already present in the person of the Emperor. Around the Emperor was ranged a whole system of government, in which Parliament had no place, for by contrast with the political structures of many other African peoples, there was no analogous institution in the traditional Ethiopian administration. There were only, on the one hand, informal consultations between the Emperor and the major figures of the realm; and on the other, the right of all Ethiopians to present petitions to the Emperor. Parliament has therefore developed, first as an institution whose inspiration was foreign and not Ethiopian, and second, as an appendage to the executive government, rather than as one of the basic repositories of the authority of the state.

When Parliament was founded in 1931, it is therefore not surprising that its powers were negligible. Legislation required only its discussion, and since it was legally bound to discuss matters referred to it, it had no veto power. Its only power of decision was that of rejecting Decrees promulgated by the Emperor during the recess, though no case of its using this power has emerged; it received further powers by the unpublished organic law drawn up at the same time as the 1931 Constitution, but the status of this is not clear. Its membership was also closely controlled by the government, the Senate being appointed by the Emperor, while the Chamber of Deputies was elected by local notables under the aegis of the provincial governors.

This Parliament could not be expected to carry out the usual functions of an elected legislature. Neither in fact nor in form was it a source of political authority; it was not popularly elected, and it made no claim to be representative. Nor was it in any way an expert body, qualified to scrutinise proposed legislation, since both chambers were largely composed of noblemen, including such great lords as Ras Seyum (28) and Ras Käbädä, whose acquaintance with written law had hitherto been slight. For most purposes it may therefore be regarded as an embryo Parliament, necessary as a symbol of Ethiopian constitutional development, for both home and foreign consumption, and also for the later growth of a more viable institution.

There was nevertheless one way in which the functions of the pre-war Parliament were related to the needs and conditions of the time, for through its aristocratic composition it served the same purpose as the council of noblemen which had earlier discussed the new Constitution. This has been very clearly explained by the drafter of the Constitution, Bäjerond Täklä-Hawariyat:[12]

> At that time, we did not want a person who could work well in the Parliament and legislate good and modern laws. We wanted the people to accept those laws which were to be legislated, and these laws could only get acceptance if they were discussed by the nobility and accepted by them first. Thus, we had brought important personalities who had considerable influence in the provinces and had them appointed in both houses according to their power of influence and importance in the public eye.

Parliament was thus used to associate the nobility with the consolidation of power under the Emperor. No adequate information is available, however, on its influence either on the laws themselves, or on their effectiveness in the country at large.

After the Occupation, Parliament reconvened in November 1942. Its powers were the same as before, and its membership was very similar, with an overwhelming preponderance of noblemen, those of higher rank being mostly in the Senate.[13] Since the 1931 Constitution provided for no parliamentary term, it sat until it was dissolved in 1957,[14] though many of its members died, retired, or were appointed to other posts; others remained for the full fifteen years. There were five deputies from each of the twelve provinces, Eritrea being added in 1952, and about thirty senators without territorial qualifications, though Eritrean representation of three senators was agreed at the time of Federation.[15]

The only meetings publicly reported were ceremonial occasions of little importance, including the annual State Opening, and the unanimous ratification of the United Nations Charter and the Eritrean Constitution;[16] these have some constitutional interest in that the 1931 Constitution gives the Emperor the exclusive right to make treaties, while the Eritrean Constitution is the only reported case before 1957 of parliamentary approval of Decree legislation passed by the Emperor during the recess. There is also evidence that Parliament took its legislative duties seriously; a few cases of parliamentary opposition to the executive have been reported from the 1940s,[17] and in the 1950s it made frequent, though usually minor, amendments to legislation. It introduced flogging as a punishment into the Penal Code of 1957; and in the Electoral Law Proclamation of 1956, it deleted a phrase allowing the Electoral Board to make *awajjoch*, or Proclamations, on the ground that these required parliamentary approval, and amended the conditions on residence for voters since the original draft was unconstitutional.[18] A readiness to reject laws is indicated by the Federal Tax (Amendment) Proclamation of 1955,[19] the preamble of which refers to imperial approval of the resolution of the Senate alone, implying that the Chamber of Deputies passed a different resolution which was rejected by the executive, while in 1956 a bill on forest conservation was so amended through the influence of the landowners in Parliament that the government refused to accept it.

These cases help to refute the assumption that Parliament was in this period simply a 'rubber stamp' for executive desires. But nevertheless, it can have made such changes as these to legislation only because the government was prepared to accept them; and these amendments, and the occasional questioning of executive officials, indicate no more than a peripheral influence. It cannot be said that Parliament had at this time acquired any significant function in the political system as a whole.

Parliament since 1957

Parliament under the Revised Constitution owes its position to the strange dialectic by which the Emperor's supreme authority has had to be reconciled with some recognition of democratic ideals. The Chamber of Deputies has since 1957 been elected by universal adult suffrage, and has thus for the first time achieved a power base independent of the Emperor; but the Senate remains directly appointed by him. Parliament also gained substantive legislative powers: each chamber may initiate and veto legislation, including taxes and appropriations, and can summon ministers for questioning and in exceptional circumstances initiate proceedings for impeachment; but the Emperor, too, can initiate and veto laws, he can dissolve Parliament, and he can legislate by Degree during the recess. Parliament is excluded from any control over the membership, policies and organisation of the executive branch. Thus the very different sources from which Emperor and Chamber of Deputies draw their authority has forced on Ethiopia a peculiar form of the separation of powers. Parliament's basic position is weak, for democratic ideals cannot be expected to take immediate root in soil to which they are so foreign; but since it stands apart from the executive, it has been able to exert pressures on it from a detached standpoint, and it shows a willingness to reject government legislative proposals which must be almost unique among the dwindling number of African legislatures. It is also unusual in having no political parties.

Elections to the Chamber of Deputies take place every four years, and have been held in 1957, 1961 and 1965. Two deputies are elected for each rural constituency, with additional representation for towns, totalling 210 deputies in 1957 and 250 since 1961. In the elections, the absence of parties immediately makes itself felt. Each candidate stands on the strength of his personal connections in the district, perhaps aided by his education, traditional authority, or ethnic affiliation, and elections are so fiercely contested that safe seats are few; 59 of the 210 sitting members (28%) were returned in 1961, and 85 out of 250 (34%) in 1965. Elections are also expensive, requiring a property qualification of about £150 in land in the constituency or £300 in moveable property, while the cost of fighting an election ranges from some £70 to £1,500 per candidate, averaging roughly £300–400;[20] this money must be found by the candidate and his friends. There is nevertheless no shortage of candidates, for the parliamentary salary of £1,300 p.a. is enough to recoup the outlay (and build up a fighting fund for the next election), and Parliament may also serve as a steppingstone to government office in Addis Ababa. A strict residence qualification for candidates, without the parties which might have given them a wider outlook, means that deputies largely represent local interests. Many of them are elected on the strength of their promises to provide their constituents with roads, schools and clinics, and many fail to be re-elected when these benefits do not appear. This is reflected in the chamber in the enthusiasm with which deputies press the executive government with local grievances and demands. They are the focus for complaints of maladministration in the provinces, and they have championed the provinces as a whole against the centripetal lure of Addis Ababa. They strongly opposed the 1959 Health Tax, which, being based on the Land Tax assessment, was generally regarded as a tax on the countryside to provide facilities in the towns, and they have constantly pressed for a higher proportion of revenues to be spent outside the capital.

The number of noblemen in the Chamber of Deputies, at first high, has dropped sharply; as a rough indication, the proportion holding traditional titles of nobility has declined from 26% in 1957 to 14% in 1965, most of these coming from the north. One result of this shift has been that Civil Code provisions on landlord–tenant relations, changed in the landlord's favour in the 1957–61 Parliament, were changed back in 1961–65.

Many deputies are former government officials, since these account for a large proportion of potential candidates with the wealth and the opportunity to stand for Parliament. Among them, the small group of schoolteachers have been especially important, as they tend to be both better educated and more radical than their fellows. They have provided several leaders of the group in the chamber most actively opposed to the government, in pressing for schools, economic development, and changes in land tenure. This group also led opposition to the Penal Code (Penalties) Decree of 1961, which permitted flogging as a punishment for certain political offences, and has been most ready to attack the government for

143

delays in promulgating laws passed by Parliament, and for deficiencies in the administration of justice. Since the 1961–65 Parliament, a majority has often been prepared to follow their lead.

In the absence of political parties, the chamber divides into more elusive groupings, which are hard to disentangle as there are no division lists, and most other records are unavailable. Such groupings vary from issue to issue, but they fall into two main kinds: 'horizontal' divisions based on social status, attitudes to economic change, and dependence on the government, and 'vertical' ones derived from ethnic, regional and religious differences.

The former have been expressed in the landowning and radical factions just noted, and in changing attitudes to the government reflected in the annual election for the chamber's President. The President is elected by and from the deputies, and in the 1957–61 Parliament his choice was government-inspired; first Lej Haylä-Maryam Käbädä, now a Minister of State, was put in to guide the chamber's first steps in democracy, and his successor after three years was the Eritrean brother of the present Minister of Public Health. This tutelage was not so marked in 1961–65; the President for three years, Lieutenant Germa Wäldä-Giyorgis, had indeed filled middle-level central government posts, but he was less clearly a government nominee, and was defeated in the 1963 election by an outsider from Gojam. Since the 1965 election, the Presidents have had a distinctly radical cast: Bayisa Jämo, a Wäläga teacher long critical of the government, was President for the first two years, but was ousted in 1967, after accepting the title of *Fitawrari*, as many members thought he had changed his front and become too favourable to the executive. His more critical successor, Tadäsä Tayé, is also from Wäläga. The presidential elections have thus reflected a steady shift towards independent criticism of the government.

Local ties are seen most clearly in the election of committees at the start of each annual session. There are seven specialised standing committees, each with fourteen members, but only one of these, the Steering Committee, is directly elected by the deputies. It then selects the members of all other standing and special committees, and also hears cases of disputed elections and disciplinary complaints against members. It is thus very important, and so it is significant that except for its first year it has always contained one member from each province. In 1962, the election failed to provide a member from Sidamo, and the Addis Ababa representative on the committee was then unseated on the ground that Addis Ababa formed part of Shoa, and his seat given to the Sidamo candidate, a case which indicates a well-established convention of representation by provinces.[21] Following the composition of the Steering Committee, other committees also tend to comprise a member from each province, and in the chamber provincial divisions often come to the surface over proposals which affect one area differently from others.

Broader regional divisions appear in the election for the two Vice-Presidents; one of these tends to come from the northern plateau, and one from the southern and peripheral areas. Deputies from the central Amhara area of Gojam, Bägémdär and western Wälo have sometimes met before the election to choose a candidate to support with their united votes. The Presidential elections, by contrast, have sometimes matched two leading candidates from the same province, and have not brought out regional differences to nearly the same extent. In some years, the Moslem deputies have supported their own candidate for the Vice-Presidency; they tend to regard themselves as representatives of their religion, and met to request assurances from the government that the Moslem courts would continue to function although these appeared to be abolished by the new legal Codes.

One difference between areas has been that while Presidents or Vice-Presidents have come from every province of the north, the southern leadership has been strongly concentrated in the two provinces of Wäläga and Harär; the Wäläga Deputies especially have been notable for their standard of education, experience and cohesiveness, and they tend to keep their seats at election time far more readily than other members. The same concentration is found in the central administration, and is probably due to educational opportunities, and to the survival in these areas of local political leadership. If the Electoral Board statistics are not completely inaccurate, the southern rather than the northern provinces have tended to be over-represented in terms of registered voters per deputy, though many members from the more backward southern provinces, especially Arusi and Gämu Gofa, have been immigrants from the north.

The Chamber of Deputies has not been content to remain a provincial pressure group and has taken a very active part in scrutinising legislation. During the first two and a half years after 1957, Parliament was largely concerned with the Civil Code, and made several important changes in it, including the removal of the section on nationality and of seventy-four of the eighty-four articles on transitory provisions for putting the Code into force. The expert who drafted the Code has written that 'this amputation may be the source of great difficulties in the application of the Civil Code',[22] but since many suggested amendments were abandoned at the government's request,[23] these changes were probably made with executive acquiescence.

Government legislation is often amended, not usually substantially, though some bills have been so changed that the government has refused to accept them, and has either returned them to Parliament for reconsideration, or has simply failed to promulgate them. Laws on the conservation of forests were twice effectively blocked in this way by the landowning interest in the early years of the elected Parliament, though they were finally passed in the session of 1964–65. One difficulty is that Parliament sometimes amends carefully drafted proposals which it has not the qualifications to appreciate; it removed the restrictions on appeal from the Courts Proclamation of 1962, in deference to the treasured Ethiopian right of unlimited appeal, although the bane of the judicial system is the fact that often so many appeals are made that no final decision is reached. It also refused to allow restrictions on appeals in the Civil Procedure Code which was promulgated by Decree in 1966 but two years later had still not received parliamentary ratification. A warning against upsetting carefully drawn up legislation was given to members by the Emperor at the State Opening in 1964.[24]

Any government attempt to levy new taxes on rural areas has been especially doggedly resisted. The Health Tax was a case in point, and during the 1967–68 session, the deputies refused to pass a bill to raise revenues for a new local government structure. Since the object of this legislation was to increase local autonomy, they might have been expected to approve it, but with an election coming up, few of them could afford to face their constituents with any new form of taxation.

Parliament thus has some power to block or modify even legislation which the government is anxious to put into effect, and in Africa, this is a phenomenon rare enough to be worth emphasising. But its capacity to obstruct is not reinforced by the qualifications needed to provide a detailed critique of technical proposals. Nor has it the influence or the expertise to establish any independent power of legislative initiative; and despite innumerable motions and proposals of legislation, the only law originating in Parliament which has so far reached the statute book has been the Members of Parliament (Salaries) Proclamation of 1962.

Documentary evidence of amendments is most clearly provided by Decree legislation enacted by the executive during the recess, since parliamentary action on these is published separately from the original legislation.[25] Decrees are theoretically limited to cases of emergency, but they have been used for routine legislation, and between 1957 and 1959 they replaced Proclamations for everything except the Budget and Fiscal Year Proclamations. The use of a Decree gives the initiative to the executive, since it remains in force until cancelled by a Notice of Disapproval, or amended by a Proclamation which must receive the imperial assent. If the two chambers of Parliament disagree, as over the Penal Code (Penalties) Decree of 1961, or if the executive does not accept the parliamentary amendments, the original draft remains in effect, whereas otherwise the government would have to make concessions to Parliament to put the law into force at all.

A Church Occasion. Haile-Selassie presiding at the celebration of the Feast of the Epiphany; seated at his right are Ras Imru, one of the bishops, and Ras Haylu Bäläw; the surrounding group include ministers, senators, and high-ranking army and Bodyguard officers; some of the Emperor's grandchildren are sitting on the steps of the throne.

The Parliament Building, Addis Ababa. The Senate chamber is on the left, with the Joint Assembly in the centre and the Deputies on the right.

There has consequently been a great deal of opposition to the by-passing of the legislature by means of the Decree power, culminating in the rejection by both chambers of the Building Materials Excise Tax Decree of 1960, a minor piece of fiscal legislation which seems to have been picked on simply as an example of the abuse of Decrees. It was finally disapproved in November 1962, and the Notice of Disapproval needed to give effect to this decision should thereupon have been published by the government in the *Negarit Gazeta*. Five months later, this Notice had still not appeared, and the Chamber of Deputies passed a motion requesting the Emperor to start impeachment proceedings against the Prime Minister. The Notice of Disapproval immediately appeared, back-dated to the previous month, and since that time the executive has been very chary in its use of Decrees. This has been one of the most notable examples of successful parliamentary pressure.

Parliament has also improved its position in the financial field; the first Budgets came out at the end of the financial year concerned and were therefore redundant, but the chambers can now examine the Budget in detail and in advance. The most active agency in this has been the Budget Committee of the Chamber of Deputies, which has been the most important of the specialised standing committees, and the only one in the selection of which provincial origins have been of little importance. Its work has consisted mostly in summoning officials to defend proposed appropriations, and though it has made very few changes, it has compelled the executive to meet sustained questioning and criticism which must now be borne in mind when the Budget is drawn up. In 1963, the Chamber of Deputies tried to raise allocations for the administration of justice at the expense of other items, but this was defeated in a joint assembly of the two chambers after a clash with the Senate. Detailed advance control of spending by Parliament has in any case been rendered ineffective by weaknesses in the appropriations machinery, which is considered in the next chapter. Parliament has been more successful in the field of loans, where the principle is now established that it should be informed of the projects for which a loan is needed before authorising it.

Parliament's right to summon ministers or their deputies for questioning has been one of its most effective weapons. Ministers may be summoned, or may attend of their own accord, whenever legislation concerning their ministries is being considered, and they are also sometimes questioned on administrative matters. The Prime Minister is responsible for more general affairs, and though he has never attended himself, except once as Deputy Prime Minister in about 1959, a senior official from the Prime Minister's office has been fully occupied with parliamentary affairs, and can often be seen addressing the chambers with such persuasive fluency that even a non-Amharic speaker finds it hard not to be convinced. A further development has been the growing tendency of ministers to visit Parliament in person, instead of leaving it to deputies, and several of them, including Yelma Derésa (35) at the Ministry of Finance, have taken pains to be conciliatory.

Deputies do not fear to press ministers as hard as they can, and the uncomfortable experience of hostile questioning has obliged officials to take account of Parliament's likely reactions. The requirements of the Constitution have also been extended by the questioning of heads of executive agencies, such as the Lord Mayor of Addis Ababa and the General Manager of the Imperial Highway Authority, and in this way the right of Parliament to examine the affairs of such agencies has been established. These enquiries have been supplemented by visits of parliamentarians to different agencies, and though these have so far amounted to little more than conducted tours, they may develop into something more. The actual effect of questioning is very difficult to establish, either in particular instances or for the practice as a whole. A few cases, such as the setting up of a branch of the State Bank at Mäqälé in Tegré, have been ascribed directly to such pressures, and in other instances they appear to have acted as a spur to the executive, but more detailed information is not available.

The government in its turn, however, has considerable sources of influence, which it may use to secure the passage of proposals which it particularly favours, or to curb the more active of its opponents. The presence of ministers in Parliament provides a channel for persuasion as well as for questioning, and some influence is exercised by the government's practice of asking the Chamber to reconsider decisions with which it disagrees, referring them back until finally its view is accepted. On one occasion, over the ratification of the Health Tax Decree early in 1960, the Emperor summoned the Deputies to the palace and requested them to pass it, as they then did, and he has sometimes called important individual opponents of the government and requested them to be more co-operative. He also asked the Deputies to hasten their consideration of the legal Codes, though no confirmation has been found for the assertion that he threatened to dissolve the chamber over this, or over the approval of the Franco-Ethiopian Railway Treaty of 1960.[26] The threat of dissolution would be a very powerful one, however, since elections are very expensive for individual members, and with the high turnover of deputies at elections, many of the sitting members would lose their seats, especially if the government was actively against them. An essential element in this process has been the power of government patronage in finding jobs for defeated deputies, and after the election of 1961, over twenty former deputies were given seats in the Senate. This did not happen in 1965, with the result that members abruptly deprived of their high parliamentary salaries were reduced to seeking posts in the administration and, often after several months of unemployment, were obliged to go wherever the government was prepared to take them. There has been no systematic government attempt to fix the elections, though individual cases have been alleged, but the instability of the deputies' position can in this way provide the executive with an important source of influence.

Day-to-day pressures have often been exercised through the Chief Clerk of the Deputies, who is appointed by the Emperor, and has carried out some of the functions of a government whip. Asratä Kasa (6), as President of the Senate from 1960 until 1964, also concerned himself with keeping the deputies in order, though his successor, Abiy Abäbä (2), has been far less inclined to do so.

But the executive lacks effective machinery for influencing or bargaining with the deputies, between mere exhortation on the one hand and heavy threats on the other. Influential deputies may receive titles or other benefits, but this often results in their losing ground with their fellows, and the chamber itself is too loosely organised to set up channels through which to mediate with the government. As Parliament develops, some such machinery may have to be devised if an open confrontation is to be avoided.

The Senate, theoretically the upper house, is in practice the less important of the two chambers. It consists of a maximum of half the members of the Chamber of Deputies, and senators are formally appointed for six-year terms, a third of the membership being due for reappointment every two years, after the manner of the United States Senate. This involves no security of tenure, however, for the Emperor has observed this term only when convenient, and senators have been dismissed, appointed to other posts, or even retired on pension, in the middle of their terms of office.[27]

The Constitution provides that a senator must be 'a Prince or other Dignitary, or a former high government official, or other person generally esteemed for his character, judgement and public services.'[28] As these qualifications suggest, the Senate consists largely of noblemen and retired civil servants; these come from every branch of the administration, and include a large number of district governors who are mostly from the nobility. The President has always been a major political figure from the high nobility. The bishops are all *ex officio* senators, but do little more than recite the prayers at the beginning of each meeting, and because so few of them turned up, a system by which two at a time attended in rotation was established in 1961. In another category are the twenty-two deputies appointed after losing their seats in the election of 1961, and there has been a tendency since 1961 to retire army officers to the Senate—particularly colonels, though several important generals were appointed in 1965.

Groupings in the Senate are difficult to distinguish, and vary greatly according to the issue. Some distinction can be made between provincial noblement prepared to assert their often very conservative views independently of the government, and civil servants who defer to the executive's wishes; but many senators fall into neither group, and some contrive to fall into both.

Despite the manner of its appointment, the Senate does not always take the government's view; this is partly because of the preponderance of noblemen, who tend to form the 'opposition' group within the governing circle, and partly because the Senate is widely used as a place of retirement and disgrace. It has provided high-ranking but virtually powerless positions for senior officials of declining powers, and for others too important either to be trusted or ignored. In the latter category, provincial noblemen and former resistance leaders are especially important. This has caused some resentment in the Senate, which cannot therefore always be relied upon to support the government, and which has occasionally taken the initiative in opposing it. It supported the deputies' rejection of the Building Materials Excise Tax Decree, partly perhaps because its President, Asratä Kasa (6), was not averse to causing embarrassment to the Prime Minister; and led by Abiy Abäbä (2), it rejected a proposed credit from Italy in 1964. This has been by far the most important political action of the Senate, and will be considered as part of a special case study. The power of appointment can nevertheless often be used to keep the Senate in order; Afä-Negus Tadäsä Mängäsha, who had been demoted from Chief Justice to senator in 1963 after taking a judicial decision which displeased the Emperor, was further demoted to a deputy governorship two years later after supporting a motion in the Senate for a measure of constitutional reform.

Unlike the deputies, however, the senators are for the most part members of the ruling group, having close links with the administration; and the occasions on which the Senate defies the government can invariably be traced back to quarrels within that group, especially between its noble and non-noble elements. But by the same token, it is usually far more sympathetic than the Chamber of Deputies to the position of the government, and on several occasions, including the Budget of 1963 and the Penal Code (Penalties) Decree of 1961, it has blocked attempts by the deputies to upset executive measures. The Senate has been far less concerned than the chamber to question and criticise, and brings far less enthusiasm to its proceedings; in place of the hubbub and frequent lapses into disorder of the deputies, there is a dignified calm, and rarely more than one senator talking at a time. This is bought at a price, however; one former deputy has told the author that while everyone can hear what you are saying in the Senate, they often do not seem to care. The excitement of partisan activity is lacking, and there have at times been great difficulties in raising the quorum of half the membership.

A rationale for the existence of an appointed Senate is not hard to find, for it clearly has a useful potential function in the representation of élite groups, such as the nobility, the armed forces, the high officials and the intelligentsia, to balance a first chamber based simply on popular suffrage. Such élite groups, both traditional and modernising, have a vital role in the maintenance equally of development and stability, and most of them are in fact represented within the present Senate. There have also been a few occasions, such as the rejection of the Italian credit, on which the Senate has represented important feelings which the executive has left out of account. One may nevertheless question whether the Senate does in fact perform such functions to any significant extent. Its few attempts at independent evaluation of government policies and practices have mostly been discouraged by the executive; and it appears that many of its members are appointed, not in order that they may perform important functions, but in order that they may be prevented from doing so.

The functions of the Chamber of Deputies, by contrast, are much clearer; the influence of the government has to some extent checked and modified its attitudes, but has not altered its basic position as a source of outside pressure on the administration. As such, it has considerable value, or at least potential value, in establishing communications between the country at large and the closed community of the central administration. Parliament is the only place where the government can openly be criticised, and where it is forced to defend its actions, since the criticisms are put directly to senior officials and have to be met if Parliament is to grant what is being asked of it. Such a process of question and answer is essential to bring to the surface some of the problems which inevitably afflict Ethiopia, and it is especially valuable in that there is a marked lack of alternative channels elsewhere in the government. Other criticism has had to be expressed either through the interplay of factions within the government, or else through subtle hinting or the cumbersome and often unsuitable machinery of a petition to the Emperor. There is no other means in the traditional system for criticism or justification, and there is therefore a tendency for criticisms to be made only behind the scenes, and to be construed, often correctly, as disloyalty. Though many of its questions and criticisms are still ill-founded or unjustified, Parliament may thus perform essential communicative functions, both upwards and downwards, for which traditional channels are now inadequate.

Parliament has a similar role in the expression of local opinions and interests, which might otherwise well be forgotten in a country whose administration is so centralised as that of Ethiopia. As the only place at which the provinces are directly represented in the central government, the Chamber of Deputies provides the only effective platform for provincial opinions. Provincial governors are little concerned to report local feelings which may well reflect on their own administration, and though central government officials from different areas to some extent represent regional interests, they are compromised by their position within the government, and have often spent too long in Addis Ababa to reflect accurately the feelings of distant provinces. The Chamber of Deputies has also helped to counteract the centralising tendencies of the administration by insisting, for instance, that a greater proportion of public health revenues be spent in the provinces. The converse of this process is the parochialism of many of the issues raised in Parliament, and the attempts of deputies to attract benefits to their constituencies to redeem their extravagant election promises. The effect of these pressures is difficult to assess, and depends largely on the attitude of the administration; but certainly through Parliament provincial interests are heard in a place where they have to be listened to.

Much of the effectiveness of the channels of communication which Parliament provides depends on the extent to which people outside Parliament take notice of happenings within, and here is perhaps the greatest weakness of the present-day position. Except for occasional spectacular debates and decisions, there appears to be little general awareness of parliamentary activities. The educated society of Addis Ababa is much more concerned with the doings of the executive government than with those of provincial representatives, for the executive branch is, after all, by far the more important; and provincial communities, more distant from and less interested in the political activities of Parliament, have so far been little rewarded by any tangible results of the deputies' efforts on their behalf. Short factual accounts of the day in Parliament appear from time to time in the press, but even the most elementary information on the issues raised and decisions reached can often only be obtained by word of mouth or through actual attendance in the public gallery.

It is at this point that the lack of a party system is most felt, since one of the essential functions of a political party is to link the people as a whole with activities in the government, and especially in Parliament. Parties could also be used for the mobilisation of the populace for social and economic development, though a strong case can be made for proceeding fairly slowly with changes which are bound to be disruptive unless very carefully handled. Other results of the absence of parties have already been noted: at the electoral level, the absence of any organisation means that each candidate must run and finance his campaign from his own resources, while the personal nature of the contest has resulted in many members being unseated at each election and often forced back on government patronage, a fact which makes them more susceptible to government pressure when in office. Within the chamber, it is very difficult without parties to present any consistent and coherent policy, which one would have thought essential for the development of Parliament beyond a certain point. If this is so, then a no-party system must restrict Parliament to a forum for the pressing of local interests, and the vocalisation of discontents.

But the absence of parties has nevertheless, at least in the short run increased rather than diminished the importance of Parliament. First, there is little doubt that were parties allowed to form of their own accord, they would do so along regional or perhaps even religious lines; not only has this been virtually the universal experience elsewhere in Africa, but provincial groupings have also been the most in evidence of the various informal factions within the Ethiopian Chamber of Deputies. The tendency to regionalism would probably be even greater in the country as a whole, where particularist appeals would be easier to press home than rather more sophisticated divisions along policy lines. It is most unlikely that any government of Ethiopia, where national unity is by no means firmly established, would permit such parties. Conversely, a single 'national' party would have the effect of reducing Parliament to central control, and so weaken or destroy the detachment of Parliament from the executive authority which has been suggested as one of its most valuable assets.

Further, the whole concept of open and loyal criticism is still a new and rather strange one, and such criticism may only be tolerable so long as it is voiced in the fairly informal manner which the no-party system permits. This reflects a general trait of Amhara society, where concessions are possible only in a fluid situation in which choices and responsibilities are not defined,[29] and a rigidly defined situation would result in direct confrontations from which Parliament would be the chief loser. It is also difficult for any modern African government to tolerate any organised body of hostile opinion, and the devising of an acceptable framework within which to meet inevitable pressures and criticisms has been one of the main problems facing the recently independent African countries. A related advantage of the rather informal and loosely organised position of the Ethiopian Parliament is that it permits a natural increase in parliamentary influence, following the play of political forces and the growth of the qualifications and experience of its members. A considerable development is clear since 1957, covering such fields as the right of questioning, the consideration of the Budget, and the position of Decree legislation; and Parliament, in my opinion, has been able to carry out its tasks the better for being able to take them on gradually. It forms in this respect a marked contrast with other African parliaments which have been launched on their way with sophisticated powers and organisations which many of them have been unable to sustain.

But finally, the usefulness of the communicative functions which Parliament can in some measure perform should not blind one to the essential weakness of its position. The social organisation of the Amhara is radically undemocratic, both in the downward communication of authority and in the lack of co-operation among equals.[30] Nor, in this respect, have recent developments countered traditional values. While the state has a firm Amhara core, the presence of a large number of other peoples deprives it of the ethnic unity necessary for a national consensus, and there is a similar lack of agreement over the desirable rate of economic and social change. The political communications and qualifications necessary for a democratic system are also absent, both in the lack of education of the masses, and in the lack of understanding of what such a system would involve among most of those who would have to run it. That Parliament has been able to develop even to its present extent has been due to the protection of an exceedingly stable system of government. Such stability is essential to the growth of representative institutions, and there has been nothing to suggest that the Parliament of Ethiopia is now well enough established to stand without it.

Chapter 11

Government Spending

•

It is a well-established maxim of political administration that the way to a government's heart is through its treasury, and that the distribution of its cash provides as good a guide as any to the internal structure of its authority. It is therefore worth taking a fairly close look at the Ethiopian budgetary system, and especially at the authorisation of government spending. Taxation, by contrast, is for our purposes a far less illuminating field, being for the most part a mere device for collecting funds to meet the government's expenses; by contrast with the more sophisticated economies of western Europe, fiscal powers are little used for economic regulation, and the revenue sections of the Ethiopian Budget are indeed no more than estimates of expected income, and have no legislative force. Money is raised through separate taxation laws, independently of the Budget, and the chief concern here, like that of the government, will therefore be with spending.

Appropriations, 1941–1960

For the first few years after the Liberation, much of the government's income came from a special British subsidy, and British advisers helped to organise the Ministry of Finance; they drew up a series of standard forms for accounting and budgeting and tried to institute a budgetary system. At first allocations were made quarterly, in principle, though in practice more probably just as need arose, and in 1943–44 the revenue and expenditure totals were totted up afterwards and termed a Budget; for 1944–45, a Budget was eventually presented for parliamentary approval and published in the *Negarit Gazeta*.[1]

But with the departure of the advisers, this system lapsed and was replaced with one more in keeping with Ethiopian methods, the basis of which was that all expenditure, for whatever purpose, required the approval of the Emperor. A minister or official wanting funds explained to the Emperor why they were needed, usually during the *Aqabé Sä'at*; if his request was approved, the Ministry of the Pen official in attendance took note, and issued the Emperor's decision as a payment order to the Ministry of Finance, authorising the payment of a given sum for a given purpose. Though the usual way of getting money was through the *Aqabé Sä'at*, the Emperor naturally granted appropriations whenever he wished to do so, not only for ordinary government spending, but also for personal benefactions, grants for special services, and anything else for which money was needed; when he initiated some project himself, he might well allocate funds for it without any need for a ministerial request.

The routine expenses of a department, such as salaries, were covered by orders which stayed in effect until revoked. Every month, each ministry applied for funds, submitting its payroll and a list of its renewable expenses, and the Ministry of Finance checked that these were in accordance with imperial payment orders before releasing the money. If the application exceeded the authority of the payment order, either in the amount asked for or in the reasons for which it was required, it was returned by the Ministry of Finance. Other payment orders authorised only a single non-repeatable allocation. These orders varied very widely in the sums which they granted and the detail in which they did so; some authorised the cost of large investment projects in very general terms, leaving the working out of details to the department concerned; others allocated tiny sums of a few pounds, for a magazine subscription or repair of a government car, when funds could not be obtained in any other way. There was every degree of variation between these two extremes, all of them requiring the Emperor's personal approval.

Appropriations were thus controlled through the ordinary government machinery for day-to-day decisions, with very close imperial supervision expressed through Ministry of the Pen orders. This strengthened the administrative tendencies of the time, by encouraging the dependence of officials on the Emperor, and impeding the growth of institutional methods and any systematic consideration of priorities. But theoretically, at least, this traditional machinery provided an adequate base for a workable system of expenditures. The Emperor's approval provided a single valid authority for spending, and his orders were very carefully kept at the Ministry of Finance, where they formed the basis of the accounting system; they were added up after the end of each financial year to form a 'budget', which for 1952–53 was published in the *Negarit Gazeta*, for information only, on the authority of the Minister of Finance.[2] Income and expenditure could be kept in equilibrium through frequent reports to the Emperor on the state of the Treasury.

In practice, however, this system was often modified by the Minister of Finance, who has consistently been one of the most important figures of the government. The present Minister, Yelma Derésa (35), has held the post throughout the 1940s and 1960s, though not in the decade in between. From 1949 until 1958, Makonnen Habtä-Wäld (19) was Minister, followed by the two-year tenure of Balambaras Mahtämä-Selassie (17). Like most of the major government offices, the Ministry of Finance has thus seldom changed hands.

Of these three, Yelma, a graduate of the London School of Economics, has been by far the best qualified, and during his first tenure of the Ministry, he had a reputation as a radical reformer, a reputation he sometimes still tries to claim. But in any case, it would scarcely have been possible for him at that time to have modernised the appropriations system. First, he was in no position to challenge either the Emperor's personal control of finance, or to offend other politicians who were then more influential than he, and that he stayed so long in office suggests that he did not try to do either. Moreover, Yelma himself was in the 1940s one of the very few officials with training enough to operate a budgetary system, which would have run counter to the whole administrative structure of the post-war years.

The heyday of the Ministry of Finance therefore belonged to the reign of Makonnen Habtä-Wäld (19), who had long been trying to obtain it, and in 1949 succeeded. Makonnen was the son of a priest, and derived such education as he acquired, and much of his limited outlook on life, from the restrictive atmosphere of the Church schools. He had been a *protégé* of the Emperor since the early days of the Regency, and held several important posts before the war; after spending the Occupation in exile in Paris, he returned to Ethiopia in 1942, and was given the portfolios of Agriculture and Commerce.

He owed much to his clerical background and his early training in intrigue. Like the Emperor, he was very hard-working and always accessible, but he had no interest or capacity in institutional methods of administration, preferring a highly personal system, operated behind the scenes through an immense number of informers and *protégés*. The rather furtive goings-on by which he was constantly surrounded gave rise to a popular belief, strengthened by his skull-like countenance, his mandarin manner, and his high-pitched squeaky voice, that he was a master of black magic; but he had redeeming qualities, in that he does not seem to have used his office to enrich himself, and like other traditional figures, he retained a pride in being an Ethiopian which many of the educated politicians have lost.

The ministries which he ran, however, were both inefficient and corrupt. The power of officials depended entirely on their relations with Makonnen; his confidants exercised great influence, whatever their formal rank, while the others were virtually redundant. This could be frustrating, as is indicated in a comment published by the Ministry of Information on the Ministry of Mines and State Domain in December 1958, when both had just been released from Makonnen's supervision:[3]

The Ministry of Mines and State Domain appeared among Ethiopia's administrative departments under its present name on the 5th of Genbot 1950 E.C. (May 1958). Before this time it was a department of the Ministry of Finance. This period was one of unpleasant memories for the Ministry of Mines and State Domain. It was a period of unfulfilled ambitions, unaccomplished plans, and unsatisfied needs of moral succour and financial support.

Such direct criticism of a ministry in the government press is unique.

Makonnen's power rested, like that of all important politicians, on the support of the Emperor, to whom he was completely and unquestionably devoted, and to whom he had access at any hour of day or night. He was a constant visitor to the palace, and in this way exerted a very great deal of influence, which underlay all his other powers, and accounted for much of the fear in which he was held in the government. He depended entirely on imperial support, having no independent or traditional base for authority.

As a result of his position with the Emperor, he was given semi-official control over a number of matters outside his ministry, among the more curious, for the son of a priest, being relations between the government and the Moslem population. He supervised contacts with the business community in Addis Ababa, and controlled the government press and information services which he took over from Wäldä-Giyorgis (33) in 1948 and incorporated into the Ministry of Finance in 1954. He also ran the Patriotic Association devoted to Ethiopian drama, a subject in which he took much interest, and which suited his own great gifts as a dramatic performer. The Association was sometimes used for political purposes, for example, when a performance criticised the Crown Prince after Makonnen had quarrelled with him while the Emperor was abroad in 1954. Here also Makonnen would receive visitors, and sit in state among his entourage of petitioners, flatterers and informers.

His rather devious methods suited his desire to exercise power while avoiding responsibility, and every form of decision-making which he favoured enabled him to carry out his wishes behind a façade involving someone else. One such façade was the Emperor himself, and Makonnen would like to say that a decision, and the whole credit for it, rested with the Emperor, unlike Wäldä-Giyorgis (33), who would be prepared to say that he had taken the decision himself. A similar device was his use of committees, to which he would invite everyone concerned with a matter to be decided. He would sometimes have several of these meeting at the same time, and would go from one to another, bringing each round to his own point of view and arguing patiently until this was accepted. The awe in which he was held, and the unwillingness of most officials to cross him, meant that the meeting would eventually end in agreement with his views, and he would then get everyone present to sign the recommendations arrived at. In this way he would anticipate the possibility of opposition, for instance before the Emperor or in the Council of Ministers, by compromising everyone in favour of acceptance. In any event, Makonnen would probably have made sure that his views had the Emperor's support before going to the meeting, and this would add further force to his persuasions.

A similarly indirect form of decision-making is found in his use of *protégés* and informers, who were placed throughout the government—often in posts of negligible official importance—in much the same way as the supporters of Wäldä-Giyorgis. They were used not only to gather information and to block the plans of Makonnen's opponents, but also as Makonnen's instruments in decisions which he did not want to take publicly himself. He would never openly block or refuse a request, but would appear to agree, and would then refer the petitioner to a *protégé* who would refuse it for him. It is important to distinguish the position of such *protégés* from that of responsible civil servants. They were not delegated particular functions, and had no independent powers of decision; they served, rather, as mouthpieces through which Makonnen's decisions were announced and his views forwarded; their positions were entirely personal, and took the traditional form of an individual's following. For the most part, they were men only little less devious than Makonnen himself, though this was often concealed behind a charming personal manner and a front of liberal efficiency, and even now they bear a distinctive cachet and are best avoided.

This long digression is justified by Makonnen's importance in the government as a whole, and in the administration of finance in particular. It is said that on entering the Ministry of Finance, he immediately cut all allowances for expenses other than salaries by half, so that ministers would have to petition either himself or the Emperor for their restoration. This would be quite in keeping with his methods, and the confusion into which the accounts were thrown that year is shown by the existence of a balancing item of $15,300,000, out of a total of $67,500,000, to account for the difference between total current expenditure and the sums which could be ascribed to given departments.[4]

His concept of finance was limited to keeping income as high and expenditure as low as possible, and whenever he could he would block or delay appropriations. It was at this point that the system of payment by imperial order broke down, since even such an order by no means ensured that the department concerned received the amount due to it, though standing orders for routine expenses would usually be paid, often after long delay. That a minister so devoted to the Emperor as Makonnen should deliberately block his orders is at first sight astonishing, but in fact he was working closely with the Emperor in doing so, and it can be taken as a first principle that he would never go against what he believed to be the Emperor's wishes. It followed from the characteristically Ethiopian methods of government embodied both in the Emperor and in Makonnen that even this part of the financial process could not lapse into an automatic matter of administrative routine. A certain amount of blockage was sometimes necessary to balance the Budget, when the Emperor granted payment orders for greater sums than there was money to cover; further, it enabled the Emperor to avoid responsibility for refusing allocations which he did not really wish to grant, while the reference back to him of orders granted in *Aqabé Sä'at* enabled him to exercise still closer control, and gave great scope for the behind-the scenes adjustments in which he excelled. In this way, the already personalised method of getting payment orders was modified by a whole range of further changes engineered through individual relationships.

Since the validity of an imperial order could not be questioned, the Ministry of Finance could not simply refuse to cash it, but would have to resort to a number of other devices. One of these was to refer the order back to the Ministry of the Pen, on the grounds that it was in some way ambiguous; in ordering a payment for a car, for instance, it might not say whether a luxury saloon was required, or simply a small and second-hand model. It was also common for the Minister himself to take the order to the Emperor for reconsideration, and suggest that the allocation be reduced, paid in instalments, or put off until the following year. The Emperor might then call in the head of the department concerned, and a process of informal adjudication would follow in which Makonnen, because of his influence with the Emperor, would usually have the upper hand.

Alternatively, the appropriation might be blocked in the Ministry of Finance itself, through a system of obstruction and delay such as officials are adept at producing behind a front of co-operative acquiescence. Makonnen would not appear personally in this, but would refer the matter to a minor official, who would put off payment from day to day with elegant excuses for doing so. The effects of this system are particularly clear in the figures for 1952–53, when actual expenditure came to $8,674,557 less than the authorised total of $89,720,040, despite the fact that revenue was $14,751,930 higher than expected, leaving a surplus of $23,426, 487.[5] The high surpluses of those years were exceptional, and were cut into as the turn in the terms of trade against commodity producers reduced the revenue from customs, but Makonnen maintained reserves in the Treasury throughout his tenure of office, and when a project arose for which some major figure was really prepared to fight, the money could always be found.

But while disregard for some imperial orders suited the Emperor's purpose, and might be necessary to balance the Budget, it was essential to pass authorisations for expenditure in which the Emperor was personally interested. In this way, imperial favour might enable a department to get a spectacular rise in its appropriations, as in 1955–56 when the Emperor was greatly interested in creating an Ethiopian Navy, and the Marine Department obtained \$2,437,710 instead of a previously allocated \$70,059.[6] Nor would a Minister of Finance be wise to block sums wanted by particularly important politicians whom it was necessary to conciliate. As a result, actual spending was to a large extent determined by the interests of the Emperor and of those ministers who were closest to him. When their requests could not be blocked, it might be necessary to compensate by delaying allocations to those less favourably placed, and at times it was difficult for some ministries to obtain enough even for routine recurrent expenses.

In this way, Makonnen's power over finance was very great, and the importance of the Ministry of Finance in the government as a whole was correspondingly enhanced. Makonnen was helped in this by the decline of the Ministry of the Pen, and the confused period after 1955; it was as Minister of Finance that he led the movement which unseated Wäldä-Giyorgis (33). But no modernising tendencies can be read into this rise in the power of financial machinery at the expense of the traditional instrument of the imperial secretariat, for it was achieved by obstruction rather than systematic control, and it is important to note that it involved neither technical knowledge nor efficient administrative machinery. Such machinery, indeed, with institutional procedures and delegation of defined powers, would weaken Makonnen's position, since the sort of control which he exercised depended on a highly personal system, without such procedures, which made it necessary for everyone and everything to come to Makonnen himself.

There remains the possibility of dispute over the extent to which this system resulted from the personal methods of Makonnen, and the extent to which it was bound to follow from the absence of officials with the education to operate more efficient machinery. Certainly, Makonnen leaned heavily on traditional traits well-suited to his officials, and the difficulties of working a modern type of budget would have been considerable; but Makonnen's own methods set the tone for the whole financial administration, both in encouraging his *protégés* and others who worked in a similar way, and in frustrating the efforts of educated economists, of whom there were quite a number by the late 1950s. This is illustrated by the developments which did take place once Makonnen's hand was removed, and by the time of his departure, Makonnen's methods were obviously anachronistic.

In May 1958, Makonnen was moved to the Ministry of the Interior, but he did not fit in there, since it involved rather different methods, and constant contact with aristocratic provincial governors who despised him. He therefore returned to his old post as Minister of Commerce later in the year, but continued to have considerable influence over finance until his death in the revolt of December 1960. This influence was exercised in a number of ways. The basis of it continued to lie in his position with the Emperor, and in the fact that officials, with the politician's unerring instinct for where the true power lies, would submit things to Makonnen rather than to the new Minister of Finance, Mahtämä-Selassie (17), who himself stood in considerable awe of Makonnen. Makonnen still operated through committees in much the same way as before, whether on an *ad hoc* basis or through more permanent creations like the Planning Board or the Economic and Technical Assistance Board, while many of his *protégés* remained in the Ministry of Finance and continued to work with him.

Mahtämä-Selassie, by contrast, was neither a forceful administrator nor particularly qualified for the post of Minister of Finance. He was noted for his habit of referring even the slightest details to the Emperor, and was probably chosen as someone who would enable the Emperor to keep a close control over financial matters. His position in the Ministry was weak, since he had to contend not only with Makonnen, but also with Yelma Derésa (35), who wanted to return to Finance and lost no opportunity of demonstrating his own knowledge of financial matters, and Mahtämä-Selassie's lack of it. The Emperor, moreover, turned for financial advice to Yelma, who eventually took over the Ministry in July 1960. Mahtämä-Selassie nevertheless had something to show for his two years as Minister. In particular, he demonstrated some determination in accepting measures to meet the Ethiopian balance of payments crisis of 1958–59; he helped to make the administration of finance slightly more efficient than it had been under Makonnen, enabling ministers to get a better idea of how much money they were likely to be allotted; and he transformed the Budget by bringing it out at the beginning of the year instead of, as hitherto, at the very end of it. With the accession of Yelma, the death of Makonnen in the 1960 revolt, and the increasing emergence of economically educated Ethiopians, this helped to produce the distinctly changed conditions of financial administration in the 1960s.

The extent of this change is clear from the fact that the times of Ato Makonnen now seem immeasurably remote; there is no longer a place in the present-day system for Makonnen's application of the methods of traditional Ethiopia to the complicated business of modern finance. Such methods might still have been viable in the years immediately after the

Liberation, but even by the time Makonnen came to the Ministry of Finance they were becoming unworkable, and difficulties were bound to increase with rising revenue and the return from abroad of trained Ethiopians. These difficulties took several forms. Systematic planning of any project was impossible, due to the uncertainty of funds; the disorganisation of the appropriations mechanism made it impossible to keep proper accounts, and led to opportunities for corruption. This disorganisation, and its consequent discouragement of institutional methods, were spread throughout the administration by the fact that every ministry had to adapt itself to Makonnen's methods in order to get its funds; and those years are still remembered with loathing by officials who spent weeks of fruitless pleading in trying to get allocations for their projects, and were sometimes reduced to tears of frustration at the end of them. An awareness of these frustrations may have influenced the Emperor's decision to move Makonnen to the Ministry of Interior in 1958.

But before expressing surprise that either the Emperor or Makonnen should have continued so long with a system which clearly did not work, it is essential to bear in mind that neither of them was particularly aware of the need to make it work. An administration of the sort that Makonnen ran was directed to no ultimate ends of administrative efficiency or economic advance, for such questions did not enter into his traditionally oriented order of things, in which there was no goal beyond the overriding requirement of loyalty to the Emperor; the concepts of means, ends and progress which are so firmly rooted in the western mind simply had no place there. In this, as in many things, Makonnen provides a clearer and exaggerated form of traits which are also present in the Emperor. A similar lack of final goals has already been noted in Haile-Selassie himself, who has equally been tied to traditional methods, in finance as in other things, which have prevented him from building up systematic machinery through which his power could be more effectively exercised. An analoguous similarity is found in the taking of decisions behind the scenes, though in this the Emperor was more subtle and more successful, in that while few doubted that Makonnen's influence lay behind the decisions of his subordinates, the Emperor was able to use Makonnen to shield himself from responsibility for practices which resulted from the methods of both of them. One of the ways in which Makonnen was most useful to the Emperor was in taking the blame for some of the less attractive aspects of his rule, so that while Makonnen was highly unpopular, the Emperor was able to remain distinct from his ministers, as the symbol of national unity. The point at which the Emperor most differed from Makonnen was in his far greater ability to adjust to changing circumstances; Makonnen was so bound up with the traditional forms described in this section as to be able to work in no other way, while Haile-Selassie, though heavily influenced by the traditional tendencies inherent in his position and upbringing, has nevertheless adapted himself to a system in which Makonnen would seem simply an anachronism.

Budget and Appropriations since 1960

The practical importance of the official government Budget before 1960 was negligible, and it has been possible to omit any mention of it from the previous section without distorting the picture of the appropriations machinery given there. For the ten years after the British advisers' Budget of 1944–45, indeed, there was no budget at all, except that the term was sometimes applied to totals either of Ministry of the Pen authorisations, or of actual annual expenditure.[7]

It was not until the financial year 1955–56 that an attempt was made to draw up a systematic Budget, based on requests for funds from the various ministries, submitted in advance, and on estimates of available income. Four foreign advisers in the Ministry of Finance formed themselves into a special committee, and completed a first draft in July 1955, two months before the beginning of the year; this draft was not accepted and was followed by others, the sixth and last being finished three months after the end of the financial year, in December 1956. This Budget had therefore no more than historical interest, but in any case the advisers had no sanguine hopes that their efforts would immediately replace the long-tried system of imperial orders, and the exercise was useful as a first step in establishing a budgetary machinery; no new method or institution can hope to spring into immediate effectiveness, and a period of probation is needed in order to get the innovation accepted, and adapt its functions to the existing framework.

The next year, 1956–57, the draft Budget was submitted to the Council of Ministers and Parliament, perhaps in deference to the procedures established by the Revised Constitution; from 1958–59 onwards it was published annually as a Proclamation in the *Negarit Gazeta*, and could formally be used as an authority for drawing funds. But these early Budgets had no financial effect, since they were only published at the very end of the year, a procedure which caused some complaint even in the appointed Parliament before 1957.[8] Meanwhile, allocations by imperial order continued undisturbed in the way already described.

The last of these shadow Budgets was for 1959–60. Thereafter, the Government was obliged by the Fiscal Year Proclamation of 1959 to present its Budget to Parliament several months before the start of the fiscal year. As well as making it necessary to produce the Budget in advance, this Proclamation laid the basis for an annual budgetary calendar, which is now well established.[9] The process of drafting begins in mid-July, nearly a year before the Budget is due to go into effect, when the Ministry of Finance sends preliminary instructions to the other departments, laying down guiding principles for the preparation of their estimates; these generally consist of exhortations to keep down spending in particular ways, while ministries whose allocations were sharply increased the previous year may be warned against applying for further rises. The estimates should be submitted to the Ministry of Finance in mid-October, nine months before the year begins, though only the smaller and more efficient departments meet this deadline, and the Ministry grants a period of grace of up to two months; if a ministry has still not presented its requests by then, it automatically receives its budget for the previous year. There is naturally a tendency for each department to inflate its requests, and some may seek the Emperor's approval for increases, to help them survive the inevitable process of scaling down which follows.

This takes place in the Ministry of Finance, where the full draft Budget is prepared by the Budget Committee, an advisory body to the Minister. It is largely composed of Ministry of Finance officials, mostly Ethiopian with one or two foreign advisers, though it has also contained representatives of the Planning Ministry since complaints that the Five Year Plan was disregarded in the drafting of the Budget. The details of the Budget, from initial drafting to final promulgation, are supervised by one of the Minister's closest personal *protégés*.

At this stage the optimistic submissions of the ministries first meet the harsh facts of available cash, and the Committee's task largely consists in deciding what to cut out. For 1962–63, for instance, requests totalling $223,550,604 were submitted by the various ministries and agencies, and reduced in the Ministry of Finance to $178,537,921. Only three or four of the smaller agencies got through unscathed, and the Ministries of Pensions, Justice and National Community Development, all of which had ambitious plans for expansion or improvement, had their requests cut by over half.[10] Occasionally, the Committee may suggest an increase, when a ministry has forgotten to include an estimate for some essential item. There is no regular system of hearings, where ministries can defend their requests, but the Committee frequently asks officials to justify increases which have not been properly explained in the written submissions.

The Committee's draft is finished early in January and submitted to the Minister, though he will already have been constantly in touch with the Committee's activities, and will have made known any particular changes which he favoured. Yelma Derésa has been especially interested in the Capital Budget, and though he has made recommendations here and there on the administrative part of the Budget, he has usually been ready to accept the views of the Committee.

In this way, the Ministry of Finance has had a controlling part in allocating funds among different projects; the Budget nevertheless remains a conglomeration of the requests of the different departments, and little attempt has been made to use it as a co-ordinated instrument of economic policy.

In mid-January, the draft is sent to the Council of Ministers, where it is submitted to a special committee. The Council of Ministers' stage is entirely concerned with the attempts of aggrieved departments to restore allocations cut out by the Ministry of Finance; a few of these requests are usually granted, especially when there were political or other reasons for a submission of which the Ministry did not take account, but there are not nearly as many changes as in the Ministry, and most of its recommendations are accepted. No new requests are made at this stage, and cuts which the ministries concerned are prepared to accept are not discussed; nor does the Council cut some allocations to release money for others, unless, as happens very occasionally, there is some isolated project which no one is prepared to fight for. Even so, the Council needs all of the two months allotted to it, with frequent and sometimes daily meetings, and a few items usually have to be held over for later discussion when the draft is rushed over to Parliament towards the end of March, on the latest possible day which the law allows.

The Budget is considered by Parliament in the same way as any other Proclamation, though as a financial measure it goes first to the Chamber of Deputies. Only a few changes have been made in Parliament, and since these are more important as indications of parliamentary opinion than for their effect on the Budget itself, they have already been considered. In any case, detailed parliamentary control of spending through the Budget is nullified by modifications in the appropriations procedure over the course of the year. The chief difference which Parliament has made to the Budget has been through its critical examination of it, especially in the Budget Committee of the Chamber of Deputies, and parliamentary reaction has always to be borne in mind in drawing up the Budget. The effect which this has is difficult to estimate, and sometimes the result may be concealment rather than change. Parliament finishes its work at the end of May or early in June, and sends the Budget up for the imperial assent. This is entirely a formality; the Emperor only affects the Budget in that projects which he is known to favour are unlikely to be cut out of it, and his influence on government spending is exercised almost entirely through special and extra-budgetary authorisations of funds.

The Budget thus published is by and large an honest assessment of expected revenue and authorised expenditure, though before 1962 the

Ministry of Finance sometimes resorted to inflation or double-counting of revenue and minimisation or ignoring of expenditure, to produce a Budget balanced at least on paper. In 1960–61, for instance, there was an entry for $10,000,000 under 'Other Revenue' which was simply a balancing item. In recent years, the tendency has been in the opposite direction, and not only has a deficit been shown, but revenue has been deliberately under-estimated so as to leave the Ministry some additional money with which to meet extra-budgetary spending. There has also been some minor falsification by individual ministries, such as the inflation of certain items so as to use the money saved on other things.

This Budget forms the basis for routine appropriations. Every month, each ministry is entitled to submit requests for a twelfth of the allocations granted to it by the Budget, and the Ministry of Finance checks that these are for the correct sums and reasons, and then issues a payment order to the Treasury. This system still has many points of similarity to that before 1960, but in practice much has changed. First, the Emperor's active participation in the process has greatly declined, and for routine expenses is now confined to the occasional adjudication of disputes between the Ministry of Finance and other departments; for the first years of the budgetary system, it appears that his formal consent was needed to release already budgeted funds, but this requirement has lapsed. Further, a single and uniform Budget is far easier to administer than were the often vague and varied imperial orders of the past.

Equally important has been a corresponding and connected change in practices within the Ministry of Finance. Payment orders for budgeted funds are issued more or less automatically; the Director-General of the Budget Department is responsible for signing monthly orders of up to $500,000, the Vice-Minister up to $3,000,000, and the Minister himself beyond that amount, which in effect means only the Ministry of National Defence. Yelma Derésa (35) does not concern himself much with day-to-day spending and delegates this to his subordinates, a great change from the time of Ato Makonnen (19); another change is that the official responsible for drawing up the Budget carries far more political weight than the official responsible for implementing it, whereas Makonnen kept his closest and most trusted *protégés* in the implementing department.

This process has thus to some extent been institutionalised, though quite a number of difficulties remain. Rarely, when revenue from taxation has been lower than expected, and the government's borrowing facilities with the National Bank have been fully drawn, the Ministry of Finance has had to cut budgeted allocations for expenses other than salaries. A more systematic cut in allocations was imposed in 1964 to pay for a rise in army salaries, which also caused the postponement of several investment projects included in the Budget. In any case, ministries very seldom get all of the

167

money allotted them in the Budget, since they often cannot use it for the purpose laid down. An investment project may be delayed, so that the money cannot be spent on it until the next year, or the Budget may grant a year's expenses for a new department which does not come into being until half-way through it, and in these and many other ways the Ministry of Finance can economise on budgeted allocations. A ministry may also draw less than allotted in the early months of the year, and then try to gain all of the remainder in a lump sum at the end, a tendency naturally resisted by the Ministry of Finance. As a result of these savings, ministries only receive a proportion of their Budget, amounting in 1962–63 to about eighty per cent; this includes sums transferred from one use to another within the ministry through the procedure described later, and the proportion often varies greatly from one ministry to another. When disputes arise, they are usually settled between Yelma Derésa (35) and the other minister concerned, though they may go for mediation to the Prime Minister or the Emperor. Although most of the routine work is now handled by vice-ministers and assistant ministers, there is no machinery for settling disputes between ministries at this level.

The system of monthly allocations gains importance from the fact that money not used during the month has to be returned to the Ministry of Finance at the end of it, and on the last day of the fiscal year the accounts of all departments are automatically closed. This very strict control is thought necessary as a check on corruption and to prevent the accounts from becoming hopelessly confused; it also enables the Treasury, which is often very short of ready cash, to take back money which is not actually being used and to distribute it where it is most urgently needed. There are nevertheless great disadvantages; ministries have to work within monthly schedules, and to use their allotted income they have to plan their spending with an efficiency of which most of them are incapable. The blocking of accounts at the end of the year even freezes funds on which cheques have been drawn but not presented, and agencies which are partly financed by foreign loans and aid find these blocked at the same time as their domestic income; they are released after scrutiny by Ministry of Finance inspectors, but this may take several months. A related problem is that work in hand continues from year to year, and a ministry may find itself having to pay for work which was budgeted for from the now-closed accounts of the previous year. In the 1959–60 Budget, allowance was made by ministries for undischarged commitments from the previous year, but this device could only be used with accuracy when the Budget was drawn up after the start of the year; various ways of meeting the problem have been considered by the Ministry of Finance, and a general fund of $2,000,000 to meet such commitments was included in the 1964–65 Budget.

But although this budgetary mechanism now accounts for by far the greater part of government spending, it still needs considerable modification and supplementation in practice. A Budget compiled so long in advance cannot possibly foresee all the requirements of the coming year, and the shortage of money makes it impossible to include margins wide enough to take care of contingencies; some machinery is therefore needed to authorise payments for urgent or unexpected expenses which arise during the year, and to transfer funds from heads under which they cannot be used to other projects for which they are wanted. Similar needs arise from the great difficulties of accurate costing and timing of operations, and from administrative inadequacies; essential matters may be left out of the Budget, or they may be sent in late so that there is no time to consider them before the Budget goes to Parliament.

A number of modifying devices have therefore been contrived. One of these is a system of authorised transfers, which first appeared in the Budget of 1962–63. Immediately after the Budget has been published, a ministry may request that funds granted to it for one purpose may be used for another; these requests are considered and authorised by the Ministry of Finance or the Council of Ministers, according to the difference between the budgeted and the requested use for the money. In theory, transfers cannot be made between ministries, or increase allocations for salaries, without amendment of the Budget by Parliament, but in fact the Emperor sometimes does authorise such transfers, and it is extremely probable that he granted transfers of all sorts before formal provision was made for them in the Budget at all; such devices are often only the means of legalising the existing practice. Since the mid-1960s, transfers have been taken increasingly to the Council of Ministers.

More interesting, and from the point of view of political development far more important, is the Allowance for Unforeseen Expenses, which is included in each Budget, and for which allowance is explicitly made in the Constitution. This amounts to between $5,000,000 and $10,000,000 a year, and is intended to cover any necessary expense not provided for in the Budget. Payments from it are authorised by the Emperor, through exactly the same system of imperial payment orders as was used for all expenses before 1960, and the Allowance thus provides a continuation, side by side with the budgetary system, of the traditional appropriations machinery. It would be impossible to abolish this machinery entirely, since the Emperor has always been accustomed to authorise spending, and no politician would challenge this right, nor be able to do so successfully. Furthermore, ministers have been used to going to the Emperor for extra expenditure, and this system still prevails for matters not covered by the Budget. These may include genuinely unforeseen expenses, like those for the Heads of State Conference of 1963, as well as projects rejected from the Budget or never submitted to it but of whose desirability the minister can persuade the Emperor, and imperial benefactions and other odds and ends which come the Emperor's way.

There is naturally a great deal of competition for these extra funds, and the Emperor usually issues orders for the payment of all of them within a few months of the start of the financial year. This does not prevent further orders from being issued, and in this way the amount of such allocations comes out at between $20,000,000 and $30,000,000 a year. The total amount has not changed significantly in recent years, though it has declined in proportion to spending as a whole. There is a special machinery for considering and dealing with these imperial orders in the Ministry of Finance, where they do not go to the Budget execution department; instead, they are sent directly to a personal appointee of the Minister, who decides whether they should be granted immediately, or whether an attempt should be made to have them delayed, reduced, or granted by instalments. If the other minister concerned disputes his decision, he usually takes it back to the Emperor, who then calls Yelma (35) to explain it; there follows a process of adjudication, the result of which depends largely on the influence of the different ministers over the Emperor and their degree of enthusiasm for the cause concerned. Yelma carries far more weight with the Emperor than most of the other ministers, and usually gets his way, but he might not care to dispute the issue with a strong ministry like National Defence, and if any minister is really determined to get funds for a particular project he usually succeeds. While this system is clearly unworkable as a general basis for expenditure, it may still have some value as a way of sorting out priorities in additional spending and reconciling the Emperor's continued powers with the need to balance the Budget.

Since the early 1960s the Council of Ministers has also made some allocations, sending payment orders to the Ministry of Finance in much the same way as the Emperor; this device has greatly increased in the mid-1960s, and now accounts for much of the activity of the Council. Whether a particular matter goes to the Emperor or to the Council probably depends on the minister concerned, and on whether it is for a project in which the Emperor is interested. Council of Ministers' allocations also accompany Council decisions to go ahead with a particular project.

The impossibility of squeezing all these allocations, from both Emperor and Council, into the Allowance for Unforeseen Expenses has been one of the reasons for the Supplementary Budget which came out towards the end of every financial year between 1961 and 1965. It has been needed, ever since the Budget started to come out in advance, in order to legalise retrospectively all of the extra-budgetary spending which has been authorised during the year. As well as payments granted by the Emperor

Figure 2

Chart of the Ethiopian Government, *c.* 1947

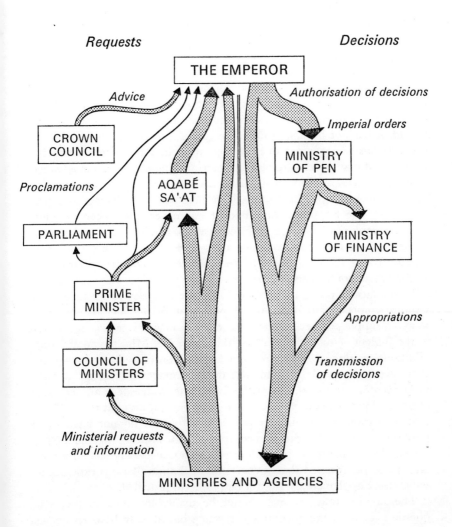

and the Council, it included ordinary budgetary estimates which were submitted too late to be considered in advance, expenses which the Council of Ministers had no time to decide on before the Budget had to be sent to Parliament, and commitments carried over from the previous year. Expenses earlier paid from the Allowance are often transferred to the Supplementary Budget so as to leave some money in reserve for the last few months of the year, and the Supplementary Budget sometimes itself creates a new allowance.

The Supplementary Budget more or less compiled itself, and its actual amount has varied from year to year between eighteen and forty million dollars, or five per cent and fourteen per cent of the original Budget. It accounts for a larger proportion of actual spending since, being drawn up mostly as a register of expenses already incurred, it is not subject to the same savings as the Budget itself. The Supplementary Budget has then gone to the Council of Ministers and Parliament in the normal way, though it has not been subject to the special procedures for the Budget itself. It has met a great deal of opposition in Parliament, which has complained that there is little use in its scrutinising the Budget in advance, when at the end of the year it will be asked to accept as a *fait accompli* a large number of expenditures for which there was no budgetary authority whatever. The Supplementary Budget has nevertheless been no more than a symptom of a whole series of weaknesses and inefficiencies, some of which have been clearly remediable, while others have sprung from administrative defects natural to an undeveloped country, or from the Emperor's use of his personal powers.

In the face of parliamentary criticism, the Ministry of Finance made some attempts to cut down the Supplementary Budget, and in order to avoid supplementary budgets altogether, a new device was introduced in the Budget of 1965–66, enabling the Council of Ministers to authorise additional spending of up to ten per cent of the ordinary Budget, provided that revenue is available. This has the advantage of securing advance parliamentary approval, but at the same time it abandons any pretence of detailed parliamentary control of expenditure; it also has the weakness that allocations from this ten per cent allowance do not have to be published, while the Supplementary Budget appears in the *Negarit Gazeta*. It has made supplementary budgets unnecessary since 1965–66, and it can be assumed that it covers all of the multifarious expenses for which the Supplementary Budget had hitherto provided.

The proviso that revenue should be available raises another vital question. If all of the government revenue has already been set against expenditure in the Budget itself, from where does the money come for all this extra spending? It is found in a number of ways. First, the Ministry of Finance is able to recoup money through savings in the execution of the

Budget, in the way explained above, which is then freed to finance non-budgetary spending. Second, the Ministry has in the Budget consistently under-estimated the revenues for the coming year, especially from Customs, due to deliberately conservative estimates designed to give it a certain amount of leeway; had a realistic figure appeared in the Budget, the Ministry would have had to pass further requests for funds, and would then have found itself without the wherewithal to meet additional expenses. Third, new taxes may come into force during the year, and in the last resort it is possible to draw on the Treasury reserves, as was done to meet a deficit of $16,000,000 in 1962–63. It has therefore been possible to meet these extra appropriations without depriving ministries of budgeted funds which they are in a position to spend.

There has thus been a considerable development in appropriations procedures since 1960, and this can be correlated with general tendencies within the government. As in the earlier period, the Minister of Finance holds a central position, linking the process to the Emperor and ministers on the one hand, and to the working of the Ministry on the other, and in this role Yelma Derésa (35) has been scarcely less important than Makonnen Häbtä-Wäld was. But whereas Makonnen could be regarded almost entirely in traditional terms, Yelma is an exceedingly astute and complex politician who combines traditional with more modern traits, and his position is therefore more difficult to assess.

As always, the relationship with the Emperor is the determining factor, and like any major politician, Yelma has a great deal of influence with him and is daily at the palace. Of all the ministers since 1960, moreover, he provides the best example of the way in which an active politician may achieve his ends by working through the Emperor, abiding by all of the conventions of the government which have already been discussed, and combining submission to the Emperor with the use of the imperial authority as the basis for all his actions. As a result, if there is any matter with which he is really concerned, it is rare for him not to be able to get his way; the Italian credit of 1964, considered later, is that rare ideal, the exception which proves the rule.

But despite this, his more modern traits are evident even in his position with the Emperor, and distinguish him from Ato Makonnen. In economic matters he has the prestige of an expert, and as such is respected by the Emperor. If an economic problem comes to the Emperor or to the Council of Ministers while Yelma is away, it is usually postponed until he returns. He is therefore not simply a servant, as Makonnen was, and his greater capacity for delegation makes him more willing and able than Makonnen to take decisions independently of the Emperor. It is also significant that he appears to be making preparations to stay in politics after the Emperor's departure, a fact which leads him, among other things, to affect the air of a fervent radical, and apparently to seek a political base among the Gallas, of which he is the leading representative on the government.

These personal matters have combined with more general tendencies to make the Emperor's part in the administration of finance very much less active than it was before 1960. He still grants appropriations in the *Aqabé Sä'at*, but these have declined from being the basis of the whole system to the status of an extra source of funds additional to the Budget. His role in the arbitration of budgetary disputes is far less important than it used to be, and though he ensures that those in charge of finance are subordinate to him, he no longer exercises any extensive control over the process. When he chooses to exercise the powers of appropriation which he still possesses, the system is modified to make room for them, but in general terms the administration has expanded beyond him, and these powers occupy a shrinking place in it.

An analogous combination of personal relations and general developments affects the place in the financial field of the other major central institutions. The role of the Ministry of the Pen has virtually disappeared, as one aspect of its general decline, but the position of the Council of Ministers and of the Prime Ministry has improved. In the Council, this is seen in its modification of the Budget, and in its increasing part in the actual implementation of appropriations through transfers and the granting of its own payment orders. The Prime Minister's Office is less directly involved, but it affects the general position through the alliance of convenience between Yelma and Aklilu (3) which has dominated the government since 1960. In this alliance, Yelma is by far the more active partner, and he is frequently able to engineer Aklilu into supporting his projects and into using his co-ordinating and reconciling powers to further them. In more routine matters of appropriations, Aklilu mediates both over the Budget in the Council, and sometimes in disputes between Yelma and other ministers over the implementation of the Budget.

The handling of matters within the Ministry is equally affected by the balance between Yelma's more modern and his more traditional characteristics. The improvement in the procedures and the efficiency of the Ministry since 1960 has been great, and much of this has been because Yelma has been prepared to delegate to his subordinates; vice-ministers and assistant ministers of Finance, exercise a power far greater than that of most of their equivalents in other ministries, and wield considerable initiative. But at the same time, they can do so because of their relations with the Minister; other officials, as competent as they or more so, have had to leave because they could not get on with Yelma. There is no senior Ministry of Finance official who holds his position independently of Yelma's approval, and the Ministry is still run, as it was under Makonnen, as part of a personal political machine. In this way, though the personality of the Minister is no longer so directly linked to the working of the financial machinery as in Makonnen's time, it remains of considerable importance.

The Italian Loan, a Case Study

Our survey of the Ethiopian government would not be complete without a particular example of the government at work, and the attempt to raise a loan of £5,000,000 from Italy in 1963–64 illustrates so many aspects of the political process that it provides the elements necessary for a detailed case study.

The reasons behind the loan were largely political. There had been discussion for some years of the possibility of some gesture of economic co-operation between Ethiopia and Italy to demonstrate that bad relations between them had finally been healed. There may also have been, on the Italian side, a desire to safeguard Italian interests in Eritrea, which came under the central Ethiopian government with the ending of Federation in 1962; and on the Ethiopian, the hope of securing Italian benevolence in the dispute with Somalia in much the same way as the French loan to the Franco-Ethiopian Railway was intended to do with France.

Certainly the Emperor favoured an agreement, though he acted largely through the Minister of Finance, Yelma Derésa (35), who championed the loan within the government and personally handled many of the details of it. He co-operated with his friend and supporter Menasé Läma, Governor of the State Bank, and they closely supervised every stage in the negotiation and discussion of the loan.

The first formal step was taken in February 1963, with the visit to Ethiopia of the Italian Minister for Foreign Trade, and the signing of an Economic Co-operation Agreement. This provided for the supply to Ethiopia of Italian machinery and technicians, and payment by the Italian government of two per cent interest on a loan of £5,000,000, to be negotiated later between Ethiopia and a consortium of Italian banks.[11] Accordingly, a team of negotiators led by Menasé Läma went to Italy in the early summer of 1963. In the resulting discussions, the Italians insisted on several conditions in the loan which the Ethiopians opposed, including the rate of interest, the form of interest payments, and the control of spending under the loan. The Ethiopians therefore left Rome without reaching any agreement.

There the matter rested for several months, until the Emperor's state visit to the United States in the autumn of 1963. There were high hopes of spectacular American aid to mark this visit, but nothing resulted, since the Americans did not think that there was any suitable project available. Rather than return home empty-handed, therefore, the Emperor revived the Italian loan project, and Menasé Läma was sent from the United States to Italy, with a grant of powers directly from the Emperor, to conclude the loan on the best terms that had been available in the summer. The Loan Agreement was accordingly signed on October 18th, 1963,[12] to the considerable surprise of those ministers, including the Prime Minister, who had not been with the Emperor in the United States and therefore knew nothing of what had happened.

The usual procedure, by contrast, is for a loan to be raised with a specific project in mind, and for the proposed terms to be studied by the Finance Credit Department of the Ministry of Finance, and often by the Economic and Technical Assistance Board. They are then submitted to the Council of Ministers, which takes expert advice and often sets up a committee of its own. If it approves, the loan agreement is initialled, and sent to the Emperor and Parliament for ratification. Instead, the Italian loan was dealt with in the Ministry of Finance personally by the Minister, and it was signed on the basis of a personal grant of powers from the Emperor, before consideration by any of the government bodies nominally existing for the purpose. It still needed to go to the Council of Ministers and Parliament, but the effect of this procedure was to present it as a *fait accompli* rather than a proposal.

Further complications arose from the commitment charge of £25,000, which had to be paid within three months of signature for the loan to go into effect. By then, the loan had still not reached the Council of Ministers, and the Minister of Finance gave the Governor of the Bank verbal instructions to pay the charge from the Treasury account, anticipating a formal authorisation. This practice seems to be fairly common when written instructions are delayed, although in this case the necessary authorisation was never sent.

The terms agreed were financially unfavourable to Ethiopia. The rate of interest payable by Ethiopia was five and a half per cent, the two per cent paid by the Italian Government having been deducted from the artificially high level of seven and a half per cent, and this interest was to be deducted in advance; with the commitment charge and other expenses, the effective rate was about six and a half per cent, significantly higher than that obtainable elsewhere. The loan was to be repaid over nine years, starting thirty months after the acceptance by Ethiopia of the first instalment, again rather worse terms than with other loans.

It is therefore not surprising that several Ethiopian economists and foreign advisers objected to the loan on technical grounds, but the objections both of Ethiopians and of advisers were muffled by the fact that the two chief supporters of the loan were in charge of the country's two main financial institutions. However, one of the Ethiopian objectors wrote a memorandum to the Prime Minister on the subject, and word of their opposition also came to the Emperor, who summoned them to the palace to hear their complaints, and appointed a commission of enquiry to investigate. This was set up in March 1964, composed of three officials from the Prime Ministry, and reported in May, largely agreeing with the criticisms already made. But its report did nothing to prevent the loan going before the Council of Ministers at about the same time, so that the commission served as a device for placating the opponents of the loan without actually affecting the issue.

Some opposition might have been expected from the Council of Ministers, particularly from members on bad terms with Yelma Derésa (35), but no one cared to join battle over a *fait accompli* supported by the Emperor, and the loan was approved in the Council without trouble. More important was the discussion of the use to which the loan should be put, and in particular of a plan to build blocks of flats on the road to Addis Ababa airport. This proposal originated with a provincial governor who was widely supposed to have a financial stake in the affair, and was rejected by the Council on the discovery that each flat would cost more to build than a detached house.

The loan was therefore submitted to Parliament without any plan for its use. The Chamber of Deputies had already refused to pass a loan from the U.S.S.R. until told why it was needed, and took a similar stand over this one, rejecting a motion for immediate acceptance by a comfortable majority on May 26th. The Ministry of Finance then hastily produced a list of projects, including a power plant and meat and glass factories.[13] Much opposition to the loan in the chamber remained, some on the ground that the list of projects should be endorsed by the Council of Ministers, and some on wider issues. A great deal of lobbying took place. The passage of the loan by the end of May was generally ascribed to the pressures brought to bear by the Chief Clerk, who was certainly very active in his role of government whip.

The opposition which the loan encountered in the Senate, to which it was then submitted, was very different from that so far discussed. There were very few senators qualified to consider either the economic justification of the loan or the uses to which it should be put, and these were former civil servants who mostly took the government side. On the other hand, there were many senators from the nobility and the Patriots who were deeply suspicious both of the Italians and of non-Amhara individuals like the Galla, Yelma Derésa (35) and the Wälamo, Menasé Läma who were chiefly responsible for the loan. This broad distinction between the civil servants who supported the loan and the noblemen who opposed it is not complete, for there were exceptions on both sides, but it is valid as a general guide.

The form which the opposition was to take was indicated in the Economic and Finance Committee of the Senate, one member of which regarded the provision in the Loan Agreement for disputes to be settled under Italian law as an infringement of Ethiopian sovereignty. This point was seized on again and again when the loan went to the full Senate on June 5th, and accompanied by invocations to those Patriots who had died to prevent Ethiopia from coming under Italian laws. Yelma was roughly treated when he went to defend the government's position and was even confronted with slanderous insinuations about his personal fortune.

Even so, there were many senators on whose votes the government could rely, and others who hesitated to oppose what appeared to be the Emperor's wishes; the loan would have been grudgingly passed had not the President, Abiy Abäbä (2), descended from the chair on June 5th and opposed the loan from the floor of the chamber. Abiy commanded great respect as a Patriot, as a member of the highest nobility, and for his personal honesty; he had also been brought up in the palace, and his loyalty to the Emperor was beyond question. His opposition to the loan therefore encouraged other senators to follow, and a motion to accept the loan was defeated. The motion was reconsidered on the insistence of the government, but on June 9th, the Senate decided to consider the question as closed.[14]

On June 25th, the Senate received a letter from the Emperor, requesting it to re-open the debate on the ground that it had not yet formally either rejected or accepted the loan. This was signed, as is usual, by the Minister of the Pen, and was strongly slanted in favour of the loan, rebuking senators for insulting government officials and regarding Italy as still an enemy.[15] The debate was therefore resumed on June 26th, and the following day the loan was formally rejected by 45 votes to 42.

After rejection by the Senate, the loan could not be put into effect, and though there were periodical rumours that the government was going to reintroduce it at the end of the parliamentary recess in November, these were not realised. At the same time, it was reported from several sources that the Emperor had let it be known that the terms of the loan had not been properly explained to him, a claim of ignorance such as often paves the way for an imperial retreat, and the loan was thereafter abandoned.

Any such exceptional case combines its peculiar features with fairly normal aspects of the government. Certainly, no incident quite like the Italian loan had previously arisen, but many aspects of it could be paralleled in other cases. It raised no new factions in the government, and those in favour of the loan were chiefly the central group of 'technician' ministers, typically non-nobles educated abroad before 1936, who were prepared to work entirely within the framework laid down by the Emperor. Into this category fall both the active supporters of the loan, Yelma Derésa and Menasé Lämä, and those like the Prime Minister who, while not particularly concerned, were prepared to grant it tacit support on the understanding that the Emperor and Yelma were for it. On the other side were the opponents of this central group, including most of those not entirely dependent on the Emperor, although only chance brought the younger educated officials into alliance with the conservative nobility. The opposition in the Chamber of Deputies was largely concerned with the Chamber's powers and was, as usual, quite distinct from that in the rest of the government; but the opposition in the Senate was closely connected with groups in the government as a whole, and also illustrates the relevance of social and provincial origins. The most extraordinary feature of the affair was that the Senate should have been so angered as to reject a measure which the Emperor favoured, and it is also now unusual for an issue to appeal directly to the Patriots; the Italian loan may well have seen their last fling as a distinct political grouping.

Given the circumstances of the loan, and the divisions of opinion which it caused, its handling within the executive was not extraordinary. It was the exception to the rule, in that it ignored procedures usually followed for loans; but this is to be expected when the Emperor is personally interested in something, since he is not bound by such procedures and works in a personal way. On the other hand, it has only been possible to establish procedures because the Emperor is not usually concerned with loans at all. Similarly, a minister with an important stake in a matter is liable to take arrangements into his own hands, as did Yelma with the by-passing of the ordinary Ministry of Finance departments and the irregular authorisation of the commitment charge. Thus, even where institutional methods are used for normal cases, they may be displaced by personal ones over controversial questions.

The handling of the economists' objections was also characteristic, and it is equally to be expected that some activities took place further behind the scenes and so escaped the author's attention. The commission of enquiry is a device often used for placating objectors by hearing criticisms which are later ignored, and the unimportance of the Council of Ministers in a case where the Emperor's inclinations were already known is not surprising. On the other hand, the Council does seem to have decided against the use of the loan for building flats, a matter in which neither the Emperor nor Yelma was particularly interested.

While the Emperor supported the loan, moreover, he was as usual careful not to take his commitment beyond the point of no return. He thus preserved himself from a possible loss of face, and he also avoided forcing opponents of the loan into direct opposition to him; as it was, they could present themselves as opponents simply of Yelma Derésa, so that the Emperor could listen to their complaints, and then refer them to a commission of enquiry. When the opponents carried the day, the Emperor could say that he had not in any case been properly informed about the loan, and disclaim all responsibility for it, leaving his Minister of Finance to shoulder the blame and put up with an ignominious defeat. In this way, the avoidance of binding commitments makes it possible to meet opposition and resolve disputes within the imperial framework.

Chapter 12
Concluding Review

The Working of the Government

The Ethiopian 'Constitution', like the English, lies not so much in written powers as in a gradually developing body of usage. The laws, and the Constitution in a narrower sense, have sometimes registered changes in usage and sometimes foreshadowed them; but they have themselves been so moulded by the conditions of government that they have had to fit themselves into the existing scheme before they could much affect developments. The fact that the working of the government depends so much on custom and so little on written laws certainly adds not only depth and interest to Ethiopian politics, but also complexity, for in the confusion of old landmarks and new institutions it is hard to distinguish what has changed from what is still the same. In particular, it is by no means obvious whether the undoubted changes since 1941 have gone to the foundations of the government, or whether they should be regarded, rather, as peripheral modifications, to a political system which remains basically unaltered.

It has already been argued that the innovations of the last half century have developed from an Ethiopian system of government which, despite variations, can broadly be described as 'traditional'. Its essentials are easily summarised. It depended first of all on the position of the Emperor. He was the keystone who held the different elements in the country together in a single polity; he was looked up to as the universal provider, whether in matters executive, legislative, judicial or military, and as the defender of the Faith and protector of the people; he had to authorise every major decision or initiative of the government; and he was constantly busy even in minor administrative affairs. Developments in this position of the Emperor would provide important indications of change.

We can look next at the Emperor's entourage—the men who wielded influence in the traditional central government. In standing, these ranged from noblemen with stature of their own in the traditional political system, to the low-born servants of the palace, but they all depended for their position on personal status and connections, whether among themselves or with the throne. To pursue their ends they employed both their personal influence and ability in manipulating court politics and the services of followings of *protégés* and retainers.

Third, we can examine the institutions of government, in so far as such institutions can be said to have existed. They were indeed feeble growths, which never achieved independence from the court; the holders of high office had no greater influence than personal qualities and imperial favour gave them; they had no effective administrative departments to supervise, and their functions were ill-defined, for like the Emperor they tended to range over every field of government. Impersonal administration by officials with defined powers was unknown.

The first innovations were indeed in the institutional field, in the pre-war establishment of ministries, a written constitution, a parliament, even a penal code. But in every case, from Menilek's time onward, the practice was to introduce a western model and then leave it more or less to chance whether this picked up significant functions. Institutions have not reflected the growth of new forces in the political system, like parties and legislative councils in the former colonies; still less were they the outcome of usage, as in England. They were simply planted in the hope that the appropriate usage would then grow into the institution. After the Liberation, likewise, the government received a modern structure before it learnt to use it. The Constitution and Parliament, with the consequent separation of executive and legislative powers, date from 1931, but neither acquired much life before the Revised Constitution of 1955 and the elections of 1957. Before 1936, the Minister of Justice and the Chief Justice were one and the same office, but even after the setting up of a distinct judicial hierarchy at the Liberation, at least one Minister continued to regard himself as a judge, and hankered for the courtroom. The Prime Ministry was established and the Council of Ministers revived in 1943, but it was many years before they acquired very much importance.

It is therefore plausible to speak, in the post-Liberation years, of a dual structure of government, in which traditional modes carried on, more or less undisturbed, behind a front of modern institutions. The Prime Minister and Parliament were simply superimposed on active traditional agencies like the Ministry of the Pen. The issues of government were still fought out between largely traditional groups, whether the nobility or the Emperor's *protégés*, each using essentially traditional methods. Despite the definition of an administrative structure and of ministerial functions, the political system continued to work through personal connections around the palace, and a powerful politician took on as many diverse functions as his influence and ability allowed.

It has sometimes been suggested that this dualism was no more than a consciously contrived façade, permitting Haile-Selassie to combine a modernising image with a reluctance to abandon traditional techniques. This is certainly one element in the situation, but I doubt whether it accounts for the whole. In the 1940s, the Emperor was surrounded by men, like himself, of generally traditional upbringing; supposedly modern institutions therefore stayed in the hands of officials who could scarcely be expected to make them work, while the most powerful politicians naturally continued to employ the methods and agencies which they were used to. It would have been unfair to ask much of a Prime Ministry under a charming old nobleman like Makonnen Endalkachäw (18), or a Parliament composed of semi-appointed country squires, least of all when their functions were pre-empted by Wäldä-Giyorgis (33) and the machinery of the palace.

Modernisation has consistently been the result of changes in the *type of official* holding the major posts, and with the disappearance of most of the old uneducated generation between 1955 and 1960, it has no longer been possible to distinguish clearly between an indigenous reality and an imported façade. Some of the present high officials have perhaps little more initiative or less subservience than their predecessors, but their *methods* are certainly different; they have fewer factional rivalries, and not many of them are very adept at intrigue; they do not employ sizeable personal followings, or depend to the same extent on personal connections. Above all, most of them have education enough to make some show of running a modern ministerial government. The Emperor's entourage has thus undergone an important, though not a revolutionary, change.

The same can be said for the institutions of government, which have expanded beyond recognition since 1941. In place of the embryo departments of pre-war days, there is now a whole range of ministries, specialised agencies and organs of government, which carry out their own defined functions in a way which would have been inconceivable even twenty years ago. This institutionalisation is naturally most effective at the lower levels, where educated younger officials have made their greatest impact; but even in the Prime Minister's office and the Council of Ministers, important indications of it are to be found, reflecting the sheer pressures of administrative development. We must not, of course, allow our enthusiasm to carry us too far: every Ethiopian institution still hums with personal undertones, and the palace is just over each minister's shoulder; but many of the changes since the Liberation—as witness the appropriations procedures—stand as evidence of solid growth.

But what of the palace? This is the most difficult and the most important problem of all. The place of the Emperor has changed, like the rest of the government, with the change in the men around him and the growth of the administration. His role in the day-to-day affairs of government has sharply declined. Even were he not so often abroad or otherwise occupied, he would not have time to attend to the details which automatically came to his attention earlier in the reign; and the powerful secretariat which made his presence felt in every corner of the government has all but disappeared. Where before he was the universal provider, a host of officials and institutions have now grown up to supplement or replace him—ministries and ministers, courts and judges, professional armed forces and their officers. Over all these he can exercise little more than general supervision, with occasional personal intervention. But his basic functions have been least affected, because for these no satisfactory replacement has been found. It is still the Emperor who authorises the major decisions of the government, since no one else has authority enough to do so; and it is still the Emperor who holds together the diverse components of the state, since no one else stands above them as he does. When the Eritrean situation threatened to get out of hand early in 1967, he himself had to spend a month there trying to calm it down, though with indifferent success. While much has been done to modernise the structure and working of the government, there seems thus to have been little basic change in the authority on which it rests, and it is for this reason that its future development still remains so much a matter for uneasy conjecture.

Government and Country

Developments in the internal working of the government may find themselves left in the air unless they keep pace with relations between the government and the country at large. Government, in a word, must look to its communications with society, for in a changing country, these communications take on far greater importance than they had in the traditional political system. There are several reasons for this. In the first place, the creation of a large state and the process of centralisation have brought to the central government a whole host of matters which were previously dealt with at the local level, often quite outside the government structure. Where previously, many of the ethnic groupings of the Empire simply ran their own affairs within their own polities, they have now to be brought into a single modern state, and even in the long-established provinces, matters now come to Addis Ababa which used to be the concern of the local ruler. A second inevitable accompaniment of modernisation is the creation of a wide range of new interests and new demands; the army, the students, the trades unions, are new political forces, often the result of the government's own policies, and they make demands of which account has to be taken; another new kind of demand arises simply from the expansion of the functions of government in recent years—there would have been little point, fifty years ago, in petitioning for a new clinic or a new road. Third, development has the effect of making old divisions far more articulate and aware of themselves than they were before, a fact best illustrated in the growth of ethnic nationalisms; by exploiting existing unities and divisions, such nationalisms can grow far more quickly and effectively than loyalties (often artificial) to a nation state. And fourth, change throws everything into a common melting-pot, creating tensions between traditional and modernising sectors, privileged and unprivileged groups, which in the past did not arise so acutely, even if they existed at all.

These pressures have created strains beneath which many African governments have collapsed, and there is more than academic interest in enquiring how Ethiopia has met them. One great advantage has been that Ethiopia has not had to meet them in so sudden or extreme a form as many of her neighbours. Much the same problems have existed—or are clearly on their way—but their impact has been transformed by the absence of colonial rule and the presence of an established traditional core. Ethiopia's frontiers, for instance, would be little less arbitrary than those of other African territories, were it not for the centralising presence of the Amhara, and the assimilation of other peoples to them. The presence of a strong established system of government, generally accepted as legitimate, has likewise prevented or postponed the problems of legitimacy which other rulers have had to face; and the extraordinary stability of this government, due to the rule of Haile-Selassie, has given Ethiopia a long period of peace during which to assimilate changes. Not the least of Ethiopia's advantages has, in my opinion, been the absence of the democratic forms which have elsewhere often led to the mobilisation of the people into political parties organised along tribal lines, and so encouraged the divisions which it is now the business of African leaders to suppress.

The traditional Ethiopian political system possessed generally adequate channels of communication between rulers and people. The more important and better established interests, such as the Church, the armed forces and the nobility were furthered through informal contacts with the Emperor and representation in the government, and could not easily be distinguished from the ordinary processes of administration. When these channels broke down, as in the reign of Lej Iyasu, the resulting pressures found an outlet in rebellion. Other interests, of a more individual and sporadic kind, were expressed through petitions to the Emperor and local governors; and if these were unsuccessful, it was possible to resort to intrigue, revolt, or withdrawal from the society.

These methods are still used, and with centralisation the process has been increasingly focused on the palace, beneath the watchful eye of the

Emperor. The representation of different groups in the government, uneven though it be, has already been noted, and the leaders of such interests as the Church and the armed forces have easy access to the throne. The right to petition the Emperor is enshrined in the Constitution of 1955, and such petitions have remained the chief overt channel for requests to the government, from pleas for individual favours to organised army demands for higher pay. Haile-Selassie has maintained and developed the traditional imperial function of redressing grievances and providing bounty. Other interests have been less directly represented, in the way that Makonnen Habtä-Wäld (19) handled relations with Moslems and the business community. Many organisations maintain contacts through some highly placed Ethiopian, often one with a seat on their board of directors, who ensures the favour of the government and where necessary takes problems to ministers or the Emperor. Members of the imperial family similarly supervise charitable concerns, and sometimes even business enterprises. In this way, communications with outside interests, like communications within the government, have been controlled, directly or indirectly, by the Emperor.

In the years since 1960, however, several types of interest group not controlled by the Emperor have developed, reflecting the inadequacy of the traditional patterns to contain the great increase in the scope and urgency of demands on the government brought about by recent changes. Economic groupings have developed with the legalisation of trades unions in 1962,[1] and since then they have grown rapidly and called several strikes; much of the leadership of these, as of other modernising ventures, has come from Eritrea. Student organisations at the University, though often at odds with one another, have grown in vigour and vocality and have launched anti-government demonstrations, one of which, in April 1968 resulted in the temporary closure of the University. Perhaps more significant are the regional organisations set up chiefly among Addis Ababans to encourage development in their home areas. These groups have not been overtly political but may very well become so, the first indication of this being the use of the Galla organisation as a political platform by Tadäsä Biru (29) and his associates in 1966. They have sometimes acted through petitions to the Emperor, but have more recently worked also with the Chamber of Deputies[2] which has become the main forum for provincial interests, and indeed for complaints of all sorts. The government has made efforts to control these new interest groups, for instance through the supervision of trades unions by the Ministry of National Community Development, the presence of ministers in Parliament, and the promulgation of laws to grant a measure of local government;[3] but the interests both of provincial areas and of the modernising sector in Addis Ababa raise pressures which it is hard for the government to accommodate, and which are likely to be increasingly difficult to maintain within the existing political system. Recent legislation has been passed to require associations to register, and to control public demonstrations.

Similar problems appear when we look at the other side of the coin—downward communication from government to society. A good deal of this also is carried out by the Emperor as part of his traditional role; he gives orders to meet the requests of petitioners, distributes charity in land and money, and offers paternal words of advice or reproof. But apart from this personal level of imperial benevolence, the downward flow of communication has been extremely weak. The newspapers have scarcely been used to inform the people on political affairs, even to the extent of putting the government's case; they usually contain little more than a record of the Emperor's activities, foreign news taken directly from agencies, and a few local items of no political significance, though exhortatory leading articles have become more common in the last few years. They found it possible to omit the slightest reference to the taking place of a general election in 1961, and information on Parliament is by the same token quite inadequate. The general factor underlying the government's inactivity in this respect is its lack of enthusiastic commitment to agreed development policies, and its unreadiness to implement programmes which call for the mobilisation and participation of the people; of such mobilisation it has indeed been more than a little suspicious.

One symptom of this is the absence of political parties—even a single government party—which have been the chief agents of mobilisation elsewhere in Africa, and this absence is no accident, for a political party would involve radical changes in the nature of Haile-Selassie's government. It would first be quite foreign to the Emperor's political techniques, since he has been used to dealing with individuals on a very personal basis, playing one off against another, and has destroyed any organisation which might have emerged as a rival to himself; the existence of a national political organisation is thus incompatible with the *methods* of palace government. Second, Haile-Selassie (like most of his people) has always regarded his power as coming from above, from God, as his political pronouncements constantly reveal; and even the most traditionalist political party would by contrast involve some acknowledgement that this power was to some extent derived from popular support, and so place the Emperor in the position of a party leader rather than that of a divinely appointed sovereign. A party system is thus equally incompatible with the *basis* of the imperial authority. These barriers to a political party will remain as long as the Emperor retains an active place in politics; it is therefore scarcely surprising that among all the schemes for modernisation and reform which have been canvassed within the government over the last few years, political parties have never, to the best of my knowledge, been seriously considered. They have, however, been suggested by intellectuals outside high office who want to see a political system very different from the present one.

The processes of political communication have thus generally been carried on through traditional channels which have so far usually managed to meet the day-to-day demands on the political system, but this has been possible only because the pressures of modernisation have not so far become acute. The inadequacies in the traditional channels which first came to the surface in the revolt of 1960 are already becoming more evident, and they are likely to be demonstrated clearly once Ethiopia is fully subjected to the inevitable pressures of a changing society. These pressures can, moreover, grow very quickly once popular political awareness has been aroused, as has happened in many other African countries, and the problem is whether new channels of communication can then be developed to meet them.

The Present and the Future

I shall not try to predict the future political development of Ethiopia, for the value of such predictions (or prophecies) is doubtful in a continent which is changing so quickly and at times as violently as present-day Africa. But the political future of Ethiopia—the perennial question, 'What will happen when the Emperor goes?'—is of such general concern that it would be ducking the issue to avoid it. And so in this final section I shall try to present the conclusions of the present so that they point, at least, towards the future.

From the central government, two distinct conclusions emerge. First, its methods have developed, with the absorption of trained administrators, to such an extent that the government even of fifteen years ago is quite inconceivable today. But the central government has failed to encourage— it has in fact deliberately impeded—the development of any alternative source of legitimate authority to supplement or replace that of Haile-Selassie. None of the institutions which we have considered shows much sign of acquiring such authority, and the same tendency is clear in the absence of central co-ordination and direction of government policies, with the resulting lack of impetus which marks all the higher reaches of the government. At the same time, inadequacies have appeared in the traditional authority under which the country has so far been governed, and these are likely to be sharply aggravated when Haile-Selassie goes, since a good deal of this authority is directly attached to his own person. The problem is then to identify alternative sources of authority in the political system, which may be able to fill the vacuum thus created, in the light of their position in the political system of today.

Of course, the fact that traditional sources of authority are no longer altogether adequate is no reason for discounting them completely; on the contrary, they remain very strong, for instance in the latent position of the Church in the Christian areas of the country, and in the residue of imperial authority which is inherent in the office and not simply a personal attribute of Haile-Selassie. Any successor government will presumably have to come to terms with these authorities, or else face, as in Yemen, the crippling effects of a civil war against them. There would therefore seem to be considerable advantages in retaining the throne, whatever the powers which it receives, although the place of traditional authorities will naturally depend also on political conditions at the time, such as the ability of the present Crown Prince.

Among alternative authorities, the Parliament has already a place in the present constitutional structure, and it may have been intended that it should, as in England, supplement and ultimately replace the authority of the Crown. This is, however, very far from the role which Parliament at present performs as a useful source of criticism and channel of communication under the ultimate protection of the central government, and for Parliament to take a central part in the political system would require developments of which there has so far been little sign. The Chamber of Deputies might perhaps gain importance as the beneficiary of a growth of political consciousness in the countryside, but this has not been the lasting result of such consciousness elsewhere in Africa and it would be optimistic to place much dependence on Parliament in Ethiopia. It is significant in this respect that among the first announcements of the rebel government in December 1960 was the adjournment of Parliament *sine die*.[4]

Another element in the present-day Ethiopian political system, and one that is likely to survive and develop, is the 'modernising élite' of civil servants and other educated classes who at present run most of the machinery of government under the supervision of the Emperor and politicians dependent on him. This group is responsible for much of the modernisation which has so far taken place, and it also commands much of the intelligence, experience and idealism in the government. As a political élite, however, it suffers from the lack of any firm foundation in political support, possessing neither the traditional authority of the Emperor, the popular election of the Parliament, or the control of physical force. A 'government of bureaucrats' is a possibility which might well be to Ethiopia's advantage, but it has to be maintained in office by

Figure 3

Chart of the Ethiopian Government, *c.* 1967

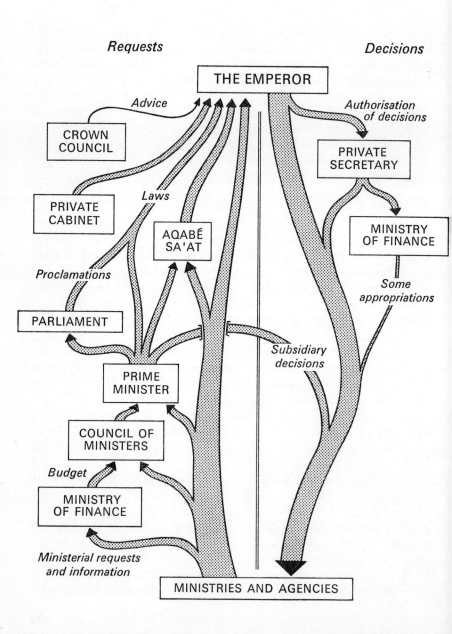

some other power, possessing the force or authority which it lacks.

Among such other powers, the armed forces cannot be ignored. The army has already seized power in some dozen African states, most of them with much smaller military establishments than Ethiopia's. The possibility of an army takeover is therefore at least a very strong one, especially if the civilian government shows signs of losing control, and many officers in the armed forces seem to be aware of its potentialities. Certainly, the only important threats to Haile-Selassie's régime since 1960 have been led by the military, and the success with which demands for higher pay were enforced in 1961 and 1964 was to a large extent the result of a latent political threat. Military régimes tend to suffer from an underlying lack of 'legitimacy', and a consequent reliance on force, but these disadvantages may be less in Ethiopia than elsewhere, as the country has no great commitment to democracy, and tacit military government can be combined, as in pre-war Japan, with the retention of the throne; a military government would probably be far more nationalist towards external enemies such as the Somalis, and far more repressive towards internal opponents such as students, than the present fairly easy-going régime. The most important question arising with the military is, however, their ability to maintain national unity, and this has been affected (or reflected) in other African countries chiefly by the unity of the military themselves. Broadly, three kinds of division are possible, all of which have been demonstrated or appear to exist in the Ethiopian armed forces. First, there may be divisions between units, like that between the army and the Imperial Bodyguard which brought the defeat of the 1960 revolt. Second, there may be divisions between the higher ranks, mostly generals trained in the wartime era with close connections with the present régime, and the post-war generation of younger middle-rank officers; this has been a factor in many of the armies of the new states, and the difference between pre-war and post-war generations gives it relevance to Ethiopia as well. Third and perhaps most dangerously, there may be divisions along ethnic or regional lines, of the kind that first openly appeared in the involvement of Tadäsä Biru (29), another brigadier general and a colonel in the Galla affair of 1966.[5]

Since the armed forces tend to have a certain commitment to national unity, such divisions among them, as in Nigeria, are likely simply to reflect similar differences in the country at large; and this raises the still unanswerable question of the unity of the Empire which has already been discussed, with some apprehension, in an earlier chapter. Here it is enough to point out that considerable dangers of disunity exist. These dangers may of course be exaggerated, and anyone who like myself has become caught up in the tradition and development of Ethiopia, must hope that they will prove to be unfounded, or at least that reserves of unity will emerge with which to meet them. This may well be so. As an old and established country, Ethiopia possesses far stronger sources of nationhood than do most of the new states of Africa, and helped by the dogged capacity for survival of existing political structures, these may be mobilised against internal divisions, and strengthened by external threats.

But we must leave these problems to wait upon events.

Biographical Appendix

1. *Abäbä Arägay*, Ras (1905–1960)
   A Shoan of Galla stock, and grandson of one of Menilek's most famous generals. He was chief of police in Addis Ababa in 1935, and fought throughout the Italian occupation as a resistance leader in northern Shoa. After the war, he was the outstanding example of a resistance leader in politics, until his death as a hostage in the 1960 revolt.
   Major posts: Governor of Addis Ababa, 1941; Governor of Sidamo, 1941–42; Minister of War, 1942–43; Governor of Tegré, 1943–47; Minister of War, 1947–49; Minister of Interior, 1949–55; Minister of Defence, 1955–60; Chairman of the Council of Ministers, 1957–60.

2. *Abiy Abäbä*, Lieutenant-General (b. 1918)
   A member of one of the leading Shoan families, and briefly husband of Haile-Selassie's youngest daughter Tsähay. He is a quiet and much respected man, formerly a friend of Wäldä-Giyorgis, and has been one of the principal noblemen in the government since 1941.
   Major posts: Governor of Wäläga, 1942–43; acting Minister of War, 1943–47; Minister of War, 1949–55; Ambassador in Paris, 1955–58; Minister of Justice, 1958–61; the Emperor's Representative in Eritrea, 1959–64; Minister of Interior, 1961–64; President of the Senate from 1964.

3. *Aklilu Habtä-Wäld*, Tsähafé T'ezaz (b. 1912)
   Born into a Shoan Church family, and brother of Akalä-Wärq and Makonnen Habtä-Wäld (q.v.). He was educated in France, where he spent the Italian Occupation, and is married to a Frenchwoman. For most of his career he has been concerned with foreign affairs, but as Prime Minister in the 1960s he has become responsible for much of the government's policy, and is probably the most influential politician in the country.
   Major posts: Vice-Minister of the Pen, 1942–43; Minister of Foreign Affairs, 1943–58, 1960–61; Deputy Prime Minister, 1957–61; Prime Minister from 1961.

4. *Andargé (Andargachäw) Mäsay*, Ras (b. *circa* 1902)
   A Shoan, educated in France during the Regency. During the 1940s, he was a bitter enemy of Wäldä-Giyorgis, and he has been married to Haile-Selassie's eldest daughter, Tänañä-Wärq, since 1944. As Representative in Eritrea, he

193

sought to reduce the autonomy of the Eritrean Government. He has been an invalid since a car accident in 1964, and has wide commercial interests.

Major posts: Governor of Harär, 1941–42; Minister of Justice, 1943–46; Governor of Bägémdär, 1946–52; the Emperor's Representative in Eritrea, 1952–59; Minister of Interior, 1958–61; Governor of Sidamo, 1961–64.

5. *Asfeha Wäldä-Mika'él*, Bitwädäd (b. 1906)
An Eritrean, educated in Italy, who acted as an interpreter during the Italian régime in Ethiopia. Thereafter, he was chiefly concerned with promoting complete union between Ethiopia and Eritrea, which was achieved in 1962. He is reputed to be an extremely astute politician.

Major posts: Chief Executive of Eritrea, 1955–62; Minister of Justice, 1963–66; Minister of Public Health from 1966.

6. *Asratä Kasa*, Ras (b. 1918)
Only surviving son of Ras Kasa (q.v.), and member of the Shoan royal house. He took the lead in co-ordinating action against the 1960 rebels, and pressed for heavy penalties against those involved. As Representative in Eritrea he has firmly opposed attempts at separatism. He has an outside chance of succeeding to the throne as a reactionary strongman.

Major posts: Governor of Bägémdär, 1942–44, 1952–56; Governor of Wäläga, 1944–46; Governor of Arusi, 1946–52; Governor of Shoa, 1956–57; Vice-President of the Senate, 1957–61; President of the Senate, 1961–64; the Emperor's Representative in Eritrea from 1964.

7. *Endalkachäw Makonnen*, Lej (b. 1926)
A Shoan nobleman, son of former Prime Minister Makonnen Endalkachäw (q.v.). He was educated at Oxford, returning to Ethiopia in the early 1950s.

Major posts: Vice-Minister of Education, 1958–59; Ambassador in London, 1959–61; Minister of Commerce, 1961–66; Permanent Representative at the United Nations from 1966.

8. *Gäbrä-Wäld Engedä-Wärq*, Ato (1905–1960)
Rather a secretive character, from a Shoan clerical family. He worked continuously in the Ministry of the Pen, both before and after the Italian occupation, and had some connection with Ras Kasa. He was killed as a hostage in the 1960 revolt.

Major posts: Director-General and Vice-Minister of the Pen, 1947–60; Secretary of the Crown Council, 1941–60.

9. *Hadis Alämäyähu*, Ato (b. 1913)
A Gojami, educated in the United States before the war. He was imprisoned by the Italians during the Occupation, and since 1941 has served largely in foreign affairs. He has a reputation as an honest and painstaking administrator, and has recently written a best-selling semi-political novel.

Major posts: Vice-Minister of Foreign Affairs, 1952–56; Permanent Representative to the United Nations, 1956–60; Minister of Education, 1961; Ambassador in London, 1961–66; Minister of Planning from 1966.

10. *Hana (Gäbrä-Hana) Jema*, Aba (1895–1960)
A Shoan priest, confessor and confidant of the Emperor, and keeper of the

Emperor's privy purse. He was custodian of the imprisoned former Emperor Lej Iyasu before 1935. He was killed as a hostage in the 1960 revolt.

11. *Haylu Bäläw*, Ras (b. *circa* 1890)
Head of the royal dynasty of Gojam. He fought in the resistance to the Italians, and was made Ras and titular Governor of Gojam at the Liberation. He is a member of the Crown Council, and has recently been given greater prominence than before on ceremonial occasions, but is of little political weight.

12. *Imru Haile-Selassie*, Ras (b. *circa* 1894)
A liberal member of the Shoan royal dynasty, he was a popular and efficient governor before the war, and one of the more successful Ethiopian generals. He was imprisoned by the Italians until 1943. Since then, he has been mostly in Addis Ababa or ambassadorial posts abroad, and he tried to serve as a go-between for discontented radicals with the Emperor in the 1950s. Because of his liberal reputation, he was declared Prime Minister by the rebels in 1960.

13. *Kasa Dargé*, Ras (1881–1956)
The greatest of the Shoan lords, whose title to the throne was at least as good as Haile-Selassie's. He held many important governorships before the war, and went into exile with the Emperor. He was President of the Crown Council, active in discussions of the Constitutions both of 1931 and of 1955, and a devout Churchman. Three of his sons were killed by the Italians; only the youngest, Ras Asratä (q.v.) survived.

14. *Kätäma Yefru*, Ato (b. 1928)
A Shoan with Harär connections, educated in the U.S.A. He has been one of the leading post-war graduates in the government, and has supported Pan-African policies as Minister of Foreign Affairs.
Major posts: Private Secretary to the Emperor, 1958–61; Minister of Foreign Affairs from 1961.

15. *Keflé Ergätu*, Däjazmach (b. 1906)
Shoan, son of a night-watchman at the French Embassy in Addis Ababa, and educated at St. Cyr. He was a close supporter of Wäldä-Giyorgis, and has been concerned with public security for almost the whole of his career.
Major posts: Director-General of Public Security, 1942–49; Vice-Minister of Public Security, 1949–55; Governor of Harär, 1955–61; Minister of State for Public Security, 1961–66; Minister of Interior from 1966.

16. *Lorénzo T'ezaz*, Blatengéta (1900–1947)
An Eritrean, educated in France, who served in the pre-war government and drafted Haile-Selassie's appeal to the League of Nations in 1936. During the Occupation, he maintained contacts between the Emperor and resistance leaders. He was a liberal politician, son-in-law of Ras Imru, and was exiled to Moscow as an enemy of Wäldä-Giyorgis.
Major posts: Minister of Foreign Affairs, 1941–42; Minister of Posts, 1942–43; President of the Senate, 1943; Ambassador to Moscow, 1943–47.

17. *Mahtämä-Selassie Wäldä-Mäsqäl*, Blatengéta (b. 1902)
Shoan, son of a former Minister of the Pen, and educated in France. He sub-

mitted to the Italians. He is something of a courtier by inclination, with a tendency to take any decision to the palace, and a close associate of the Crown Prince. He became a member of the Crown Council on his retirement from active politics in 1966.

Major posts: Private Secretary to Crown Prince, 1941–46; Vice-Minister of Agriculture, 1949–54; Minister of Agriculture, 1954–58; Minister of Finance, 1958–60; Minister of Education, 1960–61; Minister of Public Works, 1961–66.

18. *Makonnen Endalkachäw*, Ras Bitwädäd (1891–1963)

A Shoan nobleman, and lifetime associate of Haile-Selassie. He held high office as Minister of Commerce and Interior, Governor of several southern provinces, and Minister to the United Kingdom, before the war. After the war, he was a dignified and respected Prime Minister, but was not very active in politics; he preferred books, and wrote a great many of them.

Major posts: Minister of Interior, 1941–43; Prime Minister, 1943–57; President of the Senate, 1957–61.

19. *Makonnen Habtä-Wäld*, Ato (*circa* 1900–1960)

Member of a Shoan Church family, eldest of the Habtä-Wäld brothers, and lifelong devotee of Haile-Selassie. He handled financial affairs during the Regency and early part of Haile-Selassie's reign, spending the Occupation in France. He was a skilled intriguer, and wielded immense influence in the government throughout the 1940s and 1950s. He was killed as a hostage in the 1960 revolt. In addition to his formal posts, he handled many other matters, including religious and commercial affairs, information services and security.

Major posts: Minister of Agriculture, 1942–49; Minister of Commerce, 1943–49; Minister of Finance, 1949–58; Minister of Interior, 1958; Minister of Commerce, 1958–60.

20. *Mamo Tadäsä*, Ato (b. 1924)

Member of a Shoan Catholic family, educated in France and married to a Frenchwoman. One of the more influential post-war graduates, he was Chairman of the Codification Commission and closely associated with Aklilu Habtä-Wäld in the Prime Minister's Office.

Major posts: Vice-Minister and Minister of State in the Prime Minister's Office, 1958–66; Minister of Justice from 1966.

21. *Mängäsha Seyum*, Ras (b. 1927)

Tegrean nobleman, son of Ras Seyum (q.v.) and since 1960 chief of Tegré. He was not a success as a minister, but as Governor in Tegré he has taken an active part in development projects, and has built up a powerful local base. He is married to a granddaughter of Haile-Selassie.

Major posts: Governor of Arusi, 1952–55; Governor of Sidamo, 1955–58; Minister of Public Works, 1958–61; Governor of Tegré from 1961.

22. *Mär'ed Mängäsha*, Lieutenant-General (1912–1966)

A Shoan/Gojami nobleman and soldier, who fought in the resistance to the Italians. He commanded the army forces which crushed the 1960 revolt, and had considerable influence as Minister of Defence in the early 1960s.

Major posts: A.D.C. to the Emperor, 1942–47; Commander of the Second Division, 1948–56; Governor of Bägémdär, 1956–57; Deputy Minister of Defence, 1957–59; Chief of Staff, 1959–61; Minister of Defence, 1961–66.

23. *Mäsfen Seläshi*, Ras (b. *circa* 1902)
Shoan nobleman and resistance leader. He was a proud and unpopular Governor of Kaffa, where he acquired a great deal of land, and is regarded by many radicals as the embodiment of what they most dislike in the present political system.
Major posts: Governor of Ilubabor, 1942–46; Governor of Kaffa, 1946–55; Minister of Interior, 1955–57; Governor of Shoa from 1957.

24. *Menasé Haylé*, Dr (b. 1930)
A Shoan with Harär connections, who spent 1947–61 in the U.S.A. and is married to an American Negress. At the Private Cabinet, he has been chief foreign affairs adviser to the Emperor, for whom he also interprets and handles press relations.
Major posts: Head of Political Section of the Emperor's Private Cabinet 1962–68; Minister of Information, 1965–68; Ambassador to Washington from 1968.

25. *Mika'él Imru*, Lej (b. 1926)
Shoan nobleman and son of Ras Imru, educated at Oxford. He spent only two months as Minister of Foreign Affairs, before being sent to Moscow, and was with UNCTAD in Geneva from 1965 until 1968.
Major posts: Administrator of the Planning Board, 1957–59; Vice-Minister of Agriculture, 1958–59; Ambassador to Washington 1959–61; Minister of Foreign Affairs, 1961; Ambassador to Moscow, 1961–65.

26. *Mulugéta Buli*, Major-General (1917–1960)
A Sidamo Galla, trained as an army cadet at Holeta, near Addis Ababa, 1934–36. While Commander of the Bodyguard after the war he established the security system. He reached his greatest power as Chief of Staff, but his influence declined in the late 1950s and he was reputed to be planning a *coup d'état* himself. The 1960 rebels appointed him Chief of Staff, to take advantage of his popularity with the armed forces, but later killed him in the massacre of hostages.
Major posts: Commander of the Imperial Bodyguard, 1941–55; Chief of Staff, 1955–58; Private Chief of Staff to the Emperor, 1958–59; Minister of National Community Development, 1959–60.

27. *Seyum Harägot*, Ato (b. 1932)
An Eritrean, educated in the United States and married to a granddaughter of Haile-Selassie. He works as assistant to the Prime Minister, with a seat in the Council of Ministers, and is responsible for a great many of the odd jobs of administrative co-ordination.
Major posts: successively Director General, Assistant Minister, Vice-Minister and Minister of State in the Prime Minister's Office from 1958; acting Minister of Information 1964–65.

28. *Seyum Mängäsha*, Ras (1887–1960)
Chief of Tegré and grandson of Emperor Yohanes IV. He was Governor of

197

Tegré at various times from 1906 to 1960, interrupted by periods of enforced residence in Addis Ababa, and was a member of the Crown Council. He was among the hostages killed in December 1960.

29. *Tadäsä Biru*, Brigadier-General (b. *circa* 1920)
A Galla from western Shoa, who as Commander of the key police mobile column declared for Haile-Selassie in December 1960. He was interested in the National Literacy Campaign and in Orthodox Church affairs. Late in 1966 he was leader of the Galla political movement *Metcha Tulama*, and was imprisoned; after a long trial, he was condemned to death in 1968. (N.B. There is another quite different Brigadier-General with exactly the same name, appointed in 1967.)

30. *Tädla Bayru*, Däjazmach (b. 1914)
An Eritrean Protestant, educated in Italy. He was leader of the Eritrean political party favouring reunion with Ethiopia, and Chief Executive of Eritrea from the Federation until 1955, when he resigned after a quarrel with Ras Andargé (q.v.). He was given only unimportant posts by the Ethiopians, and in 1967 reversed his former policy by going over to the Eritrean Liberation Front. He is now living abroad.
Major posts: Chief Executive of Eritrea, 1952–55; Ambassador to Sweden, 1956–59; Senator, 1959–67.

31. *Täfärä-Wärq Kidanä-Wäld*, Tsähafé T'ezaz (b. 1906)
A Shoan, interpreter at the British Legation in Addis Ababa before the war, who joined the Emperor in exile. He is constantly in attendance on Haile-Selassie, for whom he often acts as secretary and interpreter.
Major posts: Private Secretary to Haile-Selassie, 1941–55; Minister of the Pen, 1955–58; Minister of the Palace from 1957.

32. *Takälä Wäldä-Hawariyat*, Afä-Negus (b. 1900)
A Shoan, first cousin of the Habtä-Wäld brothers and a life-long schemer, enemy of Wäldä-Giyorgis and critic of Haile-Selassie. He was acting Mayor of Addis Ababa in 1935, and later perhaps the greatest resistance leader. Since the war, he has interspersed high office as Mayor of Addis Ababa (1942), Vice Afä-Negus (1945–46), Vice-Minister of Interior (1955–57) and Afä-Negus (1957–61), with periods in jail for plotting against the Emperor (1942–45, 1947–54, 1961–66). He is now living quietly in Addis Ababa.

33. *Wäldä-Giyorgis Wäldä-Yohanes*, Tsähafé T'ezaz (b. *circa* 1902)
A Shoan, secretary to Haile-Selassie before the war, and the most powerful politician in the government after it. He brought the imperial secretariat to its highest peak, and has been completely excluded from government since his dismissal as Minister of the Pen in 1955. He now lives quietly in Addis Ababa.
Major posts: Minister of the Pen, 1941–55; Minister of Interior, 1943–49; Minister of Justice, 1949–55; Governor of Arusi, 1955–60; Governor of Gämu-Gofa, 1960–61.

34. *Wärqenäh Gäbäyähu*, Colonel (*circa* 1925–1960)
A Gondari Bodyguard officer, who fought in Korea and later gained Haile-Selassie's confidence as head of security. He was critical of most ministers, and

declared for the rebels in December 1960, committing suicide when the attempt failed. He was the founder and most active member of the Emperor's Private Cabinet.

Major posts: Assistant Minister of Security, 1959; Deputy Chief of Staff in the Private Cabinet, 1959–60.

35. *Yelma Derésa*, Ato (b. 1907)

A Wäläga Galla, educated in England before the war and for many years almost the only Ethiopian with training in economics. He is an active and astute politician and has been one of the most powerful ministers since 1960.

Major posts: Minister of Finance, 1941–49; Minister of Commerce, 1949–53; Ambassador to Washington, 1953–58; Minister of Foreign Affairs, 1958–60; Minister of Finance from 1960.

36. *Zäwdé Gäbrä-Selassie*, Däjazmach (b. 1927)

Tegrean nobleman, grandson of Ras Seyum and stepson of the Crown Prince. He was too independently-minded to get on as a minister, and his attempts to reform the judicial machinery were thwarted. From 1963 until 1968 he lived in Oxford, where he was educated.

Major posts: acting Minister of Public Works, 1955–57; Mayor of Addis Ababa, 1957–60; Ambassador to Somalia, 1960–61; Minister of Justice, 1961–62.

Author's Note

In a cabinet reshuffle announced on February 18th, 1969, several ministerial changes were made, too late to be incorporated in the main text of this book. The principal changes were as follows:

Bitwädäd Asfeha Wäldä-Mika'él (5), formerly Minister of Public Health, and Däjazmach Keflé Ergätu (15), formerly Minister of Interior, became ambassadors.

Ato Hadis Alämäyähu (9), formerly Minister of Planning, became a senator.

Ato Mamo Tadäsä (20), formerly Minister of Justice, became Minister of Finance.

Ato Seyum Harägot (27), formerly Minister of State, became Minister in the Prime Minister's Office.

Ato Yelma Derésa (35), formerly Minister of Finance, became Minister of Commerce, Industry and Tourism.

At the same time the Planning Office, which had become a separate Ministry in 1966, reverted to its previous position under the Prime Minister's Office, and the Tourist Organisation was moved from the Ministry of Information to that of Commerce. It is interesting that the announcement, reported in *The Ethiopian Herald*, February 19th, 1969, did not mention the 1966 Order by which ministers are theoretically chosen by the Prime Minister, but simply referred to their appointment by the Emperor.

Notes

Chapter 1: Land and People

1. No full census of Ethiopia has yet been taken. *Ethiopia Statistical Abstract 1965* gives a composite population estimate of 22,590,000
2. Levine, *Wax and Gold*, page 80
3. *The Ethiopian Herald*, June 24th, 1964
4. See, for example, Steer, *Caesar in Abyssinia*, pages 69–71
5. Perham, *The Government of Ethiopia*, page 72

Chapter 2: The Ethiopian Polity and its Development

1. Perham, *The Government of Ethiopia*, pages 69–71
2. Bruce, *Travels to Discover the Source of the Nile*, Vol. II, page 266
3. See Beckingham and Huntingford, *Some Records of Ethiopia, 1593–1646*, page 74; Ludolphus, *A New History of Ethiopia*, pages 234–5
4. Levine, *Wax and Gold*, page 32 and Chapter 5 *passim*
5. Alvarez, *Narrative of the Portuguese Embassy to Abyssinia*, pages 268–9
6. Rubenson, 'Some Aspects of the Survival of Ethiopian Independence in the Period of the Scramble for Africa', *Historians in Tropical Africa*, pages 253–66. This is the outstanding account of the whole period from 1855 to 1896. See also the same author's *King of Kings Tewodros of Ethiopia*
7. Pankhurst, 'Firearms in Ethiopian History', *Ethiopia Observer*, Vol. VI, No. 2, 1962
8. Rubenson, *Wichale XVII*, pages 59–61
9. Marcus, 'The Last Years of the Reign of the Emperor Manilek, 1906–1913', *Journal of Semitic Studies*, Vol. IX, No. 1, pages 229–34
10. Guebre Sellassie, *Chronique du Règne de Menelik II*, Vol. II, pages 527–8
11. Mahtämä-Selassie, *Zekre Nägär*, page 45
12. Notably in Mosley, *Haile Selassie, The Conquering Lion*
13. Mosley, *ibid.*, Chapter V
14. Mosley, *ibid.*, Chapter VI
15. The impression is sometimes given that the Minister of War, Habtä-Giyorgis, and the Archbishop Matéwos were conservatives completely opposed to the Regent's modernising policies. The view that they were balancers between

conservatives and reformers is suggested by Sandford, *The Lion of Judah hath Prevailed*, page 46, and recently available British Foreign Office documents. Zaphiro notes that Habtä-Giyorgis 'generally supports Taffari but does not commit himself' (PRO/FO/401/18, Bentinck to Chamberlain July 8th, 1925), and when Habtä-Giyorgis was ill, it was felt that if he died the party opposing Tafari might get the upper hand (*ibid.*, Bentinck to Chamberlain, July 13th, 1925)

16. Mosley, *op. cit.*, pages 124–5
17. Baum, *Savage Abyssinia*, page 41
18. Perham, *op. cit.*, pages 87–88; Rey, *In the Country of the Blue Nile*, page 202. See also Zaphiro, in PRO/FO/401/19, Bentinck to Chamberlain, September 9th, 1925: 'It was therefore decided that a council of elders should be appointed to advise the government on their future policy. Three-quarters of this council are Menelik's people, and consequently the Ras (Tafari) can now do nothing without the approval of the new council of advisers.'
19. Steer, *Caesar in Abyssinia*, pages 208–9
20. Farago, *Abyssinia on the Eve*, page 30
21. Farago, *ibid.*, page 215
22. The names of officials are taken from Zervos, *L'Empire d'Ethiopie*, *passim*, and the names of graduates from Pankhurst, 'The Foundations of Education . . . in Ethiopia', *Ethiopia Observer*, Vol. VI, No. 3, pages 241–90
23. Perham, *op. cit.*, page 90; Sandford, *Ethiopia under Haile Selassie*, pages 45–46
24. For example, Mosley, *op. cit.*, page 245: 'Practically every student in the country who had ever been outside Ethiopia, and at least half of those who had attained school certificate standard in Ethiopian schools, were executed.'
25. Names as in Note 22 above. Only officials with specifically military functions, such as the Minister of War, are classed with the armed forces, but each provincial governor commanded his local territorial levies, and some central government officials also took part in the fighting. Information on the fate of each of these individuals has been gathered from a great many sources, written and oral; those who have held appointments published in *Negarit Gazeta* are classed as post-war officials. The horizontal columns do not add up, since some officials were also foreign-educated
26. Greenfield, *Ethiopia, A New Political History*, pages 402–3. Greenfield deals exhaustively with the attempted *coup d'état* and gives by far the best available account, although I cannot always agree with his interpretations of it, or with his view of its place in Ethiopian history; I have discussed it in 'The Ethiopian *coup d'état* of December 1960', *Journal of Modern African Studies*, Vol. VI, No. 4, 1968

Chapter 3: The Imperial System

1. Levine, 'On the Conceptions of Time and Space in the Amhara World View', *Atti del Convegno Internazionale di Studi Etiopici*
2. Mosley, *Haile Selassie, The Conquering Lion*, pages 288–91, goes so far as to divide the ministers into 'good' and 'bad', with Ras Abäbä as the chief of the bad ones
3. Haile-Selassie, speech of April 14th, 1961, *Selected Speeches of His Imperial Majesty Haile Selassie First*, page 413

Chapter 4: The Constitutional Framework

1. The text of the 1931 Constitution has been published in Perham, *The Govern-ment of Ethiopia*, Appendix B, and in *Ethiopia Observer*, Vol. V, No. 4
2. Mängäsha Gäsäsä, *Report of an interview on the 1931 Constitution*, unpublished B.A. paper, Haile Sellassie I University, Addis Ababa
3. The text of this law has been translated and published in Dämesé Wäldä-Amanu'él, *The Constitution and Parliament of Ethiopia*, Vol. I
4. *The Ethiopian Herald*, July 22nd, 1944
5. The text of the 1955 Constitution has been published in Perham, *op. cit.*, 2nd edition, and in *Ethiopia Observer*, Vol. V, No. 4
6. Haile-Selassie, speech of November 3rd, 1955, *Selected Speeches of His Imperial Majesty Haile Selassie First*, page 407; *The Ethiopian Herald*, July 23rd, 1952
7. This report has not been made public
8. See Chapter 2, and Levine, *Wax and Gold*, Chapter 7
9. This report has not been made public
10. On an academic plane, analyses of parts of the Constitution have been pub-lished in the *Journal of Ethiopian Law* and in Paul and Clapham, *Ethiopian Constitutional Development*
11. Order No. 44 of 1966, *Negarit Gazeta*, 25th Year No. 10, March 23rd, 1966
12. Order No. 46 of 1966, *Negarit Gazeta*, 25th Year No. 23, July 27th, 1966

Chapter 5: The Emperor

1. The sort of administration which this involved is described in Sandford, *Ethiopia under Haile Selassie*, pages 45–46
2. Rey, *In the Country of the Blue Nile*, pages 29–30
3. Some of the resulting rumours are reported in Greenfield, *Ethiopia, A New Political History*, pages 180–3
4. Greenfield, *ibid.*, pages 390–1 *et al.*
5. Revised Constitution of 1955, Article 67
6. Farago, *Abyssinia on the Eve*, page 94

Chapter 6: Political Groupings

1. *The Ethiopian Herald*, January 20th, 1945, July 14th, 1951; Greenfield, *Ethiopia, A New Political History*, pages 278–9, 293–5, gives accounts of the 1944 and 1951 conspiracies which do not differ very greatly from my own notes
2. As reported in *The Ethiopian Herald*, April 18th, 1949
3. The names of these officials are taken from Zervos, *L'Empire d'Ethiopie*
4. See Levine, 'On the History and Culture of Manz', *Journal of Semitic Studies*, Vol. IX, No. 1, pages 204–11
5. Regulations for the Administration of the Church, *Negarit Gazeta*, 2nd Year No. 3, November 30th, 1942

Chapter 7: The High Officials

Foreign advisers have been noted for their discretion, and the only book written by one of which I am aware is Luther, *Ethiopia Today*. Virgin, *The Abyssinia I Knew*, gives an interesting account of an adviser's life in the immediate pre-war period.

1. Segal, *African Profiles*, page 142
2. Perham, *The Government of Ethiopia*, pages 94–95

Chapter 8: The Imperial Secretariat and its Decline

1. *Negarit Gazeta*, 2nd Year, No. 5, January 29th, 1943
2. Haile-Selassie I, speech of April 14th, 1961, *Selected Speeches*, pages 415–16
3. Bruce, *Travels to Discover the Source of the Nile*, Vol. II, page 375
4. *The Ethiopian Herald*, September 29th, 1956
5. Revised Constitution of 1955, Articles 8, 10, 11, 13, 17, 70
6. Perham, *The Government of Ethiopia*, page 89
7. *Administrative Directory*, May 1957; *ibid.*, July 1959

Chapter 9: The Growth of Central Institutions

1. *Negarit Gazeta*, 2nd Year, No. 5, January 29th, 1943; 25th Year, No. 10, March 23rd, 1966. *The Ethiopian Herald*, February 5th, 1944, July 12th, 1952
2. *The Ethiopian Herald*, November 18th, 1946, January 10th, 1959, October 21st, 1961, March 10th, 1962, March 31st, 1962
3. *Negarit Gazeta*, 3rd Year, No. 1, September 30th, 1943
4. Perham, *The Government of Ethiopia*, page 89

Chapter 10: Parliament and Legislation

The Legislative Process under the Constitution of 1955 has been described in Redden, *The Law-making Process in Ethiopia*. I have also discussed the role of Parliament in Clapham, 'The Functions and Development of Parliament in Ethiopia', *Proceedings of the Third International Conference of Ethiopian Studies*; another recent study is Markakis and Asmelash, 'Representative Institutions in Ethiopia', *Journal of Modern African Studies*, Vol. V, No. 2, pages 193–219.

Research into Parliament in Ethiopia is complicated by the fact that even the most basic records, such as the debates and votes, are not publicly available (they are also entirely in Amharic). The references to the parliamentary archives in the notes are therefore to a few documents to which it was possible to obtain informal access. Election statistics have been provided by the Central Electoral Board,

Ministry of the Interior. The largest published collection of information relating to Parliament is in Paul and Clapham, *Ethiopian Constitutional Development*, Vol. II, Chapter 7.

1. Revised Constitution of 1955, Articles 88–90
2. Revised Constitution of 1955, Articles 30, 92, 116, 119
3. Revised Constitution of 1955, Articles 27, 29, 32
4. For example, the Civil Aviation Decree and Order, *Negarit Gazeta*, 21st Year, No. 17, August 27th, 1962
5. For example, the Awash Valley Authority Charter, *Negarit Gazeta*, 21st Year No. 7, January 23rd, 1962
6. *Second Five Year Development Plan, 1963–1967*, Appendix
7. Administration of Justice Proclamation, *Negarit Gazeta*, 1st Year, No. 1, March 30th, 1942
8. Luther, *Ethiopia Today*, page 99; Monetary and Banking Proclamation, *Negarit Gazeta*, 22nd Year, No. 20, July 27th, 1963
9. Haile-Selassie I, speech on the opening of the Codification Commission, March 26th, 1954, *Selected Speeches*, page 396
10. David, 'A Civil Code for Ethiopia', *Tulane Law Review*, Vol. XXXVII, No. 2, pages 187–204
11. David, *loc. cit.*
12. Mängäsha Gäsäsä, *Report of an interview on the 1931 Constitution, loc. cit.*
13. Käbädä Engeda-Säw, *Yämeker Bétachen Edel*, pages 34–36
14. *The Ethiopian Herald*, June 27th, 1957
15. *Negarit Gazeta*, 12th Year, No. 1, September 11th, 1952
16. *The Ethiopian Herald*, October 15th, 1945, December 27th, 1952
17. Perham, *The Government of Ethiopia*, page 100
18. Archives of the Senate, File 318
19. *Negarit Gazeta*, 15th Year No. 3, November 30th, 1955
20. These figures have been gathered informally from my own investigations and are only approximate
21. *The Ethiopian Herald*, November 9th, 1962
22. David, *loc. cit.*
23. Archives of the Senate, File 100
24. Haile-Selassie I, Speech of November 2nd, 1964. *The Ethiopian Herald*, November 3rd, 1964
25. For example, *Negarit Gazeta*, 21st Year, No. 3, October 20th, 1962, which contains parliamentary amendments to six Decrees
26. Lipsky, *et al.*, *Ethiopia*, page 209; this statement has been denied both by members of Parliament and executive officials with whom I have spoken
27. Inferred from appointments in *Negarit Gazeta*, and from *Yäparlämént Zéna*
28. Revised Constitution of 1955, Article 103
29. Levine, *Wax and Gold*, page 251 *et al.*
30. Levine, *ibid.*, page 253 *et seq.*

Chapter 11: Government Spending

1. Perham, *The Government of Ethiopia*, pages 200–5
2. *Negarit Gazeta*, 13th Year, No. 4, October 31st, 1953
3. *The Ethiopian Herald*, December 30th, 1958

4. From unpublished Ministry of Finance figures. References to dollars are to Ethiopian dollars throughout; seven Ethiopian dollars equalled one pound sterling during this period
5. *Negarit Gazeta, supra,* and unpublished Ministry of Finance figures
6. From unpublished Ministry of Finance figures.
7. Luther, *Ethiopia Today,* page 62
8. Archives of the Senate, File 51
9. See Bulcha Dämäqsa, 'The Budgetary Process in Ethiopia', *Journal of Ethiopian Law,* Vol. IV, No. 2. Ato Bulcha is the official chiefly responsible for drawing up the Budget
10. From unpublished Ministry of Finance figures, compared with the published Budget in *Negarit Gazeta,* 21st Year, No. 14, June 28th, 1952
11. *Africa Recorder,* 1962–63, page 247
12. From the text of the Loan Agreement, in Archives of the Senate, File 1378
13. Minutes of the Economic and Finance Committee of the Senate, Archives of the Senate, File 1378
14. Archives of the Senate, File 1378
15. *Ibid.*

Chapter 12:   Concluding Review

1. Trades unions were already permitted in Eritrea; for their establishment in the rest of Ethiopia, see von Baudissin, 'Labour Policy in Ethiopia', *International Labour Review,* Vol. LXXXIX, No. 6, pages 551–69
2. An interesting example of this transfer of pressure from the Emperor to Parliament appears in Fäqadu Gädamu, 'Social and Cultural Foundations of Gurage Association', *Proceedings of the Third International Conference of Ethiopian Studies*
3. See the Local Self-Administration Order, *Negarit Gazeta,* 25th Year, No. 9(B), March 14th, 1966
4. This is the item which was not audible on Greenfield's tape-recording, see Greenfield, *Ethiopia, A New Political History,* page 403
5. *Adis Zämän,* February 14th, 1967

Select Bibliography

Ethiopian Government Publications

Administrative Directory of the Imperial Ethiopian Government, Institute of Public
Administration, Addis Ababa, separate editions in May 1957, July 1959,
February 1962, January 1964, July 1965, November 1966
Economic Progress of Ethiopia, Ministry of Commerce and Industry, Addis Ababa,
1955
Economic Handbook, Ministry of Commerce and Industry, Addis Ababa, 1958
Ethiopia—Liberation Silver Jubilee, Ministry of Information, Addis Ababa, 1966
Ethiopia—Statistical Abstract, Central Statistical Office, Addis Ababa, separate
editions for 1963, 1964, 1965
Negarit Gazeta, Ministry of the Pen, Addis Ababa; the official government
gazette, containing all legislation and appointments of officials of medium rank
and above, published monthly or more often since 1942
Our Land, Ministry of Information, Addis Ababa, 1963
Second Five Year Development Plan, 1963–1967, Addis Ababa, 1962

Mercha Afätsatsäm Mäglächa (Report on the Election), Central Electoral Board,
Ministry of the Interior, Addis Ababa 1961
Yä Parlamént Zéna (Parliament News), or *Yä Parlamént Mätsähét* (Parliament
Journal), Parliament, Addis Ababa, annually from 1964

Books

Alvarez, F., *Narrative of the Portuguese Embassy to Abyssinia during the years 1520–
1527*, London 1881
Atnafu Makonnen, *Ethiopia Today*, Tokyo 1960
Baum, J. E., *Savage Abyssinia*, London 1928
Beckingham, C. F. and Huntingford, G. W. B., *Some Records of Ethiopia, 1593–
1646*, London 1954
Blundell, H. J. W., *The Royal Chronicles of Abyssinia, 1769–1840*, Cambridge 1922
Bruce, J., *Travels to Discover the Source of the Nile*, Edinburgh 1790
Dämesé Wäldä-Amanu'él, *The Constitution and Parliament of Ethiopia*, translated
by S. Wright, Addis Ababa 1958
Farago, L., *Abyssinia on the Eve*, London 1935
Greenfield, R., *Ethiopia, A New Political History*, London and New York 1965
Guébré Selassie, *Chronique du règne de Menelik II*, Paris 1931

Haile-Selassie I, *Selected Speeches of His Imperial Majesty Haile Selassie I*, Addis Ababa 1967
Huntingford, G. W. B., *The Galla of Ethiopia*, London 1955
Levine, D. N., *Wax and Gold*, Chicago 1965
Lipsky, G. A., et al., *Ethiopia—Its People, Its Society, Its Culture*, New Haven 1962
Ludolphus, J., *A New History of Ethiopia*, London 1684
Luther, E. W., *Ethiopia Today*, London and Stanford, California 1958
Marein, N., *The Ethiopian Empire, Federation and Laws*, Rotterdam 1954
Mathew, D., *Ethiopia, The Study of a Polity, 1540–1935*, London 1947
Mosley, L., *Haile Selassie, The Conquering Lion*, London and New York 1964
Paul, J. C. N., and Clapham, C. S., *Ethiopian Constitutional Development*, Vol. I 1967, Vol. 2 1968 Addis Ababa
Perham, M., *The Government of Ethiopia*, London 1948; 2nd edition London 1968
Redden, K. R., *The Law Making Process in Ethiopia*, Addis Ababa 1966
Rey, C. F., *Unconquered Abyssinia*, London 1923; *In the Country of the Blue Nile*, London 1927
Rubenson, S., *Wichale XVII*, Addis Ababa 1964; *King of Kings Tewodros of Ethiopia*, Addis Ababa 1966
Sandford, C., *Ethiopia under Haile Selassie*, London 1946; *The Lion of Judah Hath Prevailed*, London 1955
Segal, R., *African Profiles*, London and New York 1962
Skordiles, K., *Kagnew, the Story of the Ethiopian Fighters in Korea*, Tokyo 1954
Steer, G. L., *Caesar in Abyssinia*, London 1936
Trevaskis, G. K. N., *Eritrea, a Colony in Transition*, London 1960
Trimingham, J. S., *Islam in Ethiopia*, London 1952
Ullendorff, E., *The Ethiopians*, London 1960; 2nd edition London and New York 1965
Virgin, E., *The Abyssinia I Knew*, London 1936
Zervos, A., *L'Empire d'Ethiopie*, Athens 1936

Käbädä Engeda-Säw, *Yä Meker Bétachen Edel*, Addis Ababa 1960/1
Mahtämä-Selassie Wäldä-Mäsqäl, *Zekre Nägär*, Addis Ababa 1957/8

Periodicals

Adis Zämän, daily, Addis Ababa
Ethiopian Herald, daily, Addis Ababa
Ethiopia Observer, quarterly, Addis Ababa and London
Ethiopie d'Aujhourd'hui, monthly, Addis Ababa
Journal of Ethiopian Law, twice yearly, Addis Ababa
Journal of Ethiopian Studies, twice yearly, Addis Ababa
L'Ethiopie, Bulletin d'Information, monthly, Paris

Collected Conference Papers

Atti del Convegno Internazionale di Studi Etiopici, Rome 1960
Journal of Semitic Studies, Vol. IX, No. 1, Manchester 1964 (containing papers delivered at the Second International Conference of Ethiopian Studies)
Proceedings of the Third International Conference of Ethiopian Studies, Addis Ababa 1968–9
Historians in Tropical Africa, Salisbury, Rhodesia 1960 (containing papers delivered at the Leverhulme African History Conference)

Articles

(Excluding those in the above periodicals)

Clapham, C., 'The Ethiopian *coup d'état* of December 1960', *Journal of Modern African Studies*, Vol. VI, No. 4, 1968

David, R., 'A Civil Code for Ethiopia: Considerations on the Codification of the Civil Law in African Countries', *Tulane Law Review*, Vol. XXXVII, No. 2, February 1963, pp. 187–204

Hambro, E., 'The Rebellion Trials in Ethiopia', *Bulletin of the International Commission of Jurists*, No. 12, November 1961

Hess, R. L., 'Ethiopia', in Carter, *National Unity and Regionalism in Eight African States*, Ithaca 1966

Levine, D. N., 'Haile Selassie's Ethiopia—Myth or Reality?', *Africa Today*, May 1961

— 'Ethiopia: Identity, Authority, and Realism', in Pye and Verba, *Political Culture and Political Development*, Princeton 1965

Markakis, S., and Asmelash, Beyene, 'Representative Institutions in Ethiopia', *Journal of Modern African Studies*, Vol. V, No. 2, pages 193–219

Von Baudissin, Georg Graf, 'Labour Policy in Ethiopia', *International Labour Review*, Vol. LXXXIX, No. 6, pp. 551–69

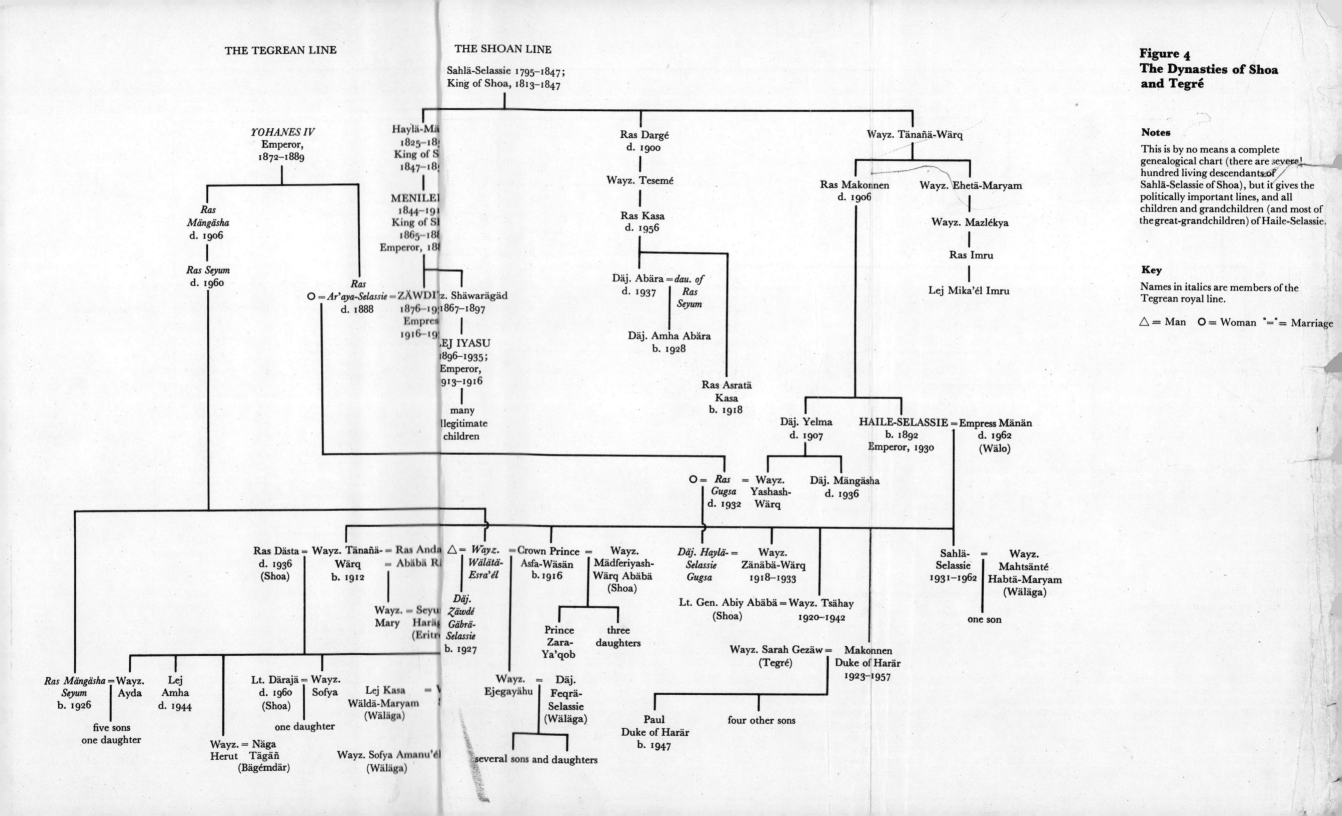

Figure 4
The Dynasties of Shoa and Tegré

THE TEGREAN LINE

THE SHOAN LINE

Notes

This is by no means a complete genealogical chart (there are several hundred living descendants of Sahlä-Selassie of Shoa), but it gives the politically important lines, and all children and grandchildren (and most of the great-grandchildren) of Haile-Selassie.

Key

Names in italics are members of the Tegrean royal line.

△ = Man   O = Woman   ˙=˙ = Marriage

Sahlä-Selassie 1795–1847; King of Shoa, 1813–1847

YOHANES IV Emperor, 1872–1889

Haylä-Mä... 1825–18.. King of S... 1847–18..

Ras Dargé d. 1900

Wayz. Tänañä-Wärq

Ras Makonnen d. 1906

Wayz. Ehetä-Maryam

Ras Mängäsha d. 1906

MENILE... 1844–191. King of Sh... 1865–188. Emperor, 188.

Wayz. Tesemé

Wayz. Mazlékya

Ras Imru

Ras Seyum d. 1960

Ras Kasa d. 1956

Lej Mika'él Imru

O = *Ar'aya-Selassie* = ZÄWDI... d. 1888 1876–191. z. Shäwarägäd 1867–1897 Empres... 1916–19..

Däj. Abära = *dau. of* d. 1937   *Ras Seyum*

Ras

.EJ IYASU 1896–1935; Emperor, 913–1916

Däj. Amha Abära b. 1928

many illegitimate children

Ras Asratä Kasa b. 1918

Däj. Yelma d. 1907

HAILE-SELASSIE = Empress Mänän b. 1892   d. 1962 Emperor, 1930   (Wälo)

O = *Ras Gugsa* d. 1932   = Wayz. Yashash-Wärq

Däj. Mängäsha d. 1936

Ras Dästa = Wayz. Tänañä- = *Ras Anda...* d. 1936   Wärq   = Abäbä R... (Shoa)   b. 1912

△ = *Wayz. Wälätä-Esra'él*

= Crown Prince = Asfa-Wäsän b. 1916

Wayz. Mädferiyash-Wärq Abäbä (Shoa)

Däj. Haylä-Selassie Gugsa

Wayz. Zänäbä-Wärq 1918–1933

Sahlä-Selassie 1931–1962

= Wayz. Mahtsänté Habtä-Maryam (Wäläga)

Wayz. = Seyu... Mary   Har... (Eritr...

Däj. Zäwdé Gäbrä-Selassie b. 1927

Lt. Gen. Abiy Abäbä = Wayz. Tsähay (Shoa)   1920–1942

one son

Prince Zara-Ya'qob

three daughters

Ras Mängäsha = Wayz. *Seyum*   Ayda b. 1926

Lej Amha d. 1944

Lt. Däräjä = Wayz. d. 1960   Sofya (Shoa)

Lej Kasa = V... Wäldä-Maryam ... (Wäläga)

Wayz. = Däj. Ejegayähu   Feqrä-Selassie (Wäläga)

Wayz. Sarah Gezäw = Makonnen (Tegré)   Duke of Harär 1923–1957

five sons one daughter

one daughter

Paul Duke of Harär b. 1947

four other sons

Wayz. = Näga Herut   Tägäñ (Bägémdär)

Wayz. Sofya Amanu'é... (Wäläga)

several sons and daughters

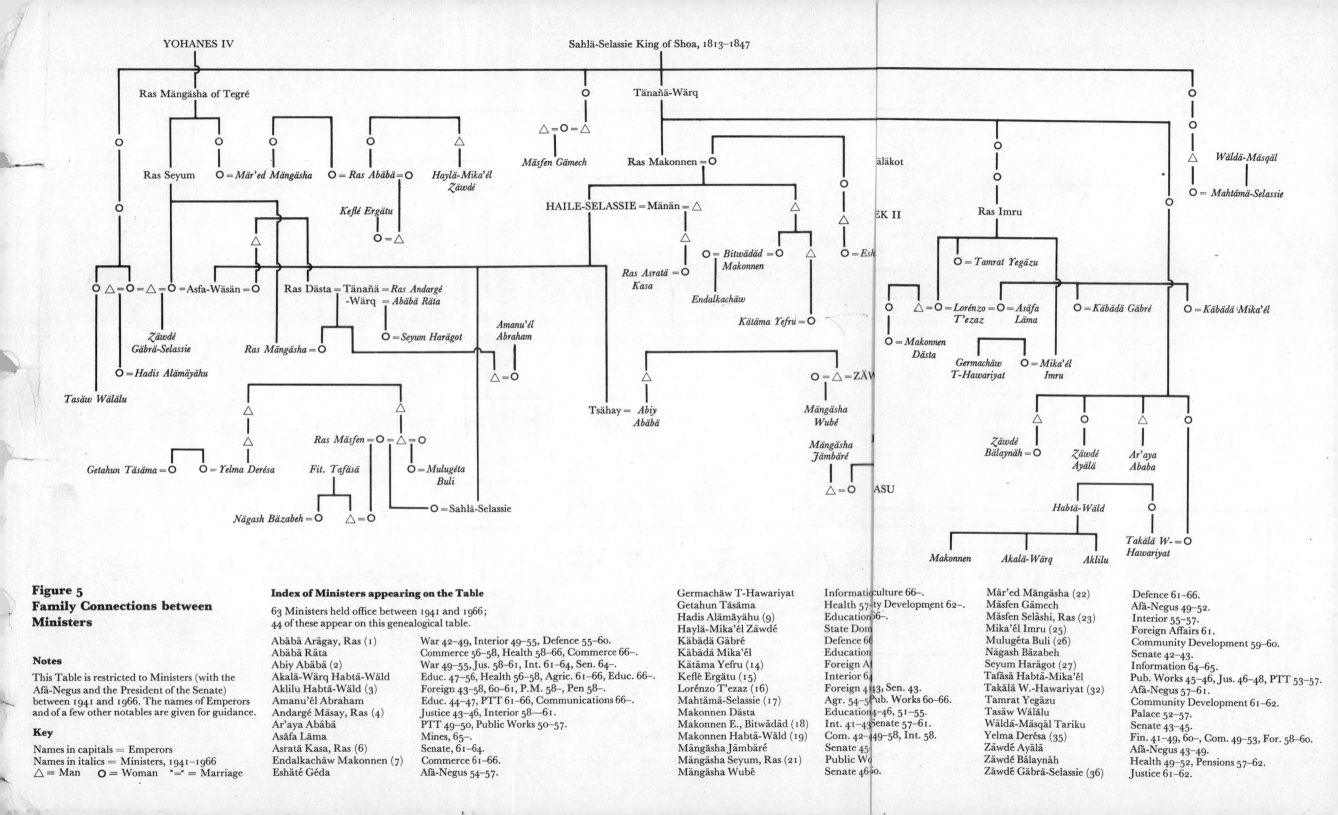

YOHANES IV

Ras Mängäsha of Tegré

Ras Seyum = Mär'ed Mängäsha = Ras Abäbä = Haylä-Mika'él Zäwdé

Keflé Ergätu

= Asfa-Wäsän = Ras Dästa = Tänañä = Ras Andargé -Wärq = Abäbä Räta

Zäwdé Gäbrä-Selassie

= Hadis Alämäyähu

Tasäw Wälälu

Ras Mängäsha = Seyum Harägot

Amanu'él Abraham

Getahun Täsäma = = Yelma Derésa

Ras Mäsfen = = = Mulugéta Buli

Fit. Tafäsä

Nägash Bäzabeh = = = = Sahlä-Selassie

Sahlä-Selassie King of Shoa, 1813-1847

Tänañä-Wärq

Mäsfen Gämech   Ras Makonnen =   äläkot

HAILE-SELASSIE = Mänän

Ras Asratä Kasa   Bitwädäd Makonnen   = Esh

Endalkachäw

Kätäma Yefru =

Wäldä-Mäsqäl

= Mahtämä-Selassie

Ras Imru

= Tamrat Yegäzu

= Makonnen Dästa

= Lorénzo T'ezaz = Asäfa Läma   = Käbädä Gäbré   = Käbädä Mika'él

Germachäw T-Hawariyat   = Mika'él Imru

Tsähay = Abiy Abäbä

= ZÄW

Mängäsha Wubé

Mängäsha Jämbäré

ASU

Zäwdé Bälaynäh   Zäwdé Ayälä   Ar'aya Ababa

Habtä-Wäld

Makonnen   Akalä-Wärq   Aklilu

Takälä W-Hawariyat

Figure 5
Family Connections between Ministers

Notes

This Table is restricted to Ministers (with the Afä-Negus and the President of the Senate) between 1941 and 1966. The names of Emperors and of a few other notables are given for guidance.

Key

Names in capitals = Emperors
Names in italics = Ministers, 1941–1966
△ = Man   O = Woman   "=" = Marriage

Index of Ministers appearing on the Table

63 Ministers held office between 1941 and 1966; 44 of these appear on this genealogical table.

Abäbä Arägay, Ras (1)   War 42–49, Interior 49–55, Defence 55–60.
Abäbä Räta (2)   Commerce 56–58, Health 58–66, Commerce 66–.
Abiy Abäbä (2)   War 49–55, Jus. 58–61, Int. 61–64, Sen. 64–.
Akalä-Wärq Habtä-Wäld   Educ. 47–56, Health 56–58, Agric. 61–66, Educ. 66–.
Aklilu Habtä-Wäld (3)   Foreign 43–58, 60–61, P.M. 58–, Pen 58–.
Amanu'él Abraham   Educ. 44–47, PTT 61–66, Communications 66–.
Andargé Mäsay, Ras (4)   Justice 43–46, Interior 58—61.
Ar'aya Abäbä   PTT 49–50, Public Works 50–57.
Asäfa Läma   Mines, 65–.
Asratä Kasa, Ras (6)   Senate 61–64.
Endalkachäw Makonnen (7)   Commerce 61–66.
Eshäté Géda   Afä-Negus 54–57.

Germachäw T-Hawariyat   Information culture 66–.
Getahun Täsäma   Health 57–ty Development 62–.
Hadis Alämäyähu (9)   Education 66–.
Haylä-Mika'él Zäwdé   State Dom
Käbädä Gäbré   Defence 66
Käbädä Mika'él   Education
Kätäma Yefru (14)   Foreign A
Keflé Ergätu (15)   Interior 6
Lorénzo T'ezaz (16)   Foreign 4143, Sen. 43.
Mahtämä-Selassie (17)   Agr. 54–5 Pub. Works 60–66.
Makonnen Dästa   Education 4–46, 51–55.
Makonnen E., Bitwädäd (18)   Int. 41–43 Senate 57–61.
Makonnen Habtä-Wäld (19)   Com. 42–449–58, Int. 58.
Mängäsha Jämbäré   Senate 45
Mängäsha Seyum, Ras (21)   Public Wo
Mängäsha Wubé   Senate 46 0.

Mär'ed Mängäsha (22)   Defence 61–66.
Mäsfen Gämech   Afä-Negus 49–52.
Mäsfen Seläshi, Ras (23)   Interior 55–57.
Mika'él Imru (25)   Foreign Affairs 61.
Mulugéta Buli (26)   Community Development 59–60.
Nägash Bäzabeh   Senate 42–43.
Seyum Harägot (27)   Information 64–65.
Tafäsä Habtä-Mika'él   Pub. Works 45–46, Jus. 46–48, PTT 53–57.
Takälä W.-Hawariyat (32)   Afä-Negus 57–61.
Tamrat Yegäzu   Community Development 61–62.
Tasäw Wälälu   Palace 52–57.
Wäldä-Mäsqäl Tariku   Senate 43–45.
Yelma Derésa (35)   Fin. 41–49, 60–, Com. 49–53, For. 58–60.
Zäwdé Ayälä   Afä-Negus 43–49.
Zäwdé Bälaynäh   Health 49–52, Pensions 57–62.
Zäwdé Gäbrä-Selassie (36)   Justice 61–62.

Index

Major references are in heavy type. f/4, f/5 refer to Figures 4 and 5.

Abäbä Arägay, Ras (1), 22–25, 31, 60, 70, 88, 96, 100, 113–17, 121–6, **193**, f/5.
Abäbä Räta, Ato, 63, f/4, f/5.
Abiy Abäbä, Lieut.-General (2), 62, 67–69, 72, 89, 96, 99, 101, 115–16, 125, 149–50, 178, **193**, f/4, f/5.
Adäfresäw, Ras. 123–5.
Addis Ababa, 1–5, 14–18, 21, 24–25, 34, 36, 47, 50, 53, 67, 76–79, 87, 94, 105, 117, 127, 139, 143–4, 152, 177, 186.
Addis Ababa Municipality, 5, 50, 52, 142.
Adisgé family, 67.
Admasu Räta, Blata, 53.
Administrative Court, 130.
Advisers, *see* Foreign Advisers.
Adwa, 3, 13–14.
Afä Negus, 11, 15, 89, 150, 182; *see also* Judiciary.
Africa Hall, 50
African Countries: compared with Ethiopia, 1, 19, 51, 75, 80, 82, 87, 103, 139–40, 153, 185–8, 191–2; *see also* Foreign Policy, Heads of State Conference.
Agäñähu Engeda, Ato, 114.
Agencies, governmental, 46, 104, 148.
Agriculture: Minister, 157; Ministry, 45.
Ahmad Grañ, 11–13, 84.
Akalä-Wärq Habtä-Wäld, Ato, 113, 115, f/5.
Aklilu Habtä-Wäld, Tsähafé T'ezaz (3), 25–26, 29, 57, 68, 74–75, 87–90, 93, 96, 101, 109, 113, 115, 118, 120–1, 126, **130–4**, 174, **193**, f/5; *see also* Prime Minister.
Aksum, 1, 3, 8–9.
Alexandria, Patriarch, 82–83.
Amanu'él Abraham, Ato, 85, f/5.
Ambassadors, 52, 76; *see also* London, Moscow, Paris, etc., Embassy.
Amdä-Mika'él, Däjazmach, 123.
American influences, 23, 37, 60, 73, 80, 103–6, 127, 175–6.
Amharas, 1–2, 14, 59, 76, 79–81, 145; social structure, **4–7**, 9, 42, 153–4.
Amharisation, 14, 81, 185.

Andargé Mäsay, Ras (4), 24, 62, 67, **73**, 111–14, 117, 124, **193–4**, f/4, f/5.
Anglo-Ethiopian Agreements, 1942 and 1944, 21–22, 27, 113, 131.
Antiquities Proclamation, 138.
Appointments, 32, 46, **94–96**, 132, 148–9; *see also* Recruitment.
Appropriations, 127, **155–75**; *see also* Budget.
Aqabé Sä'at, 52, 60, **108–10**, 119, 130, 133, 156, 160, 171, 174, 190.
Ar'aya Abäbä, Lej, f/5.
Archbishop, 16, 83, 123–5.
Armenians, 103.
Army, Armed Forces, 21, 24–27, 30, 35, 39, 80, 93–94, 98, 113–14, 134–35, 184, 186, 191–2; *see also* Bodyguard, Navy.
Arusi, 3, 78, 116, 145; Governorship, 72, 115–16.
Asäfa Läma, Major, f/5.
Asfa-Wäsän, Crown Prince, 18, 24, 28–29, **59–62**, 73, 109, 113, 123, 125, 129, 158, 189, f/4, f/5.
Asfeha Wäldä-Mika'él, Bitwädäd (5), 73, 79, 85, **194**, 199.
Asratä Kasa, Ras (6), 25, 29, 66–70, 149–50, **194**, f/4, f/5.
Auditor General, 130.
Authority figures, 5–7, 10–11, 30, 55, 58, 124, 187.
Ayälä Gäbré, Ato, 72.
Ayalew Biru, Däjazmach, 18.
Ayänäw Adal, Qänazmach, 54.

Bägémdär, 2, 3, 58, 145; Governorship, 61, 114; representation in government, 59, 76–77.
Balé, 3, 78.
Banking: laws, 137; *see also* Investment, National and State Banks.
Basiliyos, Patriarch, 86; *see also* Archbishop.
Bayisa Jämo, Fitawrari, 144.

Bell, J., 103.
Béza family, 67.
Bishops, 83, 129, 149.
Bodyguard, 24, 30, 113–14, 191;
Commander, 22, 24, 53–54, 75, 96, 114.
Boräna, 114.
Brazil, 24.
British influences, 13, 16, 19, 21–22, 104, 155.
Bruce, J., 115.
Budget, 41, 43, 57, 105, 127, 135, 138, 146–7, 150, 153, 155, 162, **164–75**;
Allowance for Unforeseen Expenses, 169–72; Budgetary Transfers, 169;
Supplementary Budget, 170, 172; *see also* Appropriations, Finance, Parliament.
Building Materials Excise Tax Decree, 147, 150.
Bulga, 79.

Central Personnel Agency, 46, 64, 94n, 121, 128, 130, 133, 136.
Chamber of Deputies, *see* Parliament.
Chief of Staff, 24, 54, 116, 120–1.
Chief of Police, *see* Police.
China, 80.
Christianity, 2, 81, 83, 85; *see also* Lutherans, Orthodox Church, Roman Catholicism.
Church, *see* Orthodox Church.
Civil Aviation Decree, 137.
Civil Code, 27, 83, 138, 143, 145.
Civil Procedure Code, 138, 146.
Code Napoléon, 138.
Codification of Laws, 23, 27, 50, **138**;
Codification Commission, 138;
see also Civil Procedure, Commercial, Criminal Procedure, Maritime and Penal Codes.
Collaborators with Italian Occupation, 19–21, 30, 51, 72–73, 93.
Commerce: Minister, 63, 157, 162;
Ministry, 17, 45, 115.
Commercial Code, 27, 138.
Commissions of Enquiry, 177, 179.
Committee for Administrative Reform, 137.
Communications: Minister, 85; Ministry, 45; *see also* Political Communications, Press.
Communism, 80.
Constitution: of 1931, 17, **34–36**, 82,

135, 140–1, 182; of 1955 (Revised Constitution), 9, 23, 27, 34, **36–44**, 82, 123–4, 135, 142, 164, 169, 182, 186;
Constitutional Commission, 37–38;
Constitutional Revision Committee, 42–43.
Consultative Committee for Legislation, 137.
Corruption, 30–31, 70, 117, 157, 177.
Council of Ministers, 28, 118, 159;
Origins, 15–19, 22, 27, 126, 182;
Composition, 45–46, 85, 98, 121, 126, 131–3; Powers, 38–39, 42, 126; Working, 33, 102, 109–10, **127–9**, 137–8, 164, 166, 169–79, 183, 190.
Coups d'état (and attempted *coups d'état*):
of 1916, 15–16; of 1928, 16; of 1944, 70; of 1947, 22, 60, 70; of 1951, 22, 27, 70; of 1960, 24–28, 32, 42, 50, 54–55, 67–69, 96, 106, 117, 121, 132, 162, 188–91.
Courts Proclamation of 1962, 136, 146.
Crown Council, 28, 37, 39, 60, 86, **123–5**, 129, 171, 190.
Crown Prince, *see* Asfa-Wäsän.
Criminal Procedure Code, 138.
Customs dues, 17, 173.
Cuba, 80.

Danakil, 2.
Dästa, Ras, 61–62, f/4, f/5.
Debteras, 86.
Decrees, *see* Legislation.
Defence (National Defence): Minister, 24, 31, 53, 69, 71, 99, 101, 116, 132;
Ministry, 45, 89, 96, 100, 167, 170; *see also* War.
de Gaulle, General C., 134.
Delegation, 6, 10–11, 26, 31, 66, 111.
Deputies, *see* Parliament.

Ecclesiastical Affairs Department, *see* Private Cabinet.
Economic and Technical Assistance Board, 162, 176.
Education, 17, 19–20, 23, 56, 76–77, 84–86, **87–91**, 93, 97; Minister, 56, 85, 97, 115; Ministry, 45.
Egypt, 13.
Elections, *see* Parliament; Electoral Board, 141, 145; Electoral Law, 141.
Elites, 64–65, 87, 151, 189–91; *see also* Graduates, Ministers, Nobility, etc.

Emperor: office of, 2, **6–12**, 181; powers, 9–12, 35–36, 38–42; succession, 9, 14, 38–39, 59, 86, 188–92; *see also* Haile-Selassie, Menilek, Téwodros, Yohanes.
Endalkachäw Makonnen, Lej (7), 67, 69, **194,** f/5.
Eritrea, Eritreans, 1, 3, 11, 14, 57, 67. 72, 85, 186; Federation, 22–23, 27, 36–41, 73, 112–13, 116, 129, 131, 138; Governorship, 29, 62, 66, 114; representation in government, 29–30, 63, 73, 76–77, 79, 83, 93, 133, 141, 144; separatism, 4, 23, 27, **80–81**, 184.
Eskender Dästa, Lej, 62, f/4.
Ethiopia, *passim*; geography, 1–4; history, 8–27.
Ethiopian Air Lines, 46, 57, 104, 127.
Ethnic groups, 1–4, 59, **75–82**; *see also* Amharas, Eritreans, Gallas, Regional Groups, etc.

Family connections, 33, 59–63, 66–67, 73–74, 77–78, 92, 94, f/4, f/5.
Federal Tax Proclamation of 1955, 142.
Federation, *see* Eritrea.
Finance: Minister, 29, 34, 60, 89, 114, 128, 132, **155–80**; Ministry, 24, 45, 79, 96, 100, 109, 115, 148, **155–80**, 190; Budget Committee, 165–6; Budget Department, 167; Finance Credit Department, 176; Financial System, 19, 21, 40, 56, 79, 110, 155–75.
Fiscal Year Proclamation, 146, 164.
Five-Year Plan, 23, 27, 91, 129, 165.
Foreign Advisers, 18–19, 21, 37, **103–7**, 136–9, 155, 164.
Foreign Affairs: Minister, 25, 29–30, 32, 52, 97, 115, 122, 130–1; Ministry, 15, 17, 45, 69, 110–11.
Foreign influences, 72–73, 133; *see also* American, British, French, etc., influences.
Foreign policy, 25, 35, 39, 48, 50, 56, 84, 91, 122, 128.
Franco-Ethiopian Railway Treaty, 148.
French influences, 13, 16, 73, 131, 133, 175.

Gäbrä-Wäld Engedä-Wärq, Ato (8), 86, 113, 118, 123, 125, **194.**
Gallas, 2, 11, 14, 16, 177; representation in government, 27, **77–79**, 83, 114,

119; separatist movement, 27, **80–82**, 96, 186, 191.
Gämu Gofa, 3, 78, 145; Governorship, 62, 117.
Gänät Le'ul Palace, 28n.
Gäräsu Duki, Däjazmach, 70.
Germa Wäldä-Giyorgis, Lieutenant, 144.
Germachäw Täklä-Hawariyat, Däjazmach, f/5.
Germamé Neway, Ato, 24.
Gershkowitz, L., 106, 120.
Getachäw, Ras, 73.
Getahun Täsäma, Ato, f/5.
Ghana, 8.
Gojam, 2–3, 22, 68; dynasty, 67, 124; Governorship, 18; representation in government, 59, 70, **76–78**, 144–5.
Gondar, 1, 3, 12, 59.
Goré, 61.
Governors-General, 52, 129; *see also* Governorships, under each province.
Graduates, 20, 23–25, 29, 32, 87–91, 93.
Grañ, *see* Ahmad Grañ.
Greeks, 103–4.
Groupings, political, **64–91.**

Hadis Alämäyähu, Ato (9), 97–98, **194,** 199, f/5.
Haile-Selassie I, Emperor, *passim*; rise to power, 16–17, 47–49; early reign, 17–18; exile and return, 6, 18–19, 21, 61; family, *see* Imperial Family; personal characteristics, **47–51**; methods of government, 24–25, 28–33, **51–59**, 163–4; centralising policies, 18, 21–22, 35, 40–41, 57, 67, 71–73; modernizing policies, 10, 17–18, 35–36, 41, 49, 58; political role, 30, 32, **55–58**, 183–44; speeches, 105; state visits, 24, 50, 60, 122, 132, 175–6; *see also* Emperor, Tafari.
Haile-Selassie I Foundation, 115.
Haile-Selassie I Prize Trust, 50.
Haile-Selassie I University, 62, 87, 119, 139, 186.
Haile-Selassie Gugsa, Däjazmach, 19, 73, f/4.
Hana Jema, Aba (10), 53, 86, **194–5.**
Harär, 2–3, 57, 85–86; Duke of, *see* Makonnen, Prince; Governorship, 47–48, 61, 116; representation in government, 77, 79, 83, 145.
Harrell, V., 104.
Haylä-Maryam Käbädä, Lej, 144.
Haylä-Mika'él Zäwdé, Fitawrari, f/5.

Haylu of Gojam, Ras, 18, 59, f/5.
Haylu Bäläw, Ras (11), 67, 123–5, **195**.
Heads of State Conference of 1963, 48, 50, 56, 169.
Health Tax, 143, 146, 148.
Heruy Wäldä-Selassie, Blatengéta, 17.
Hobbes, T., 58.

Ilg, A., 103.
Ilubabor, 3, 77–78.
Impeachment, 39, 147.
Imperial Bodyguard, see Bodyguard.
Imperial Chelot, 28, 57, 60.
Imperial Court: Minister, 29, 118; Ministry, 45–46, 89, 118.
Imperial Family, 9, **59–63**, 77, 81, 123, 186, f/4.
Imperial Highway Authority, 148.
Imperial Orders, 39, 108–12, 130, 135, 156, 159–60, 169–70; see also Legislation.
Imperial Secretariat, 22–23, 28, 46, 64, 69, 74, 93, 102, **108–23**, 130, 161; see also Pen, Private Cabinet.
Imru Haile-Selassie, Ras (12), 18, 24, 66, 69, 97, 124–5, **195**, f/4, f/5.
India, Embassy, 67.
Information: Minister, 122; Ministry, 45, 158; see also Press.
Innovation, 6, 10, 12, 14, 18, 35, 48–49, 87, 103, 107, 182–4.
Institute of Public Administration, 134, 136.
Institutionalization, 84, 89, 102, 130, 134, 164–7, 179, 183.
Interest Aggregation/Articulation, 29–30, 32, 55, 58, 61, 75–76, 79–80, 85, 119, 143, 151–2, 184–88.
Interest Groups, 186–7.
Interior: Minister, 62, 69, 71, 96, 99, 112–16, 130, 162–63; Ministry, 45, 54, 89, 96, 100–1.
Intrigue, 5, 7, 48, 54–55, 157–9
Investment Bank, 79.
Islam, 8–11, 15, 23, 37, 80–85, 138, 145, 158, 186.
Italian influences, 13–14, 16, 103; Occupation of 1935–41, 17–21, 62, 66, 72, 82, 84, 103, 157; proposed loan of 1963–4, 27, 71, 150–1, 173, **175–80**.
Italian Somaliland, 129.
Iyasu, Lej, Emperor, 15, 18, 28, 53, 59, 78, 185, f/4, f/5.

Japan, 50, 191; Constitution of 1889, 34–35.
Jerusalem, projected crusade to, 12.
Jesuits, 12, 84–85.
Jibuti, 3, 14.
Jubilee Palace, 28.
Judiciary, 25, 35, 38, 40–41, 43, 97, 136, 150.
Justice: Minister, 15, 66, 69, 72–73, 97, 112, 115, 133, 182; Ministry, 45, 54, 96, 100–1, 136, 165.

Käbädä Gäbré, Lieut.-General, 101, f/5.
Käbädä Mängäsha, Ras, 140.
Kafa, 3, 78.
Kasa Dargé, Ras (14), 18, 21–22, 25, 27, 29, 37, 66, 68, 71, 86, 88, 109, 111, 113, 123–5, **195**, f/4.
Kasa Wäldä-Maryam, Lej, 62, 119, f/4.
Kätäma Yefru, Ato (14), 29–30, 32, 118–19, 122, **195**, f/5.
Keflé Ergätu, Däjazmach (15), 113–16, **195**, f/5.
Korea, 23, 106.

Lake Tana, 3, 12,
Lalibela, 1, 3.
Land Reform, 25, 91; Land Reform and Development Authority, 46; Ministry, 45–46.
Land Tax, 143.
Lasta, 59, 76.
Leadership, 5–7, 11, 16, 77.
League of Nations, 18.
Legislation, 127, 133, **135–9**, 141–2, 145–7; Decrees, 40, 135–8, 140–2, 146–7, 152; General Notices, 136; Legal Notices, 136–7; Ministerial Circulars, 136; Notices, 136; Notices of Disapproval, 146–7; Orders, 39, 44–45, 135–8; Proclamations, 135–8, 146, 164.
Legitimacy, 9, 24–25, 51, 58, 65, 187–9, 191.
Lej Iyasu, see Iyasu.
Liberation of 1941, 19, 21, 27.
Ligaba, 11.
Litigation, 5.
Loans, 38, 40, 127, 135, 147, 176; see also Italian Loan, Russian Loan.
Local Government Reform, 146, 186.
London: Embassy, 97; London School of Economics, 157.

Lorénzo T'ezaz, Blatengéta (16), 18, 114, **195**, f/5.
Lutherans, 85.

Mäba 'a-Selassie Alämu, Ato, 122.
Mahdists, 13.
Mahtämä-Selassie Wäldä-Mäsqäl, Blatengéta (17), 53, 72, 86, 99, 125, 157, 162, **195–6**, f/5.
Makonnen, Prince, Duke of Harär, 27, 59, **61–62**, 123, 125, f/4.
Makonnen of Harär, Ras, 47, 79, f/4, f/5.
Makonnen Dänäqä, Brigadier-General, 113.
Makonnen Dästa, Däjazmach, f/5.
Makonnen Endalkachäw, Ras Bitwädäd (18), 37, 67, 88, 113–14, 117, 123–6, 130–1, 183, **196**, f/5.
Makonnen Habtä-Wäld, Ato (19), 17, 22–25, 52, 54, 68, 74, 79, 86–89, 96, 100–2, 113, 115, 118, 121–4, 131, **157–64**, 167, 173—4, 186, **196**, f/5.
Makonnen Wäldä-Yohanes, Ato, 117.
Mamo Tadäsä, Ato (20), 72–73, 85, 101, 133, **196**, 199.
Mänän, Empress, 59, **61**.
Mängäsha Jämbäré, Bitwädäd, 70, f/5.
Mängäsha Seyum, Ras (21), 29, 62, 66–68, **196**, f/4, f/5.
Mängäsha Wubé, Bitwädäd, f/5.
Mängestu Neway, Major-General, 24, 96.
Mänz, 79.
Mäqälé, 148.
Mär'ed Mängäsha, Lieut.-General (22), 78, 89, **196–7**, f/5.
Maritime Code, 27, 138.
Marsé-Hazen Wäldä-Kirkos, Blata, 85.
Mäsfen Seläshi, Ras (23), 67, 70, 116, 124, **197**, f/5.
Massawa, 3, 13.
Mathew, Sir Charles, 42.
Members of Parliament (Salaries) Proclamation, 144.
Menasé Haylé, Dr (24), 30, 56, 73, 101, 122, **197**.
Menasé Läma, Ato, 175–7, 179.
Menilek II, Emperor, 13–18, 28, 47–48, 58, 66–67, 70, 87, 103, 108, 182, f/4, f/5.
Menilek Palace, 28, 123.
Metemma, 13.
Mika'él of Wälo, Negus, 15, 59, 78.
Mika'él Imru, Lej (25), 70, 97, **197**, f/4, f/5.

Miliyon Näqneq, Ato, 97.
Mines, Ministry, 45, 158.
Ministers, 15, 29, 31, 39, 45, 51–53, 95, **98–102**, 126, 136; Ministers of State, 46; Ministers (Definition of Powers) Order of 1943, 19, 108; Ministerial Circulars, see Legislation; Ministerial Responsibility, 31, 97–98; see also under individual Ministries.
Ministries, 17, 45; Ministry of Finance, etc., see Finance, etc.
Modernisation, see Innovation.
Moja family, 67, 123, 125.
Moslems, see Islam.
Moscow Embassy, 97, 114.
Mulugéta Buli, Major-General (26), 22–25, 54, 65, 68, 78, 88, 93, 96, 101, 114–16, 120–1, **197**, f/5.

Nägash Bäzabeh, Bitwädäd, 70, f/5.
National Bank, 167.
National Community Development: Minister, 121; Ministry, 45, 165, 186.
National Defence, see Defence; National Defence Council, 60.
Nationalism, 80, 82–85, 157, 191–2.
Navy, 50, 62, 161.
Nazrét, 115.
Negarit Gazeta, 19, 27, 95, 108, 118, 133, 147, 155–6, 164, 172.
Nkrumah, K., 50.
Nobel Peace Prize, 50.
Nobility, Noblemen, 11, 15, 21, 29–32, 35, 37, **65–71**, 92, 100–1, 113, 123–5, 140–1, 149, 177–9.
Notice of Disapproval, see Legislation.

Ogaden, 3, 121.
Opposition, 6–7, 11, 68, 128, 141, 143, 145–8, 150–4, 176–80; see also Coups d état, Revolts.
Orders, see Imperial Orders, Legislation.
Organisations, political, see Groupings, Parties, Political Pressures, Protégés, Regional Associations.
Orthodox Church, 2, 7–10, 13, 15, 21, 27, 37, 40, 61, 65, 71, **82–86**, 157, 186, 189.

Palace, 28; Palace Government, 15–17, 28–33, 51–58, 75, 100; Minister, Ministry, see Imperial Court.

Paradis, D. E., 42, 106, 133.
Paris Embassy, 72, 116.
Parliament, 28, 169, 171, 182–83, 189–90; under 1931 Constitution, 17, 21, 27, 35–36, **140–2**; under 1955 Constitution, 27, 38–44; legislative activities, 135, 137, 141–2, 145–7, 164, 166, 172; relations with executive, 26, 130, 133, **147–50**, 177–9; Chamber of Deputies, 26, 33, 35, 40–44, **140–54**, 166, 177, 179; Budget Committee, 147, 166; composition, **141-4**; elections, 23, **142-4**, 149, 187; functions, **151–4**, 186, 189; groupings, 144–5; President, 144; Senate, 26, 40–41, 99, 140–54; composition, 35, 38, 95, 141, **149–50**; Economic Committee, 178; functions, 150–1, 177–9; President, 50, 66, 71, 89, 123, 125, 130, 149.
Parties, political, effects of absence, 30, 32, 42, 75, 142, 152–3, 187–8.
Patriarch, 25, 86, 125; see also Alexandria, Archbishop.
Patriots (resistance fighters), 22, 30, 70–73, 93, 113, 124, 177–9.
Patriotic Association, 158.
Pen: Ministry, 22, 28, 45–46, 100, **108–19**, 123, 134, 136, 156, 160–1, 171, 174, 182; Minister, 15, 24, 27, 72, 95, 100, **108–19**, 126, 129, 133, 178; see also Aklilu Habtä-Wäld, Täfärä-Wärq, Wäldä-Giyorgis.
Penal Code, 27, 138, 141; Penal Code (Penalties) Decree, 143, 146, 150.
Pensions, Ministry, 165.
Perham, M. F., 105, 123, 127.
Planning: Board, 46, 104, 129, 134, 162; Minister, 97; Ministry, 45–46, 165, 199; see also Five-Year Plan.
Plowden, W., 103.
Police, 113; Chief of Police, 24, 54, 96.
Polish advisers, 104.
Political Communications, 53–55, 112–113, 151–4, 185–8.
Political Parties, see Parties.
Political Pressures, 23, 30–32, 151, 184–8.
Politicians, 46, 57, 62–63, **64–102**; see also under individual names and offices.
Portuguese, 11–12, 84, 103.
Posts: Minister, 15, 69, 83; Ministry, 45, 96.
Press and Newspapers, 152, 158, 187; see also Information, Private Cabinet.
Prime Minister, 25, 60, 67, 69, 73–75, 86, 106, 109–10, 114, 150, 176; activities, 29, 37, 50, 52–53, 56, 95, 97,

101–2, 118, 120, 122, 128, **130–4**, 147, 168, 171, 190; powers, 41, 44–45, 64, 126, 130–4; 1966 increase in powers, 26–27, 32, 42–43, 45–46, 94, 132, 134; see also Aklilu Habtä-Wäld, Makonnen Endalkachäw.
Prime Minister's Office, 29, **129–34**, 174, 177, 183; establishment, 22, 108, 130, 182; legislative activities, 44, 127, 133, 136–7, 139; officials, 63, 126, 133–4.
Private Cabinet, 27, 54, 86, 106, 117, **120–3**, 190; Ecclesiastical Affairs Dept., 86, 121; Imperial Chronicles Dept., 37, 120–1; Judicial Dept., 121; Press and Information Dept., 120, 122; Special Branch, 120–1.
Private Secretary to the Emperor, 116–19, 190.
Proclamations, see Legislation.
Protégés, 74–75, 87, 100–1, 113, 116–17, 123, 157, 159.
Provincial Government, 10–12, 18, 21, 68, 99, 134; see also Governors-General, and individual provinces.
Public Health: Minister, 42, 144; Ministry, 45, 73.
Public Security Department, 54.
Public Works, Ministry, 45, 69.

Ramadan, 85.
Rasses, 67–68, 123–4; see also under individual names.
Rea, G., 104.
Recruitment, 2, 83, 87–89, 92–98; see also Appointments.
Red Sea, 2, 13.
Regency: of Lej Iyasu, 15; of Ras Täfäri, 16–18, 34, 49, 87, 157.
Regionalism, 29, 59, 75–82, 92, 144–5, 152, 184–6; see also Ethnic Groups.
Regional Associations, 78–79, 81, 186.
Regulations for the Administration of the Church, 82.
Religion, 82–86; see also Christianity, Islam, Orthodox Church.
Resistance to Italian Occupation, 19; see also Patriots.
Revised Constitution, see Constitution of 1955.
Revolts, 22, 81; see also Coups d'état, Gallas, Eritrea.
Rhodesia, 56.
Rights, constitutional, 35, 39, 41–42.
Roman Catholicism, 9, 12, 85, 103, 133.
Russian Loan, 177.

Sahlä-Selassie, Prince, 62, f/4.
Salah Henit, Ato, 83, 85.
Schoolteachers in Parliament, 143-4.
Security, 24, 54-55; Chief of Security, 24, 54, 96, 120; see also Private Cabinet, Public Security Department.
Senate, see Parliament.
Seyum Harägot, Ato (27), 63, 133, **197**, 199, f/4, f/5.
Seyum Mängäsha, Ras (28), 18, 25, 29, 61, 66, 123-5, 140, **197-8**, f/4, f/5.
Shoa, Shoans, 2-3, 11, 13, 18, 83, 113; representation in government, 4, 14-15, 29-30, 59, 67, **75-79**, 81, 92, 124, 144.
Shum-Shir, 31, 95-96.
Sidamo, 3; Governorship, 48, 70, 72, 117; representation in government, 77-78, 144.
Social origins of politicians, **71-75**; see also Nobility.
Solomonic Legend, 9, 38.
Solomonic Restoration, 8-9.
Somalia, Somalis, 2, 27; representation in government, 77, 83; Somali problem, 2, 4, 80, 84, 121, 129, 133, 138, 175, 191.
Sovereignty, 39-40.
Spencer, J. H., 37, 106.
State Bank of Ethiopia, 104, 148, 175-6.
Students, 25, 186, 191.
Sudan, 4, 13, 80.
Suez Canal, 13.
Supreme Court, 29, 43.
Swedish advisers, 104.

Tadäsä Biru, Brigadier-General (29), 81, 96, 186, 191, **198**.
Tadäsä Mängäsha, Afä-Negus, 150.
Tadäsä Nägash, Liqämakwas, 114, 116-17.
Tadäsä Tayé, Ato, 144.
Tädla Bayru, Däjazmach (30), 81, **198**.
Täfärä-WärqKidanä-Wäld,TsähaféT'ezaz (31), 29, 99, 116-18, **198**.
Täfäri, Ras, 16-18; see also Haile-Selassie I.
Täfäri Makonnen School, 49.
Täfäri Sharew, Ato, 115.
Tafäsä Habtä-Mika'él, Fitawrari, f/5.
Tajura, Gulf of, 13.
Takälä Wäldä-Hawariyat, Afä-Negus (32), 70, 75, 114-17, **198**, f/5.
Täklä-Hawariyat, Bäjerond, 34-35, 141.
Tamrat Yegäzu, Colonel, f/5.

Tänañä-Wärq, Princess, 62, 111, f/4, f/5.
Tasäw Wälälu, Ligaba, f/5.
Taxation, 146, 155.
Tegré, Tegreans, 1-3, 13-14, 22, 27, 68, 124, 148; dynasty, 29, 59, 61, 66-67, 77, f/4; Governorship, 29, 66, 70, 96, 114-15; representation in government, 59, **76-81**.
Teleq säw, 5.
Téwodros, Emperor, 12-14, 25, 58, 103.
Theofilos, Bishop, 86.
Theological College, Addis Ababa, 84.
Tokyo Embassy, 97.
Toleration, 85.
Tourist Organization, 199
Trades Unions, 23, 43, 105, 184, 186.
Tradition, 8, 51, 181-2.
Treasury, 156, 160, 167-8, 173, 176.
Tsähafé T'ezaz, 10, 15, 22, 108; see also Pen.
Tsähay, Princess, 62, f/4, f/5.

United Nations, 23, 36, 67, 136, 141.
United States Constitution, 40; see also American influences.
University College of Addis Ababa, 23, 27, 85, 87; see also Haile-Selassie I University.
Unkulal bét, 28.

Vatican, 85.
Vice-Ministers, 46, 126.

Wäläga, 2-3, 85; representation in government, 29, 59, 62, 77, 79, 83, 119, 144-5.
Wälamo, 177.
Wäldä-Giyorgis Wäldä-Yohanes, Tsähafé T'ezaz (33), 17, 22-24, 27, 57, 60, 68-69, 72-75, 79, 87-88, 95-97, 100-1, 106, **110-19**, 121-4, 128-31, 158, 161, 183, **198**.
Wäldä-Mäsqäl Tariku, Tsähafé T'ezaz, f/5.
Wälo, 2-3, 15-16, 67; Governorship, 59-61; representation in government, 59, 78, 83, 145.
War Minister, 16, 100, 115; see also Defence.
Wärqenah Gäbäyähu, Colonel (34), 24-25, 54, 120-3, **198-9**.

Washington Embassy, 67, 115, 122.
Wubnäh Täsäma, Ras, 67.

Xenophobia, 103.

Yelma Derésa, Ato (35), 29, 68, 73–74,
77, 79, 87, 89, 95–96, 101, 114–15,
148, 157, 162, 165–70, **173–5**, 177–80,
199, f/5.
Yemen, 189.

Yohanes IV, Emperor, 13–14, 18, 66, f/4,
f/5.
Yohanes Kidanä-Maryam, Ato, 119.
Yugoslav influences, 104, 106, 120.

Zänäbä-Wärq, Princess, 62, f/4.
Zäwdé Ayälä, Afä-Negus, f/5.
Zäwdé Bälaynäh, Blatengéta, f/5.
Zäwdé Gäbrä-Selassie, Däjazmach (36),
66, 70, 97–98, **199**, f/4, f/5.
Zäwditu, Empress, 16, 28, 38, f/4, f/5.
Zimbabwe, 8.